IMAGES
of America

TIPTON COUNTY

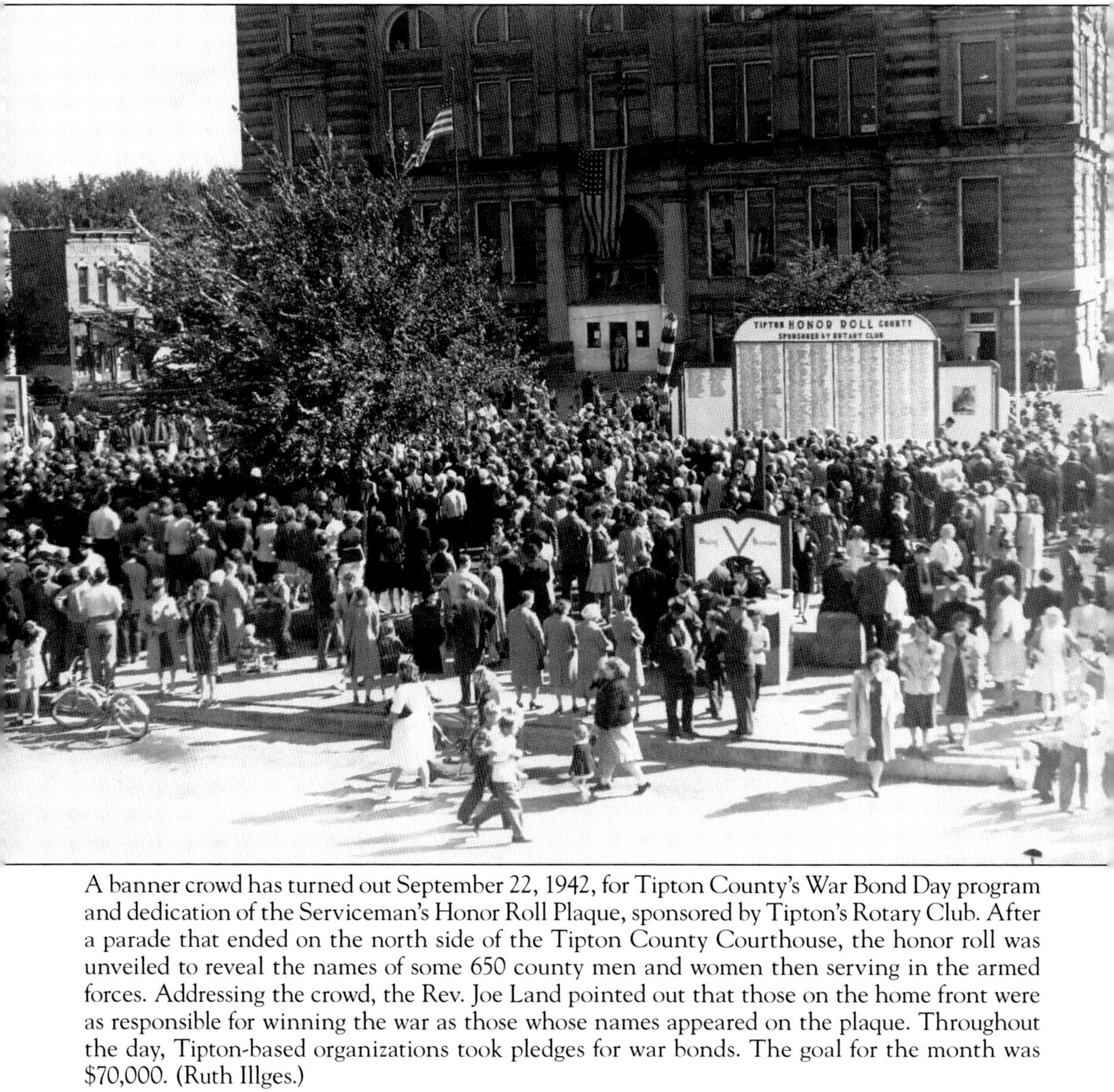

A banner crowd has turned out September 22, 1942, for Tipton County's War Bond Day program and dedication of the Serviceman's Honor Roll Plaque, sponsored by Tipton's Rotary Club. After a parade that ended on the north side of the Tipton County Courthouse, the honor roll was unveiled to reveal the names of some 650 county men and women then serving in the armed forces. Addressing the crowd, the Rev. Joe Land pointed out that those on the home front were as responsible for winning the war as those whose names appeared on the plaque. Throughout the day, Tipton-based organizations took pledges for war bonds. The goal for the month was $70,000. (Ruth Illges.)

On the Cover: This photograph was taken on a Saturday in April 1949 at the annual Children's Play Day, hosted by local businessman Eugene C. Baranowski at the Tipton Municipal Park. Here, Baranowski stands at the top of the baseball diamond bleachers pitching handfuls of coins to the eager children below. In addition to the "penny toss" event, the picnic featured numerous games, such as the shoe scramble, sack race, and the rooster catch. The picnics were held each spring from 1949 through 1954 for some 300 kids, consuming more than 1,000 hot dogs, 41 cases of soft drinks, and 20 gallons of ice cream. (Gene Baranowski, with permission of the *Indianapolis Star*.)

IMAGES
of America

TIPTON COUNTY

Janis Thornton and the
Tipton County Historical Society

ARCADIA
PUBLISHING

ISBN 978-0-7385-9398-2

Published by Arcadia Publishing
Charleston, South Carolina

Printed in the United States of America

Library of Congress Control Number: 2012939069

For all general information, please contact Arcadia Publishing:
Telephone 843-853-2070
Fax 843-853-0044
E-mail sales@arcadiapublishing.com
For customer service and orders:
Toll-Free 1-888-313-2665

Visit us on the Internet at www.arcadiapublishing.com

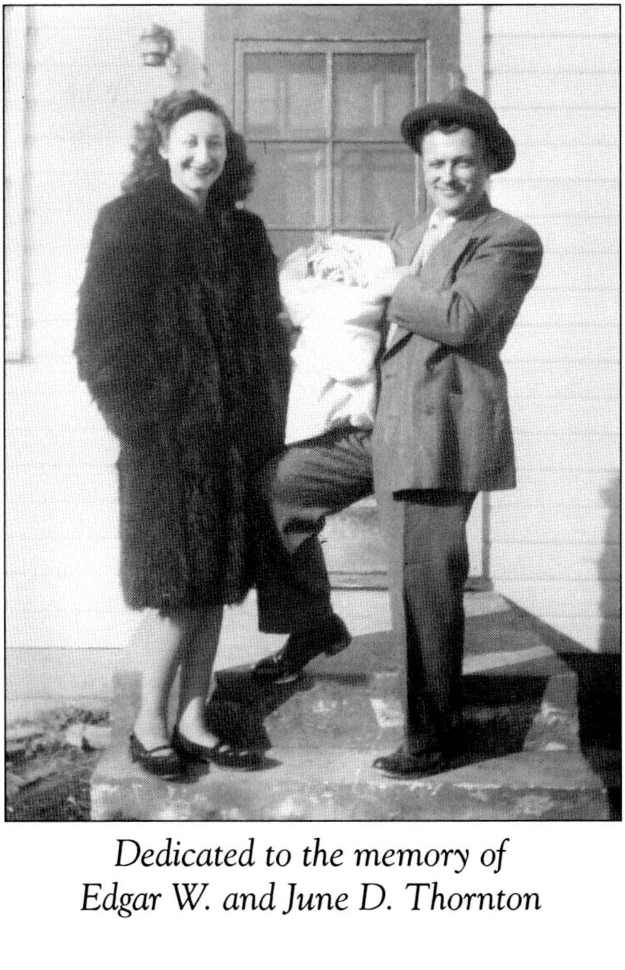

Dedicated to the memory of
Edgar W. and June D. Thornton

Contents

Acknowledgments		6
Introduction		7
1.	Founding and Founders	9
2.	Railroads	25
3.	Business and Industry	33
4.	Agriculture	63
5.	Faith and Community	69
6.	Schools and Sports	85
7.	Events and Celebrations	101
8.	Patriots and Presidents	111
Bibliography		127

Acknowledgments

The historical photographs and anecdotes in this book belong to the many members of the Tipton County community, who dug into their family albums and allowed their personal pictures and memorabilia to be reproduced in print. The following pages are a testament to their generosity.

I am deeply indebted to the Tipton County Historical Society for its partnership in this project and thank Jill Curnutt Howerton, Esther McMath, Don Manlove, and Reba Howery, in particular. I also am grateful to the Tipton County Public Library—primarily Beau Cunnyngham, Sheryl Nierswick, and Kendra Hummel—for providing accessibility to the library's many resources. Appreciation goes to Jackie Henry of the *Tipton Tribune* and Vicki Warner of the Tipton County Chamber of Commerce for their assistance in communicating the need for photographs. I also thank friends Jim Bush for copyediting and Cathy Shouse for the nudge, guidance, and continual encouragement.

While it is impossible to acknowledge everyone who helped with this project, special thanks go to the following people and organizations for providing photographs and other essential contributions: Madonna Alderson, Gary Amos, Gene Baranowski, Joann Boes, Sandra Bridgewater, Evelyn Brooks, Deborah McIntosh Bussy, Ron Byal, Jennifer Wiggins Cels, Virginia Chambers, Shawn Clements, Rosemary Comer, Redmon Conwell, David Cox, Rick Curnutt, Stephen Doi, Janet Driver, Gary Ertel, Catherine and William Funke, Melinda Goodnight, Richard Harvey, Helene Heath, Ruth Illges, Delores Jones, Viola Jones, Paul Julius, Judy Kendall, Tom Lett, Heather Magee, Penny Manier, Gae Matchette, Terry McIntosh, Fred and Julie Miller, Bill Moore, Bob Nichols, John O'Banion, Jim Paikos, Linda Peters, Elaine Phelps, Dave Reasner, Selita Reichart, Alice Ricketts, Jeanie and Bob Robinson, Larry Rump, Sharon Shupperd, Tom Smith, Morris Stillabower Jr., Deb and Ray Tharp, Bill Tidler, Garry Tidler, Tipton Police Department, *Tipton Tribune*, Joe Van Bibber, John C. Walker, Susan Ramsay Warren, Joe Watson, Joan Wray, and Ken Ziegler.

Photographs listing no source are from the archives of the Tipton County Historical Society or my own collection. I regret that I could not use all the photographs submitted.

Introduction

The pioneers who founded Tipton County were hardy, hardworking, determined, and brave. Responding to a promise of inexpensive land, they migrated from the east and south, traversing an uncharted, primitive landscape amid unknowable, life-threatening hardships.

In 1830, Allen Goodpasture walked all the way from Fort Wayne to secure title to real estate in what would become Tipton County. On the long, lonely return trip through the wilderness, Goodpasture encountered a severe snowstorm that lasted all night and obliterated the trail. To ensure that he would not lose his way, he walked round and round a small sapling next to the path throughout the night. When dawn finally came and the snowfall ceased, he could see the blazed road and reached home safely. Soon after, he returned to his newly acquired land, where he lived until his death in 1865.

When Sarah McCullough migrated to Tipton County from Kentucky as a young girl in 1831, her family brought a wagonload of flax for weaving cloth for their garments and cured meat from 13 head of hogs.

William Wimer hiked to Tipton County from western Virginia in 1843. Paths were few, and the rugged journey took him six weeks. Through hard work and grit, he eventually was able to buy land, build a home, and raise a family with his wife in Tetersburg.

Mary Ann and George Brown came to the county in 1864 in search of affordable land on which to build a home. Settling south of Windfall, they found nothing but a few houses planted in a great swamp. However, they stuck it out, clearing and "ditching" 100 acres on which they built a home and farmed.

Tipton County was still a wilderness in 1841 when Zerelda Ellen Jones and her family settled into the Normanda area. Throughout her long life, she often spoke of those early years when wolves howled outside her home. Like Jones, Sylvanus Bilby, born in 1828, reported at the 1911 Old Settler's Meeting a time when hordes of "wild animals of about every description" lived in the forests and swamps of Tipton County. "The nights were made hideous with the soul-racking howls of the wolves," he said.

Although the Indiana Territory was somewhat populated in 1816 when Indiana became the 19th state, there is no record of permanent settlements for that time in what would become Tipton County—and little wonder. The land was largely composed of swamps and nearly impenetrable forests that never felt the warmth of sunlight on their floors. Besides that, wild animals—bears, wolves, bobcats, and even panthers—posed a continual threat to the well-being of anyone who dared penetrate their territory.

Despite the natural hazards, an increasing number of settlers were arriving, placing pressure on Gov. James B. Ray (1825–1831) for substantive "internal improvements" in the form of roads and navigable waterways. Ray, like many Hoosiers, believed the surest means to that end was securing rights-of-way through Indian land, and once obtained, growth and commerce would follow. To achieve that end, Ray proposed a treaty with tribal leaders.

Enter a highly regarded, 40-year-old Indian agent named John Tipton, who earned his reputation fighting Tecumseh at the Battle of Tippecanoe. Tipton, the namesake for both the county and the county seat, was born in eastern Tennessee in 1786 and migrated to southern Indiana in 1807. Two years later, at the age of 23, he joined a militia company of mounted riflemen. By the time his military service came to an end seven years later, he had progressed to the rank of general, prompting an appointment as Indian agent by Pres. James Monroe in 1823.

In 1826, when Governor Ray needed a facilitator to oversee treaty negotiations with the Wea, Ottawa, Potawatomi, and Miami tribes, he called on General Tipton. Thanks to Tipton's tough bargaining skills, in little more than a month, the Mississinewa Treaty was signed. As a result, the government acquired the northwest part of Indiana, including land that would become the northern segment of Tipton County. The southern portion, however, would remain under the jurisdiction of Hamilton County until 1844, when the Indiana State Legislature recognized the new county of Tipton.

By then, settlers were arriving steadily, forging new lives, forming communities, starting businesses—like barrel factories, cabinet shops, and wagon and boat manufacturing—and drawing resources from the extensive forestland. Swamps were drained to allow the county's vastly fertile soil to be farmed. Consequently, agriculture soon became integral to the county's identity and its lifeblood.

Like farming, the impact of railroads on Tipton County's development cannot be overstated. Rails brought people, commerce, and jobs. They connected the local economies to the nation. During the early part of the 20th century, passenger trains arrived in Tipton three times a day, every day—at 8:40 a.m., 1:50 p.m., and 8:50 p.m. Hobbs, Goldsmith, Jackson Station, Kempton, Sharpsville, and Windfall had their own depots, too, and experienced growth. The introduction in 1899 of the electric interurban system increased business in downtown Tipton and the county as well. More business brought more opportunities, which in turn brought more people, families, schools, culture, and churches. The community was blossoming.

For a while, Tipton was a microcosm of a sophisticated, metropolitan city, offering many of the same amenities. Today, although empty lots occupy spaces on which thriving businesses once stood, the county's vibrant past can still be sensed—the almost constant rumblings of steam locomotives; public gatherings on the courthouse square, from balloon ascensions to war bond rallies; the awe-inspiring staircase leading to the main floor of the cavernous and unforgettable Carnegie library; the live theatrical productions, from classic opera to bawdy vaudeville on the Martz Theatre's stage or at some makeshift venue under the stars; 10¢-a-week newspapers with reporting so thorough that an out-of-town dinner guest was worthy of page 1; 15¢ roast beef dinners; pin boys; Blue Devil sundaes; county basketball tourneys; Hal Roach comedy carnivals; and packed churches.

Rather than a detailed, in-depth exploration of Tipton County's rich history, the 200-plus photographs filling the following pages are meant to provide readers an overview—a glimpse—of Tipton County's past and how it arrived at its present. Enjoy the journey!

One

FOUNDING AND FOUNDERS

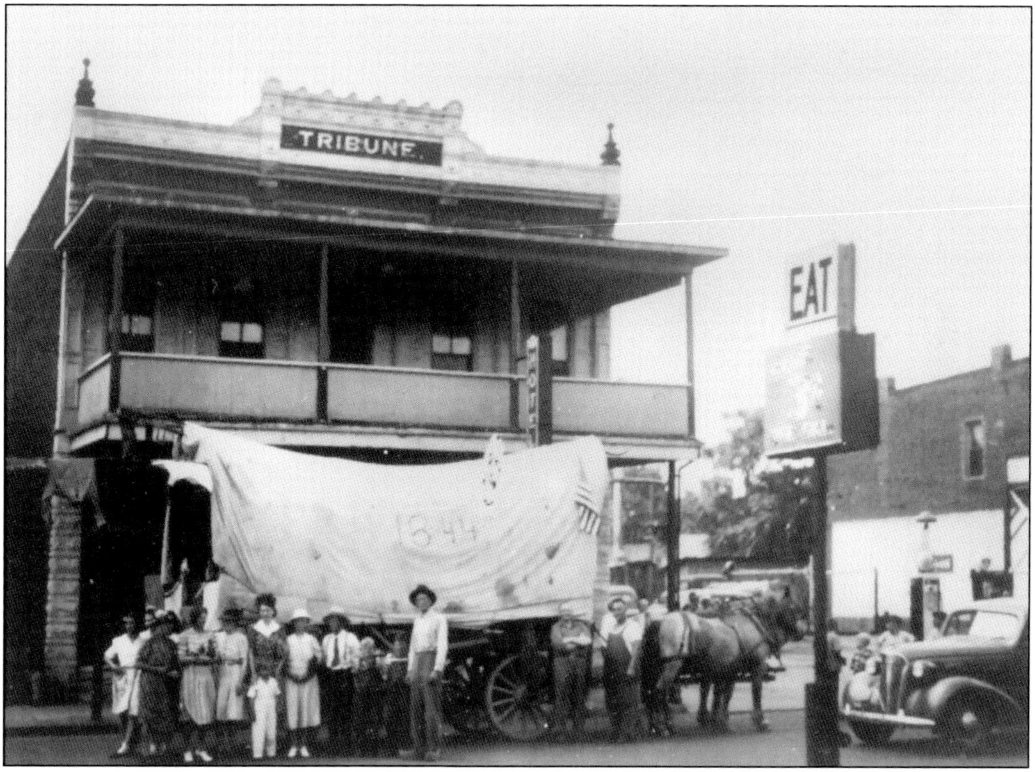

Tipton County's centennial celebration in 1944 featured Roscoe Shockney's covered wagon, which he drove into Tipton from Windfall. Besides Shockney, the pioneer vehicle transported nine passengers and an array of pioneer farming tools and implements. The 12-mile journey took the wagon more than four hours. It is parked here in front of the *Tipton Tribune*'s East Jefferson Street office. (John O'Banion.)

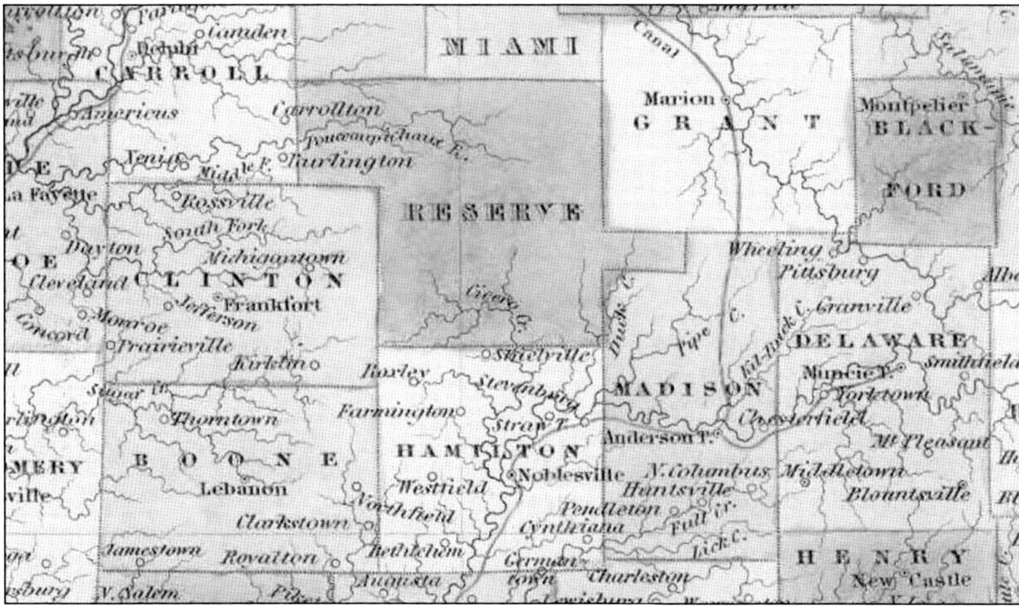

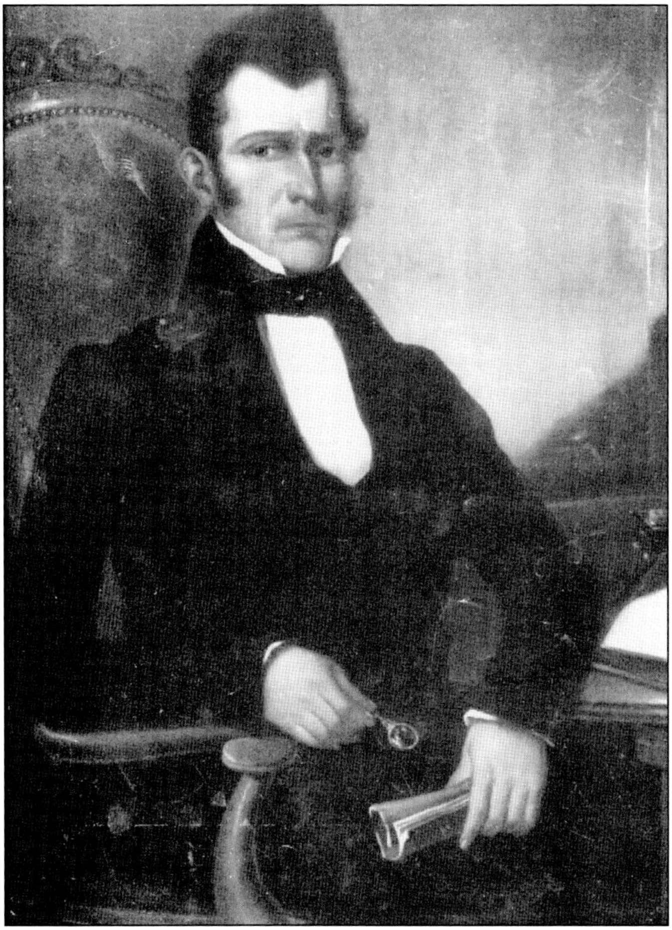

An act of the Indiana General Assembly on January 15, 1844, carved a new county from the Miami Reserve. The county and the county seat were named for Gen. John Tipton, who came to prominence fighting with the Indiana militia in the 1811 Battle of Tippecanoe, for which he earned the rank of brigadier general. After his military service, Tipton became Harrison County sheriff, 1816–1819, and a member of the Indiana House of Representatives, 1819–1823. He was elected to the US Senate in 1828, filling the vacancy resulting from the death of James Noble. Tipton was reelected in 1831 but declined to run again. He died at the age of 52 in 1839 in Cass County. Renderings by artist George Winter in 1837 depict the only known likenesses of Tipton. (Above, David Rumsey Map Collection; left, Tipton County Historical Society.)

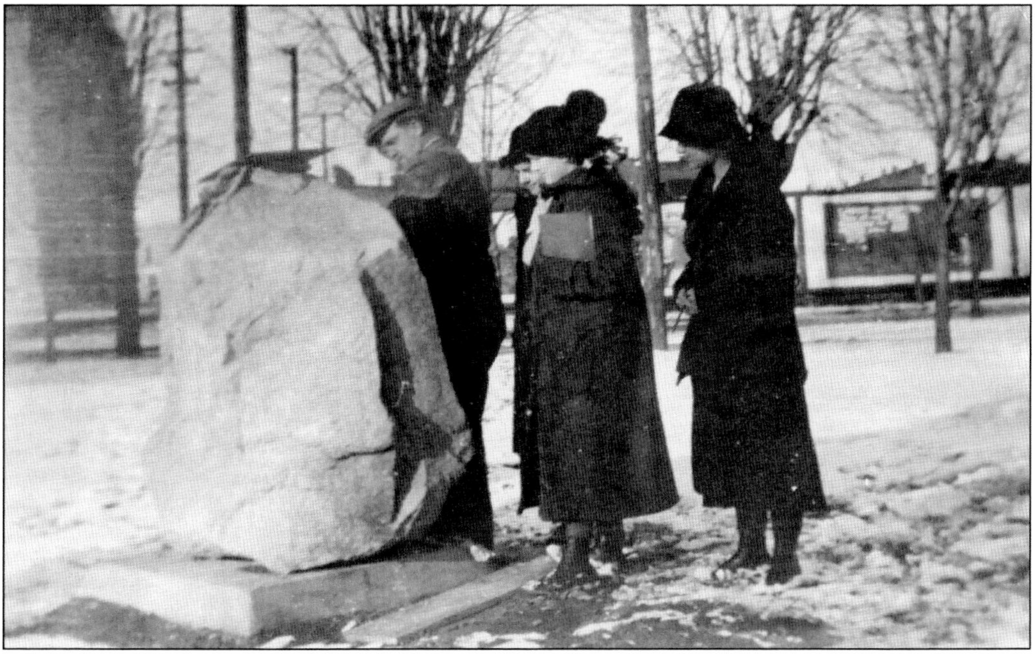

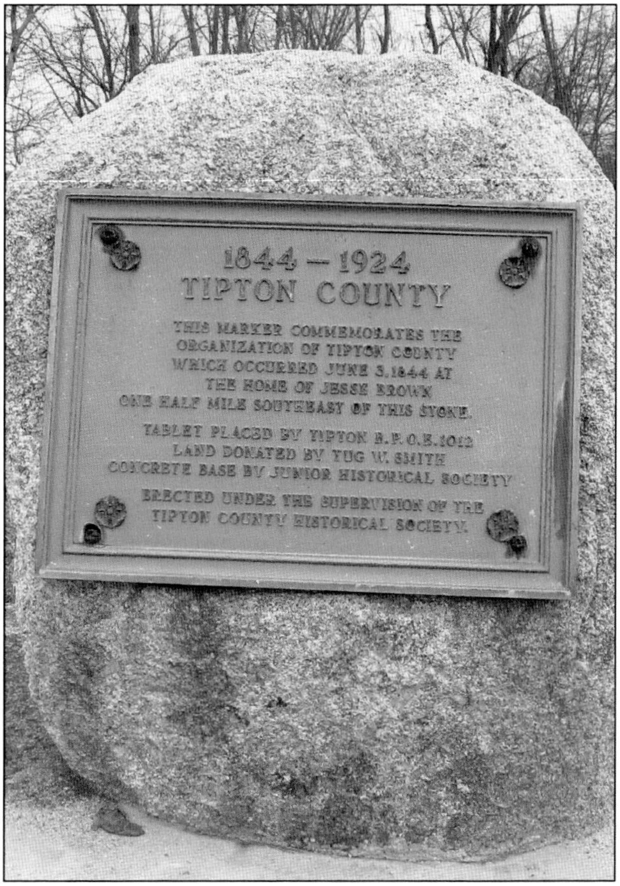

Above, Ruth and Eunice McGraw, Marie Purvis, and an unidentified gentleman preview the bronze tablet and boulder honoring Gen. John Tipton at the Tipton Public Library on December 11, 1916. It was a project of the Tipton County Historical and Junior Historical Societies, headed by librarian Ida Matthews and dedicated as part of the state's centennial celebration. The tablet reads, "General John Tipton, 1786–1839, Pioneer Leader, Hero of Tippecanoe, Indian Agent, Statesman, Centennial Memorial 1816–1916." The boulder came from the farm of Ora Richardson, who hauled it into town on a mud boat. The monument was relocated to the courthouse lawn when the library was razed in 1980. Right, the Jesse Brown marker, commemorating the organization of Tipton County, stands on the corner of County Roads 300 South and 100 West on land donated by Tug W. Smith. (Above, library archives; right, author's collection.)

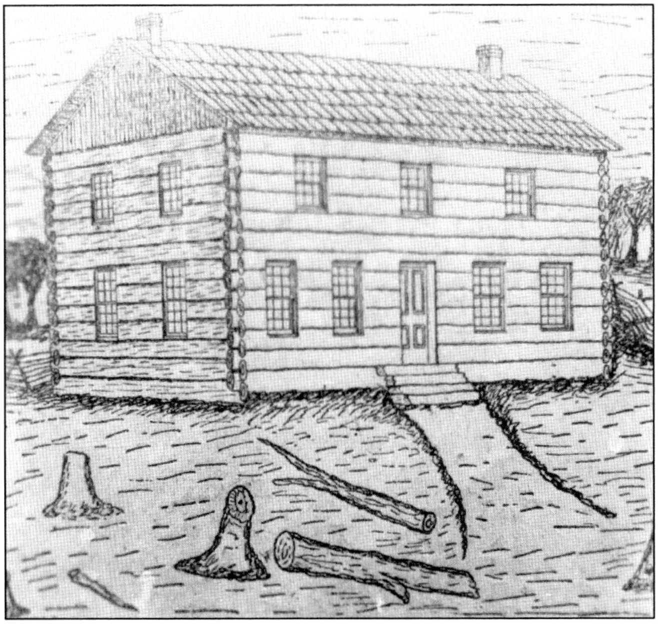

Early in 1845, the Tipton County assessor, Jesse Brown, advertised for sealed proposals for a two-story frame courthouse, 20 feet wide by 24 feet long, to be completed by June. The bid went to George Tucker. The total cost—which included surveying, clearing land, finishing the rooms, labor, materials, and furnishings—was approximately $1,200. This sketch illustrates the finished building. It was destroyed by fire in 1857. (Library archives.)

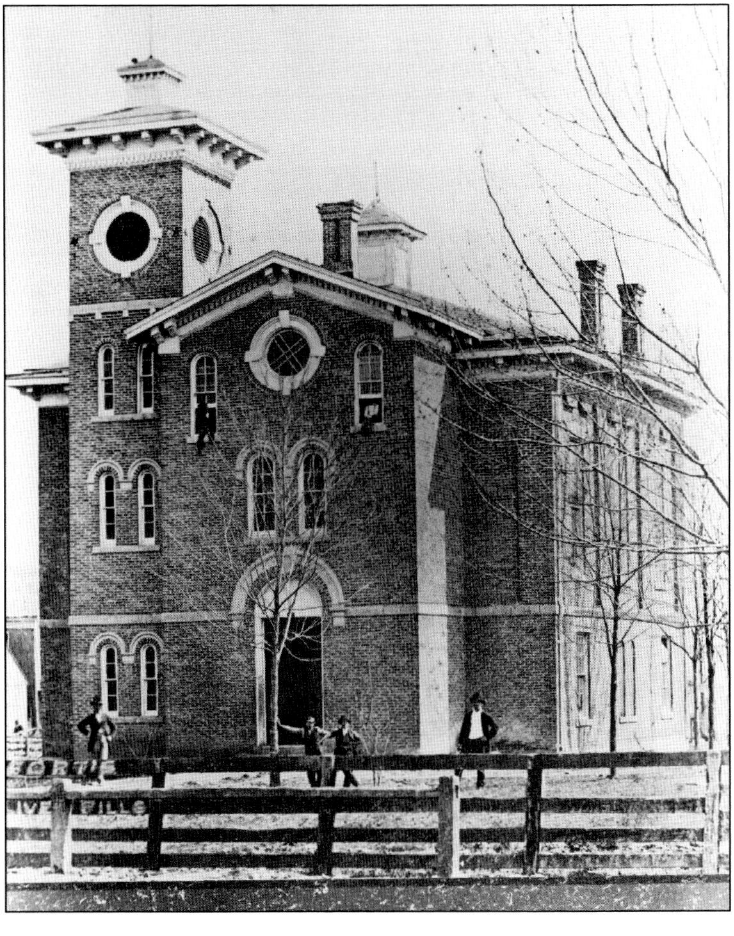

Tipton County's second courthouse was built of fireproof brick and limestone in 1858–1859 by a Hamilton County contractor for $10,000. The building's first floor housed the county offices, and the upper story contained the courtroom. The structure was torn down in 1892 to make way for a new, modern courthouse. N.S. Martz of Tipton bought the used bricks for the construction of his Fame Canning Company. (John O'Banion.)

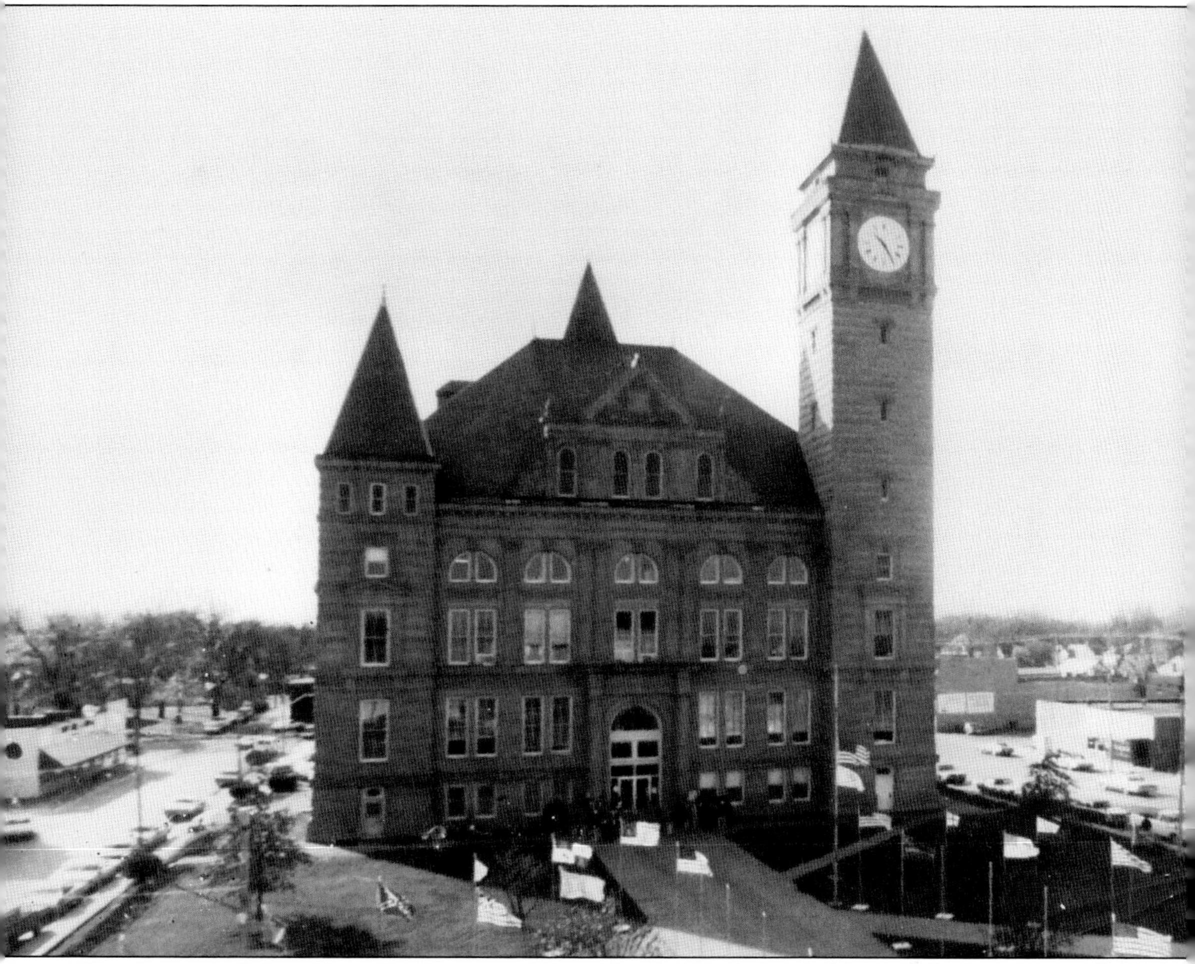

Construction of the current Tipton County Courthouse was completed in 1894 for $183,000, and it has stood as a quiet sentry over the community for the nearly 120 years since. Its 206-foot-high clock tower defines the Tipton skyline and serves as the city's landmark, recognizable for many miles in every direction. The building contains 45 rooms on three floors. County offices occupy the first floor, and the second is dedicated to the judiciary, with two courtrooms, judges' quarters, and meeting rooms. The top-of-the-line Seth Thomas clock cost the county $1,425, well below the market price at that time. Its dial is 10 feet in diameter, and its bell weighs 3,000 pounds. Although the community initially accused the commissioners of corruption for spending more than $8,800 for the building's elegant furnishings and elaborate fixtures, the community later admitted that anything cheaper would have been a pronounced mistake. (John O'Banion.)

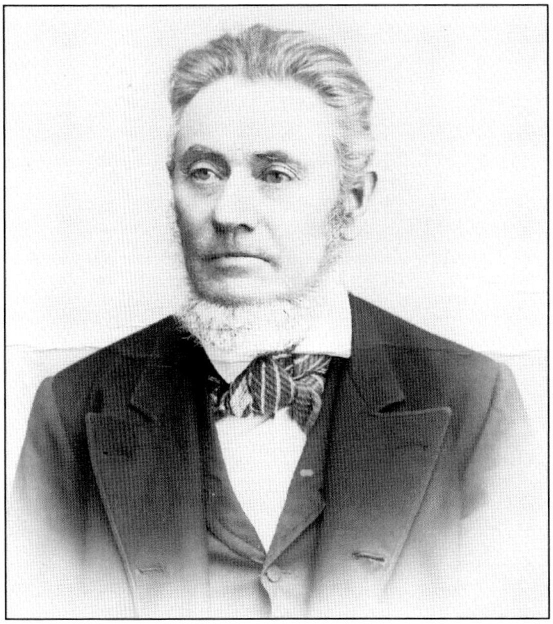

Harrison A. Woodruff of Tipton was born in 1819. He moved his family to Tipton County from Johnson County in 1842. Shortly after settling into the county, he established a tavern at the corner of Jefferson and Main Streets and later owned a hotel, which was occupied by the Independent Order of Odd Fellows. (Library archives.)

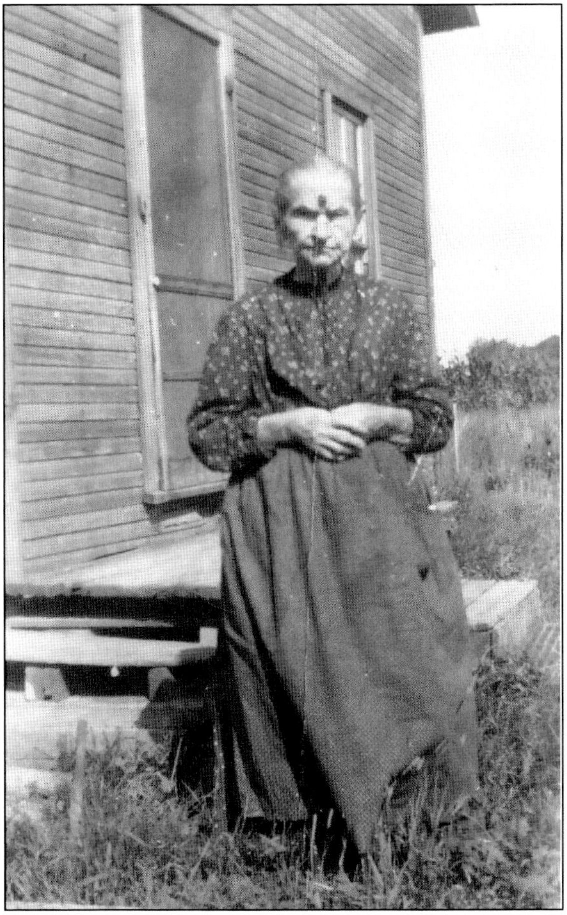

Zerelda Ellen Montgomery Jones was born in Jay County in 1833. She moved to Tipton County with her family in 1841 and married Thomas B. Jones in 1851. Later in life, she was known throughout the county as Grandma Ellen and often spoke of her early pioneer life in the wilderness. This photograph was taken at the Old Settler's Meeting September 1, 1923. She died the following month. (Library archives.)

This photograph of Amy M. Ruddick Stewart, wife of Stephen Stewart, is dated February 21, 1896. She was 72. Amy was born in Bartholomew County, where she and Stephen married in April 1848. They settled in Tipton County in 1855, acquiring land along Normanda Pike. They donated a plot of land to the township for a cemetery, which still bears their name. (Linda Stewart Peters.)

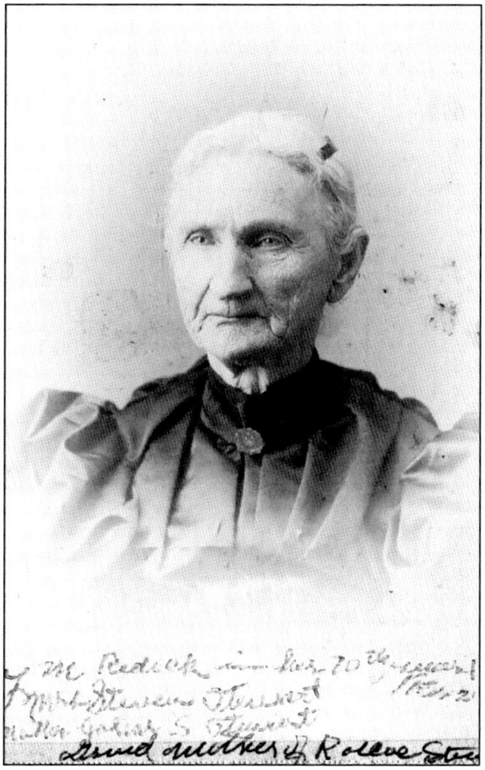

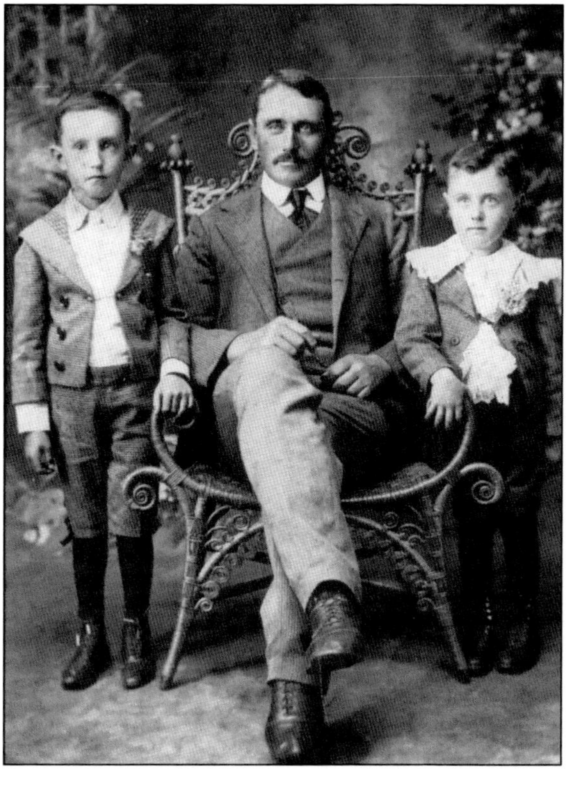

Stephen and Amy Stewart were parents to eight children, seven of whom spent their lives in Tipton County working and developing the land. They were Robert O., William P., Catherine, Amy, Mary Jane, Laura, and John, who is pictured here with his two young sons, Rosco, left, and Otis. (Linda Stewart Peters.)

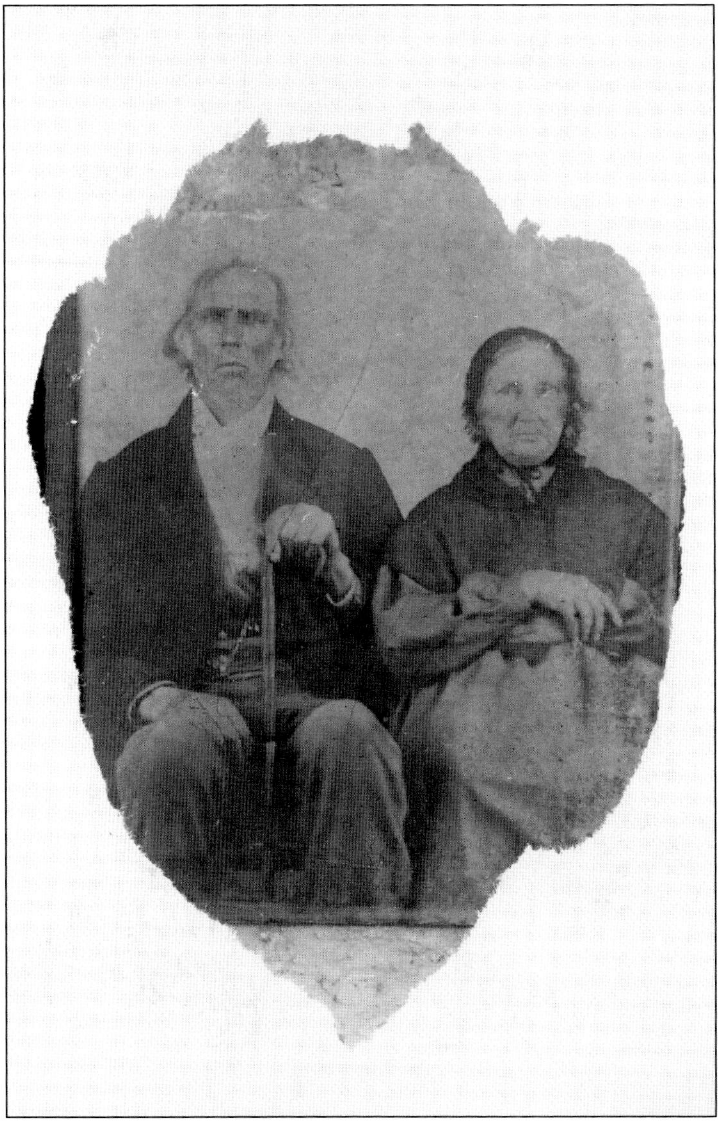

John F. and Sarah Walmsley Newkirk migrated from Pennsylvania to Tipton County in 1848, settling on property that is now County Road 100 West, just north of 300 South. John was born in 1799 in Pennsylvania, and Sarah was born in 1804 in Ohio. The Newkirks died in Tipton County and are buried in Sumner Cemetery. They had 10 children.

George W. Bragg, taller of the two bearded gentlemen near the center, was a Civil War veteran, who lost his left hand in the Battle of Missionary Ridge. In 1866, at 22, he became Hamilton County sheriff. He later settled in Windfall, married Laura Rush, and farmed. He became a preacher for Hazel Dell Friends Church. George was part of the crew that built Tipton County's first brick courthouse. (Morris Stillabower Jr.)

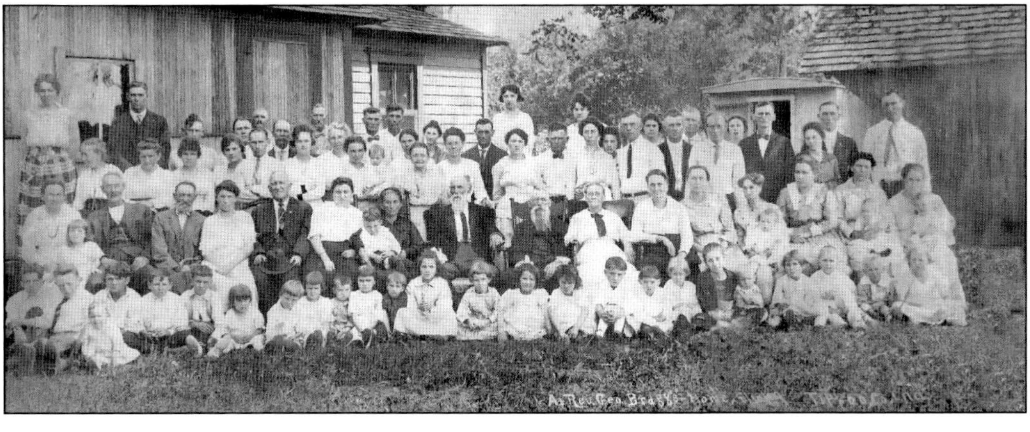

Mary Jane Beam Sharp poses for this photograph outside her house in Shilo, located in the county south of where 900 West crosses 400 South, around 1920. She was married to James "Mack" Madison Sharp. (Penny Manier.)

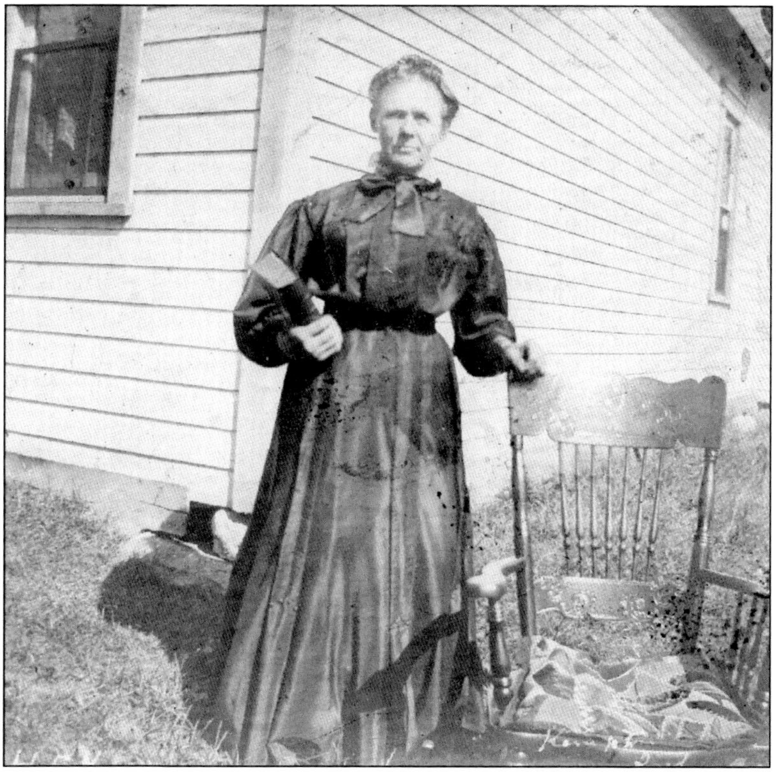

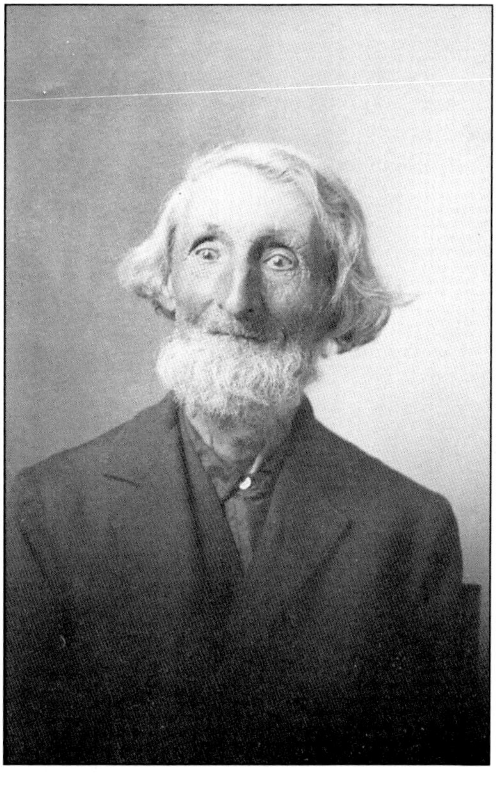

A native of Kentucky, James "Mack" Madison Sharp arrived in Ekin in 1849 at the age of 19. At the outbreak of the Civil War, he joined the 75th Indiana Regiment, Company B, serving as a cook. He fought in several battles and was shot once in the hand. He married Mary Jane Beam. At the time of his death in 1923, he lived southeast of Kempton and was thought to be the oldest man in that part of the county. He was 93. (Penny Manier.)

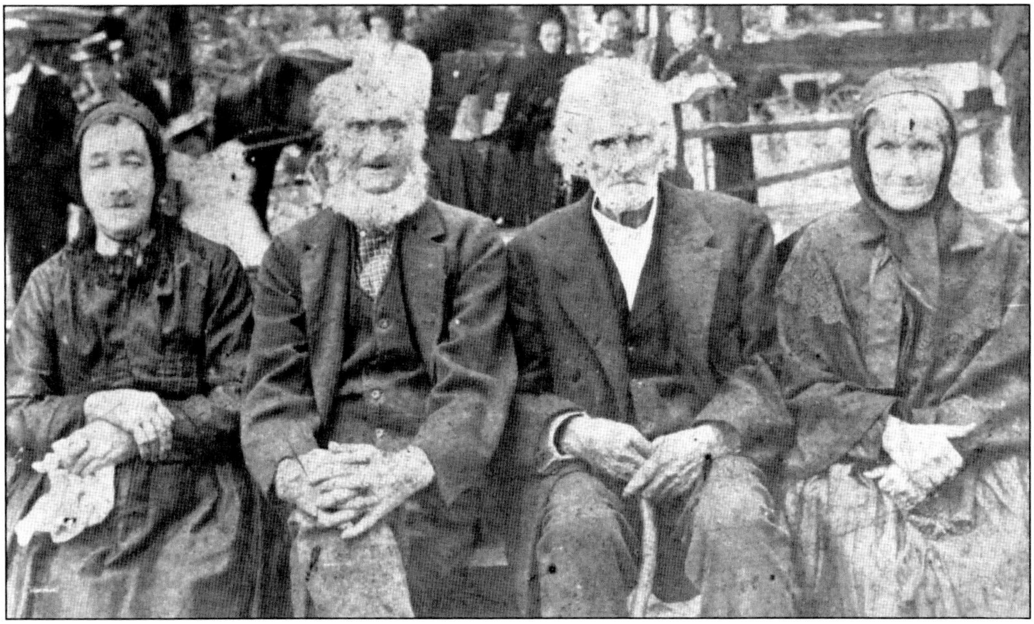

The Small family members are, from left to right, Eliza and Jessie Small and Archibald and Mary Ann Coats Small. Archibald settled in Jefferson Township, near the county line, in 1837. He later donated the land that became Small Cemetery. His first wife died in 1839 and was the first reported death in Jefferson Township. His marriage two years later to Mary Ann was the first in that township. In his later years, Archie was county recorder and auditor. He died in 1902 at age 93. Because of his immense popularity throughout the county, his body was placed in the courthouse, where friends and associates paid their last respects. The Smalls raised seven daughters. Pictured below are, from left to right, (sitting) Lucinda, Melinda Ann, and Sarah Ellen; (standing) Hettie Rosetta, Josephine "Piney," Marinda Olive, and Marietta. (Both, Penny Manier.)

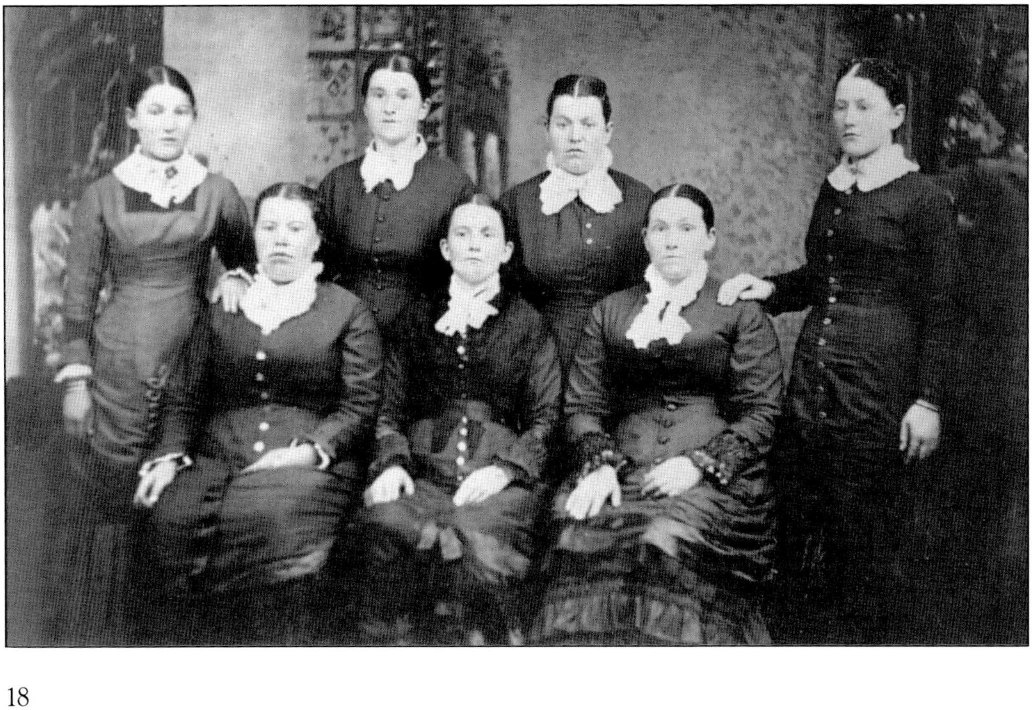

William Wimer hiked to Tipton County from western Virginia in 1843. He worked for various farmers and purchased a homestead from John Longfellow in Tetersburg for $50, which he earned by splitting rails at $1 per hundred. Wimer then paid the government $1.25 per acre for the 160-acre tract. He married Julia Wolford, and the young pioneer couple produced 10 children. William died in 1891, and Julia died in 1906. They are buried in the Wolford Cemetery at Goldsmith. (Viola Jones.)

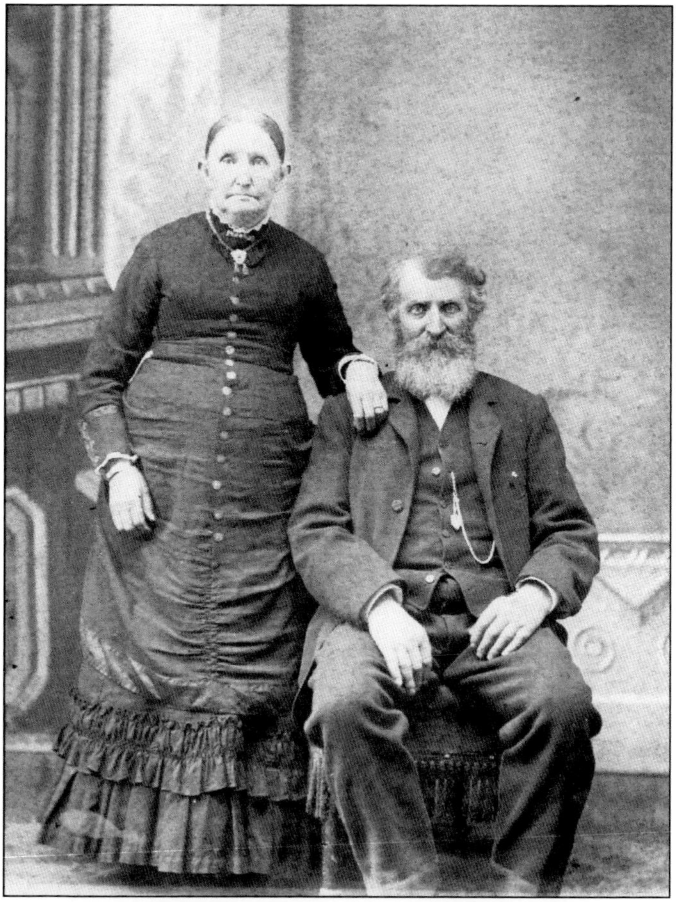

Elizabeth Goodykoontz was one of Tipton County's pioneer schoolteachers. She was born in Hamilton County in 1847 and married John W. Goodykoontz, who died in 1876. Her only child, a son, Beecher Goodykoontz, died in 1928. Elizabeth died October 26, 1933. (Janet Driver.)

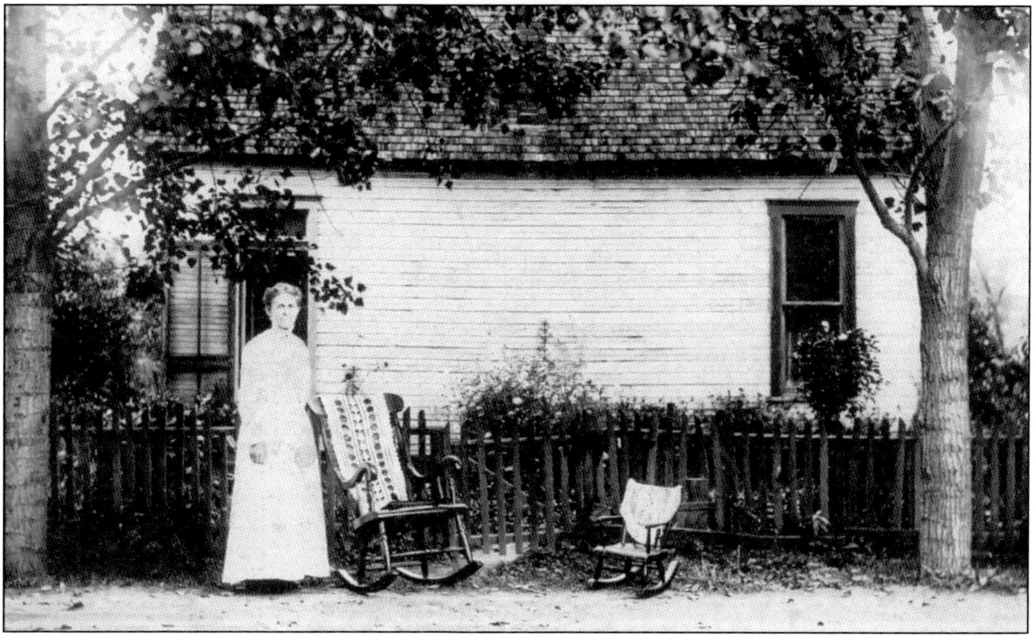

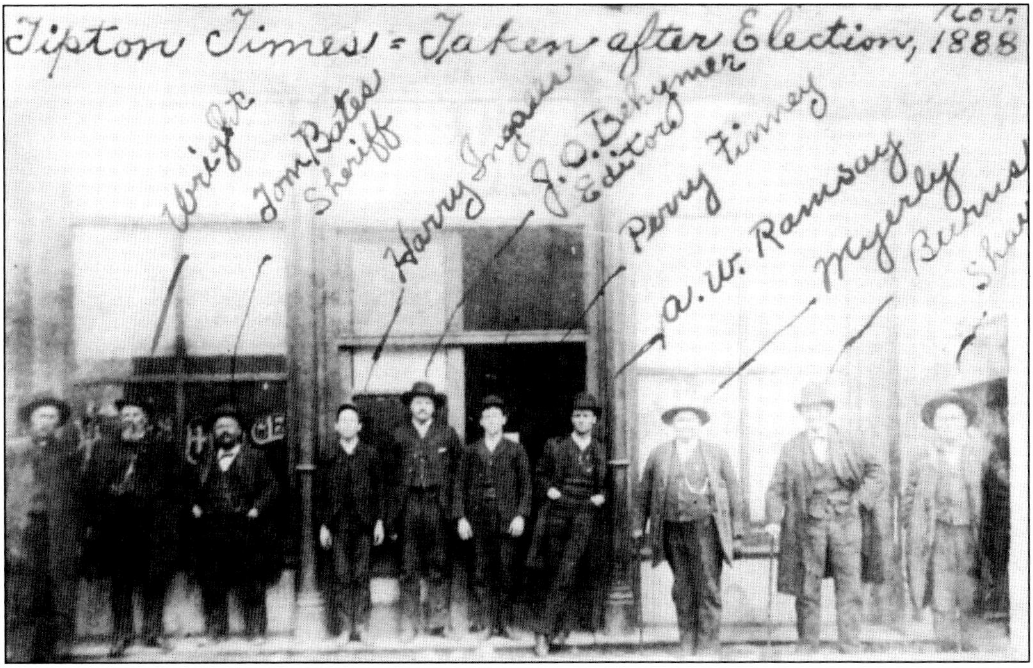

This photograph, taken outside the home of the *Tipton Times* following the general election of November 1888, was mentioned in a 1946 'Round Town column. The article identified some of the men, from left to right, as follows: unidentified, Morgan Wright, Sheriff Tom Bates, *Times* employee Harry Ingalls, *Times* editor J.O. Behymer, *Times* pressman Perry Finney, *Times* publisher Arch Ramsay, Tipton County treasurer George W. Myerly, ? Burns, and ? Shaw. (Library archives.)

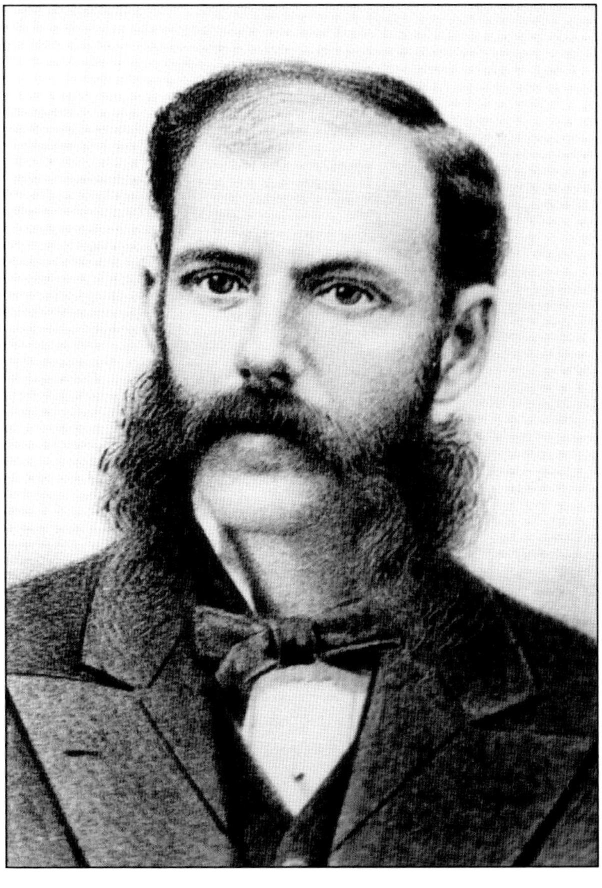

Today's *Tribune* evolved from the city's first newspaper, *Tipton County Democrat*, started in 1855. To compete, Marvin W. Pershing founded the Republican-slanted *Tipton Advocate*. He ran it until becoming postmaster in 1901. Pershing authored two local history books before moving to Indianapolis in 1916 to work for the secretary of state. He continued writing for the *Tribune* until his death in 1942. He is buried in Fairview Cemetery. (Rick Curnutt.)

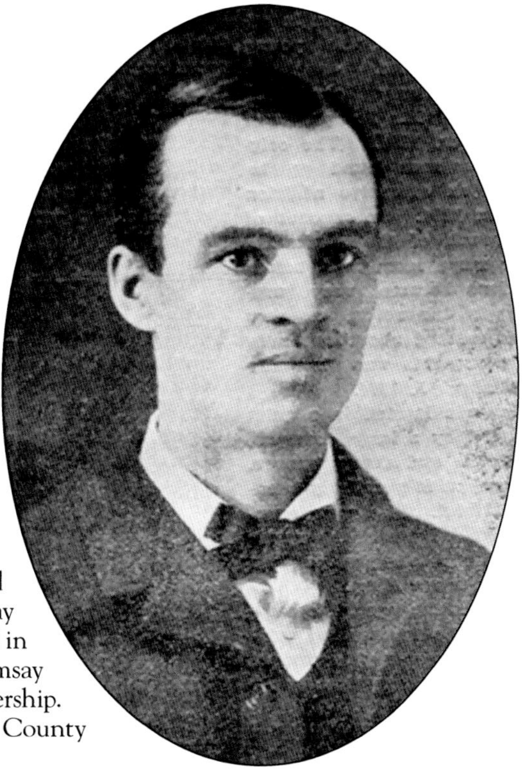

It was as if ink ran through the veins of Archibald W. "Arch" Ramsay Jr., right, born in Tipton in 1865. He was the son of the *Democrat's* first printer, Arch Ramsay Sr. Arch Jr. learned the printer's trade at the *Advocate* and honed the rest of his journalism skills at other publications. In 1895, he and J.E. Anderson launched the *Daily Tribune* amid several other newspapers that served the county. Ramsay's future partner, Ira M. O'Banion, below, was born in 1859 in Madison County. While serving as Tipton County clerk, he bought Anderson's interest in the *Tribune* in 1898. O'Banion tended to circulation and advertising sales, leaving Ramsay to concentrate on editorial matters. Ramsay died in 1928; O'Banion died in 1950. Their sons F.N. Ramsay and C.L. O'Banion succeeded them in the partnership. (Right, Susan Ramsay Warren; below, Tipton County Historical Society.)

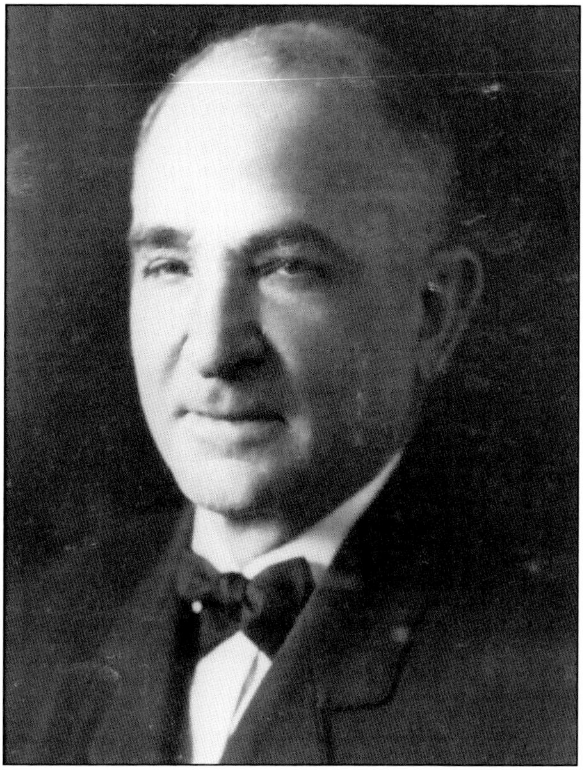

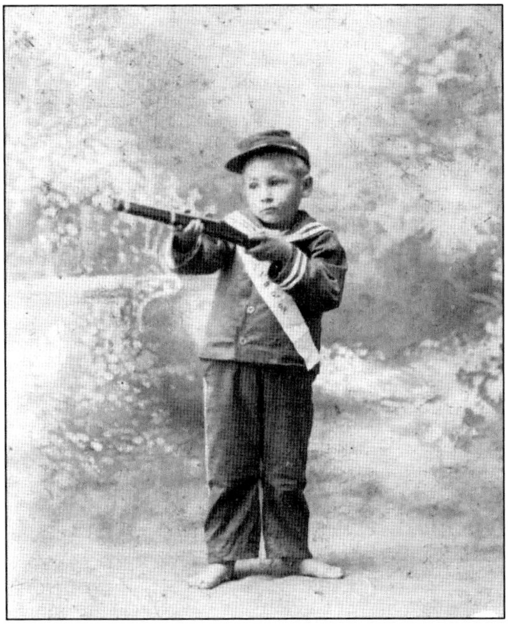

C.L. O'Banion, son of *Tipton Tribune* publisher Ira M. O'Banion, demonstrates his fine sharpshooting form. The photograph is dated 1898, the same year Ira entered partnership with Arch W. Ramsay Jr. at the *Tribune*. At the close of World War I, C.L. and Floyd N. Ramsay jointly purchased the business from their fathers. The two remained partners in the business until Floyd's death in 1943. (John O'Banion.)

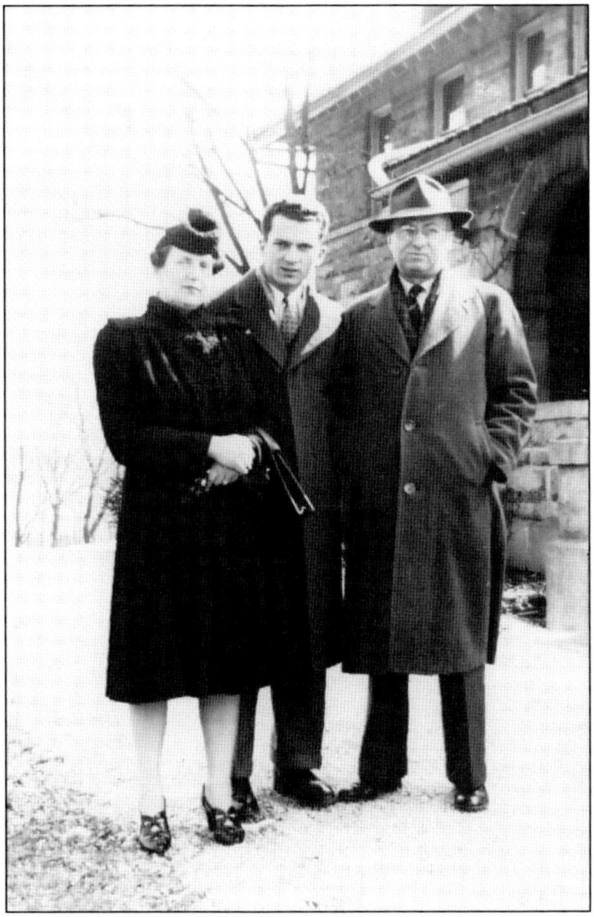

Former *Tribune* owner/editor Floyd N. "F.N." Ramsay, right, poses with wife Lilly and their son Jack at Indiana University, Bloomington, around 1942. F.N., born in 1890 in Tipton, met Lilly during his World War I Army service while stationed near Nantes, France. They married in 1919. Jack continued the family's tradition with Ramsay Printing Company, which he sold in the 1990s to his daughter and son-in-law, Susan and Ron Warren. (Susan Ramsay Warren.)

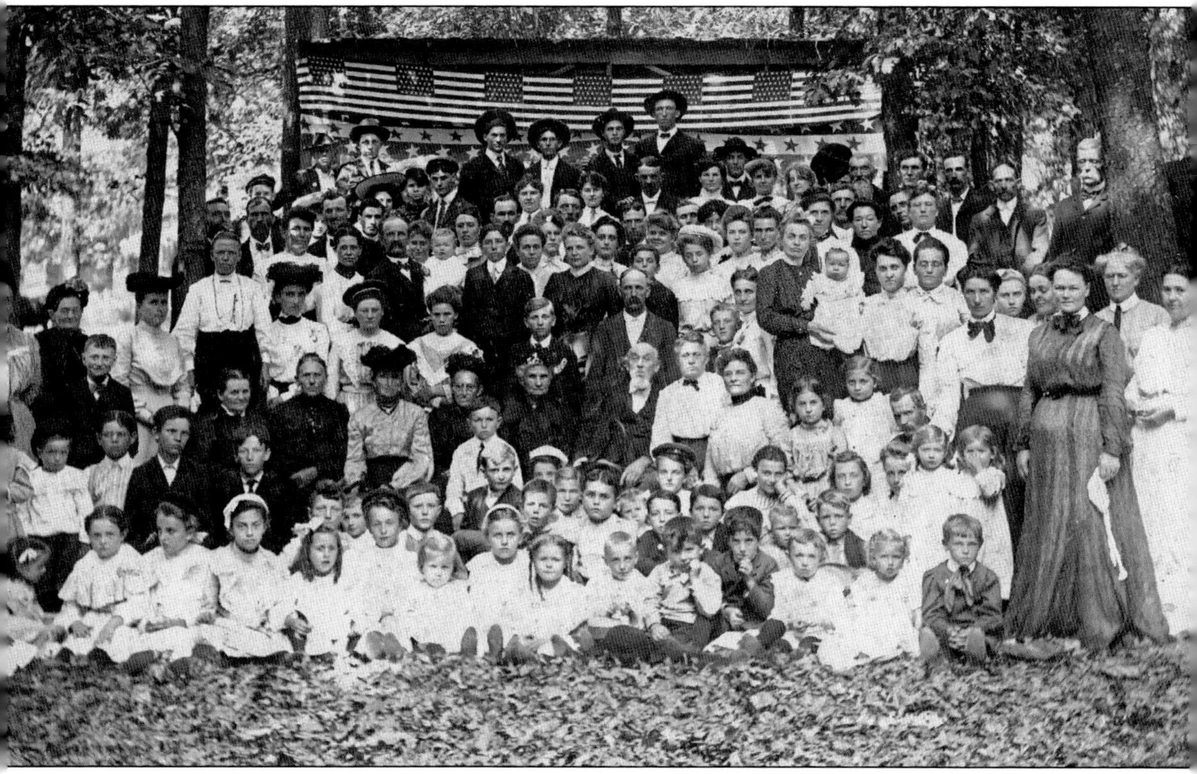

This photograph is believed to have been taken at an Old Settler's Reunion around 1900. When the first annual reunion met in 1883, real pioneers still lived in Tipton County. For the first few events, the early settlers were among the hundreds flocking to the Magnett Grove Woods in Goldsmith the first Saturday in September. However, when this photograph was taken, the number of pioneers was dwindling, but those who could continued to attend as long as they were able, renewing acquaintances and sharing memories of days past. The events featured music, food, games, speeches, sermons, and storytelling about pioneer days. When the last of the original old settlers passed, their children carried on the tradition and stretched the event from one to three days in later years. Old Settler's held its last reunion in 1991. (Viola Jones.)

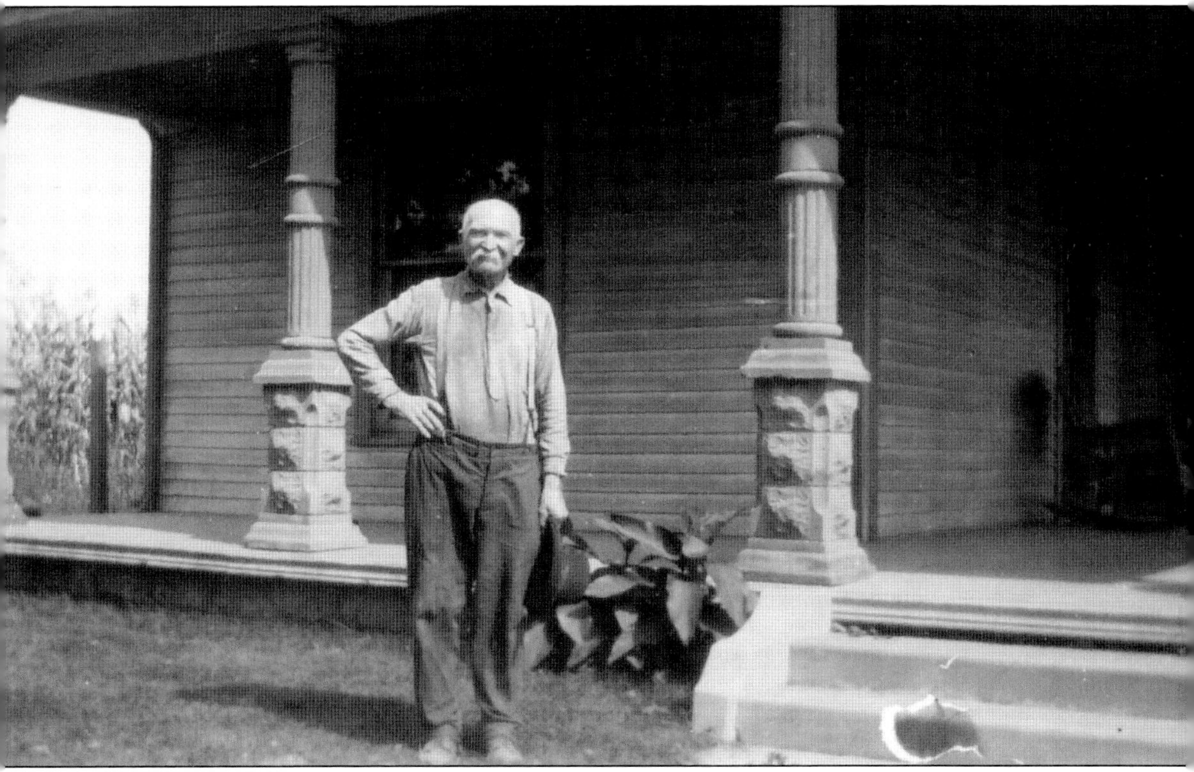

When Lafayette Jackson died July 4, 1929, at age 89, he was Tipton County's oldest native-born resident. Born April 25, 1840, near New Lancaster in a brick house built by his father, he moved to a farm northeast of Hobbs in 1869 after he married Amanda Carr. Jackson was highly respected and well liked, according to his obituary, which also states the following: "He was absolutely honest and reliable, his word being a bond." Jackson was a large landowner and one of the county's best-known stockmen. He is buried next to his wife in Cook Cemetery, located in the southeast corner of the county. Ida Matthews took this photograph in 1923. (Library archives.)

Two

Railroads

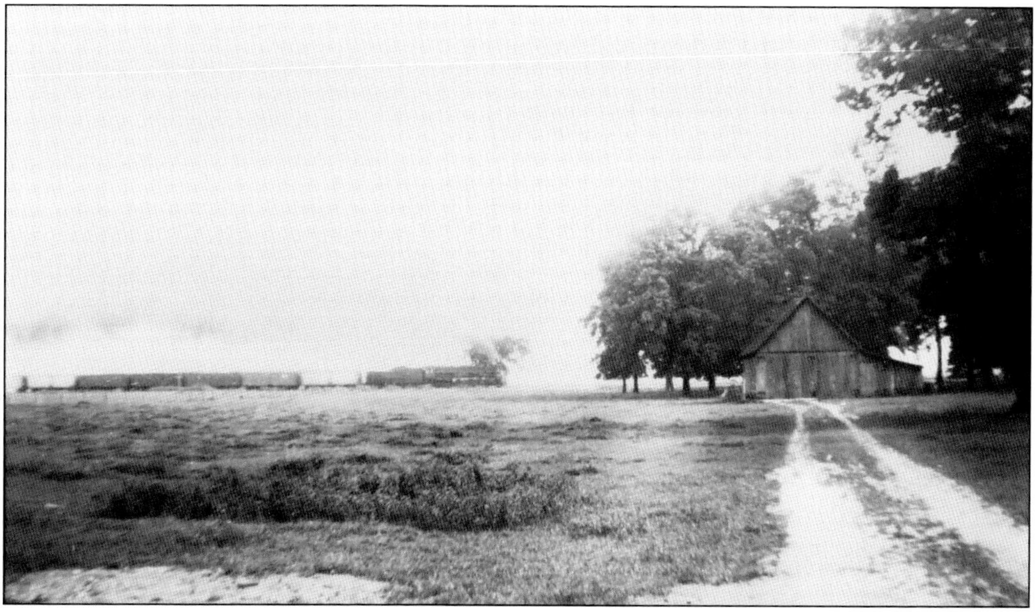

In the late 1840s, Tipton Countians lived an isolated life, but the railroads—and change—were coming. Tipton's first train reportedly ran to Indianapolis on August 4, 1853, over wooden rails that started near the East Madison Street bridge over Cicero Creek. Although the passengers paid their fares, they were expected to climb off the train whenever the cars derailed and set them back on the track. (Ken Ziegler.)

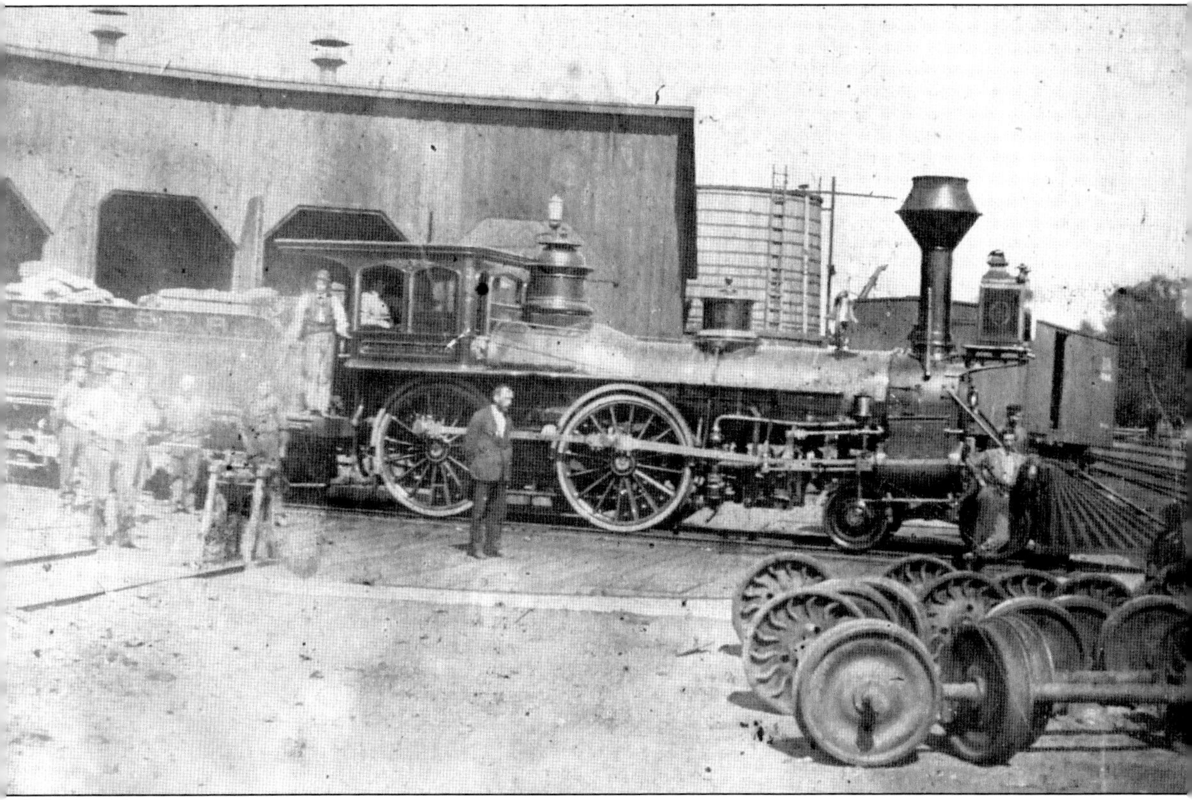

The Indianapolis, Peru & Chicago tracks arrived in Tipton in 1852. So eager were farmers to get their grain to market by rail that they donated rights-of-way, despite some old pioneers who insisted nothing could ever replace a good team of horses. The north-south tracks helped stimulate Tipton's growth, and when the Lafayette & Muncie Railroad laid east-west tracks through the county in 1875, railroad networks were generating local economies throughout the state. At the time the north-south and east-west tracks formed a junction, the area was undeveloped. By the turn of the century, the junction supported four hotels, four restaurants, four barbershops, and a grocery store. Tipton had become a division point with a 12-stall roundhouse, an icehouse, a coal house, and holding pens for livestock. Passenger trains, arriving from each direction, met at the junction three times a day. (Library archives.)

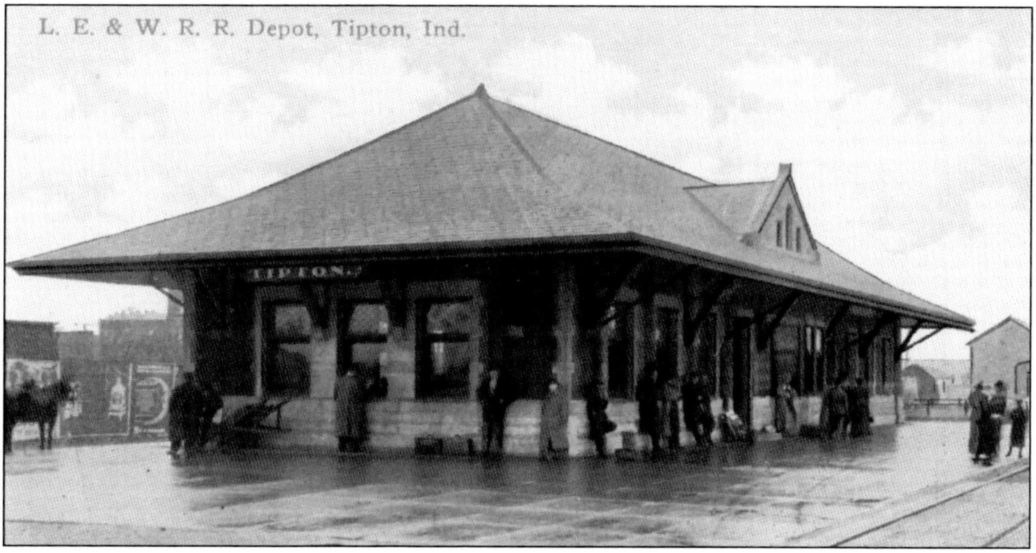

At the turn of the 20th century, the north-south Lake Erie & Western Railroad was under control of the New York Central. The design of the Tipton depot's styling is typical of New York Central, and similar depots were found in Lafayette, Frankfort, and Bloomington, Illinois. Built in 1902, Tipton's passenger depot (above) was an exquisite brick and concrete facility with marble floors, copper sheathing on the roof, brass downspouts, and leaded glass. It was in use for many decades, but after the Nickel Plate Railroad abandoned passenger service through Tipton, with north-south service ceasing to operate in 1932 and the east-west run ending in the mid-1950s, the building was put to use as office space and storage. Other towns in Tipton County boasting their own depots were Curtisville, Hobbs, Goldsmith, Jackson Station, Kempton (below), Sharpsville, and Windfall. The depots brought commerce, people, jobs, and growth to the communities. In many cases, depots were the towns' lifeblood, connecting them to the rest of the world. (Above, Alice Ricketts; below, library archives.)

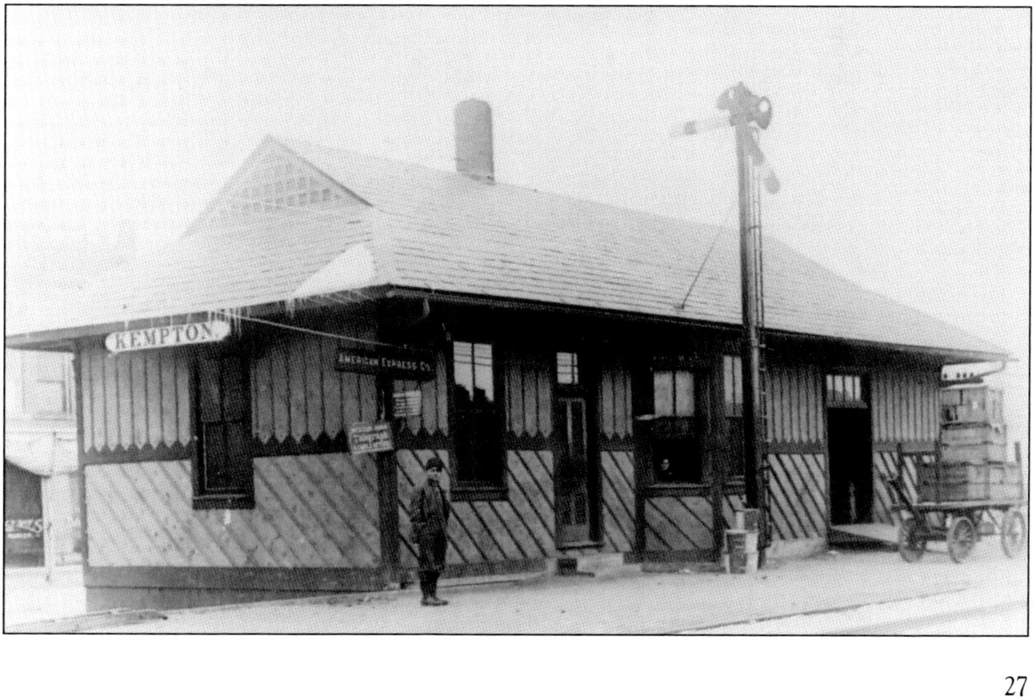

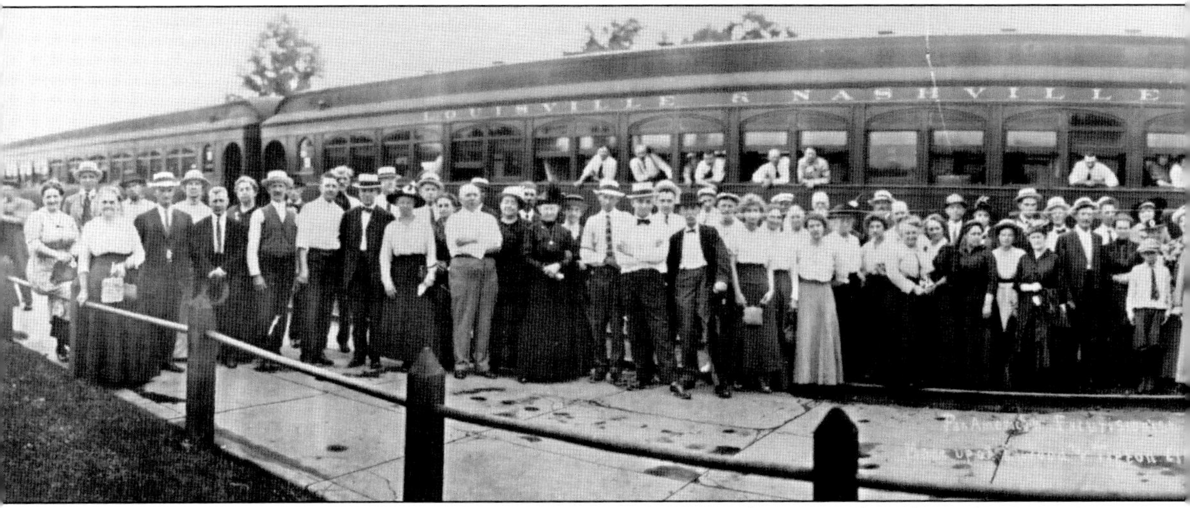

One hundred fifty-two passengers gathered at Tipton's LE&W depot on Thursday, July 15, 1915, to board five passenger coaches for a six-week, luxury excursion. The *Tipton Daily Tribune* reported that a crowd of hundreds was there to send off the "Pan-American Excursionists" making the trip under the auspices of the Elwood Fishing and Touring Club. After departing Tipton, the train made stops in Indianapolis, Louisville, Birmingham, Mobile, New Orleans, Houston, El Paso,

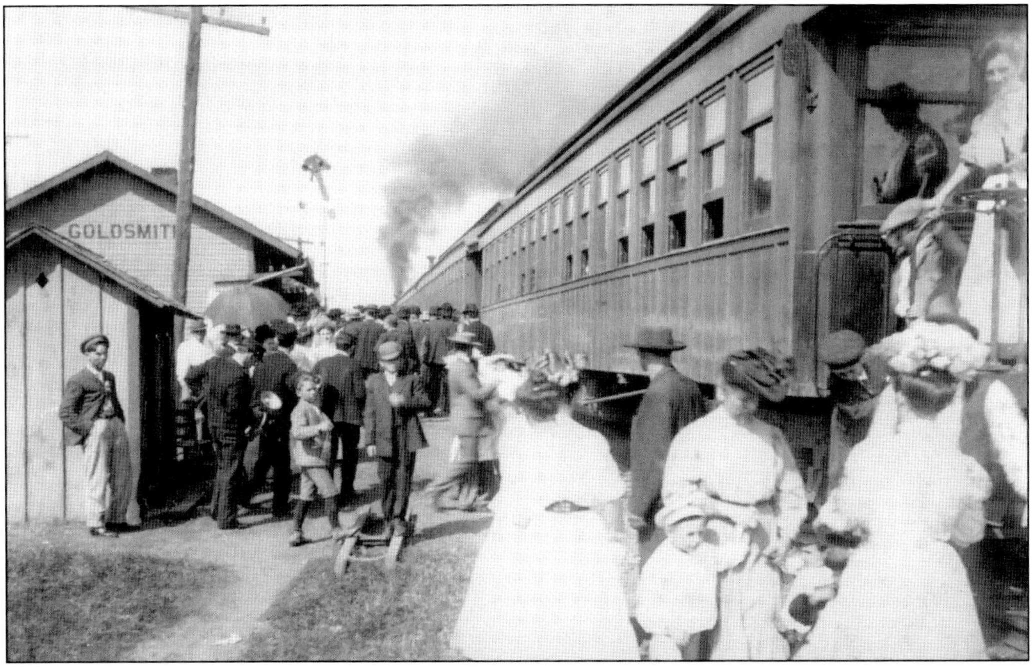

This undated photograph depicts the festive atmosphere experienced in Goldsmith when a trainload of passengers arrived at its depot. The westbound train, with its steaming locomotive, could have been headed to Frankfort or perhaps it brought visitors for the Old Settler's Meeting, held annually on the second Saturday of September. A band, likely the Goldsmith Band, greeted the arriving passengers. (Jeanie and Bob Robinson.)

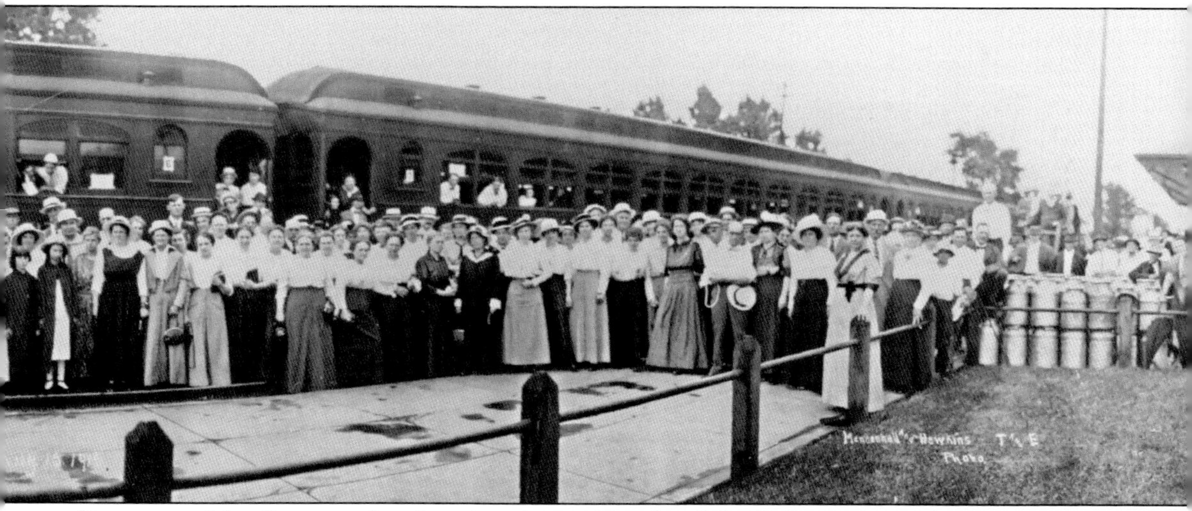

Tucson, and finally arrived in Los Angeles on Tuesday, July 27. From there, the Excursionists journeyed to San Diego, San Francisco, and Sacramento before leaving the Golden State and heading for home. They arrived back in Tipton on August 25. (Library archives.)

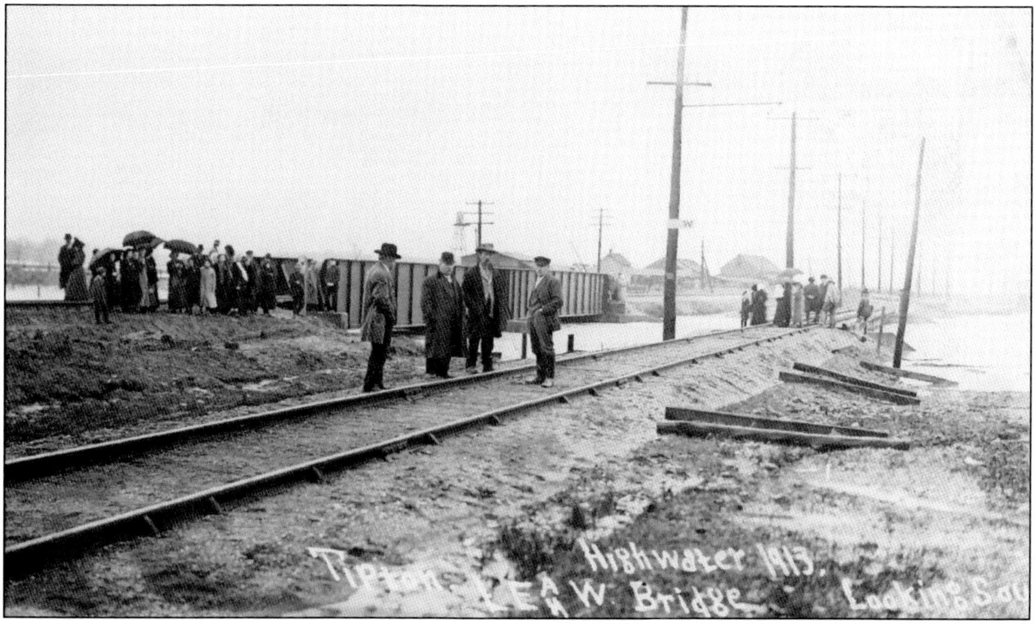

In the aftermath of the great storm that ripped through central Indiana March 21–23, 1913, railroad officials and others observe the flooded, impassable Lake Erie & Western Bridge, located south of Tipton. Although the bridge withstood the assault, rail and traction service was halted for at least two days while waiting for the floodwaters to recede. For more about the storm, see page 62.

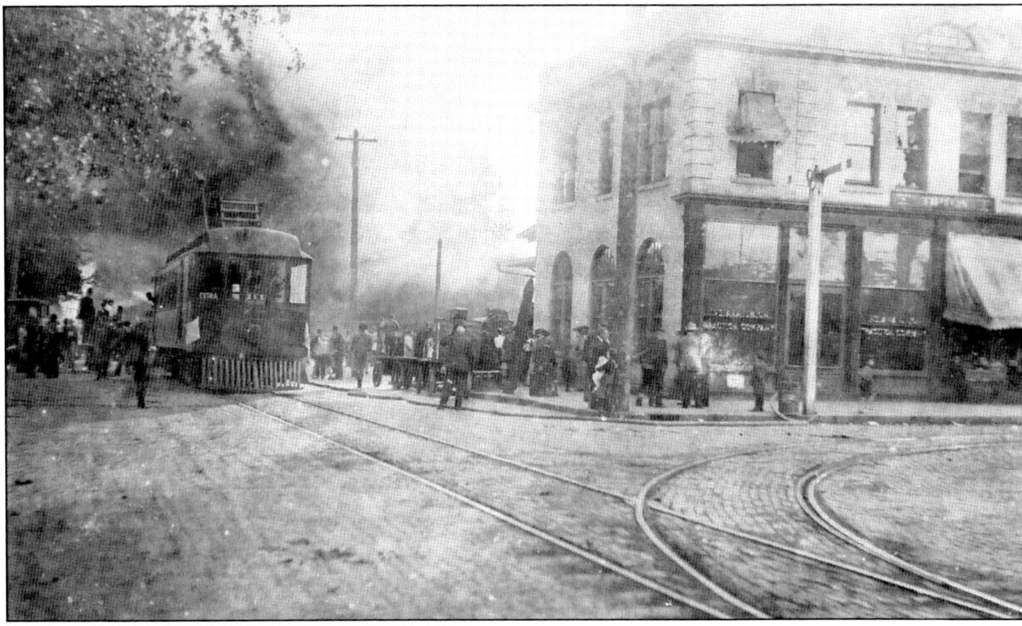

Introduction of the electric interurbans in 1899 gave steam-powered trains a run for their money. Offering efficiency and cheaper fares, interurbans quickly gained popularity, particularly for short trips, although the service connected communities throughout Indiana. The Depression and tougher competition from the railroad drove the interurbans out of service by the late 1930s. Tipton's interurban depot and freight office occupied the corner of Main and Madison Streets. (Tom Lett.)

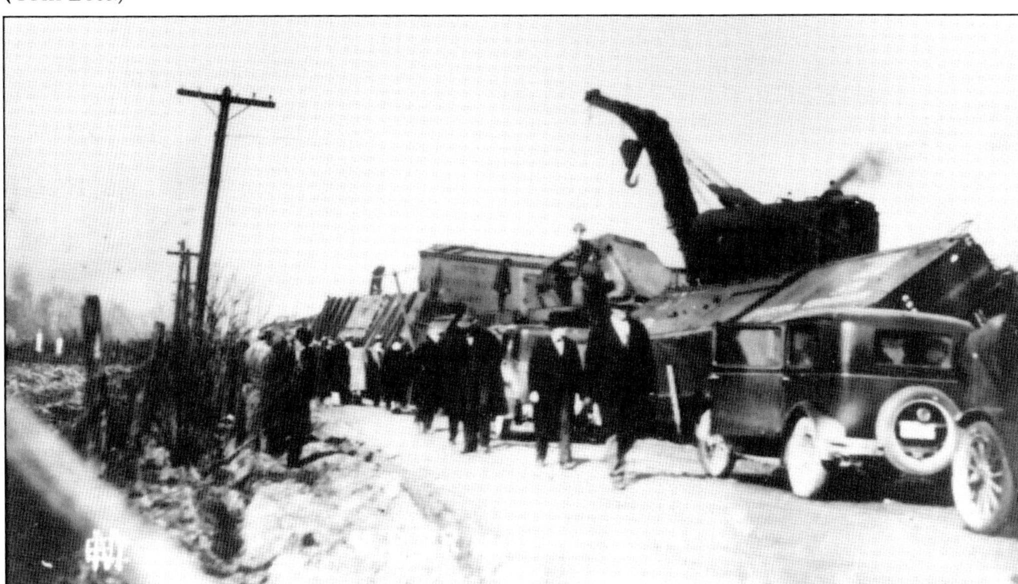

Two Nickel Plate Railroad crewmen, brakeman George Howard and conductor M.H. Maish, lost their lives in this early-morning wreck east of Tipton on March 12, 1928, when a speeding eastbound freight train slammed into the back of a slow-moving freighter pulling 50 loaded cars. Momentum sent the engine down a steep embankment where it overturned. Both victims had been riding in the caboose. They died instantly. (Library archives.)

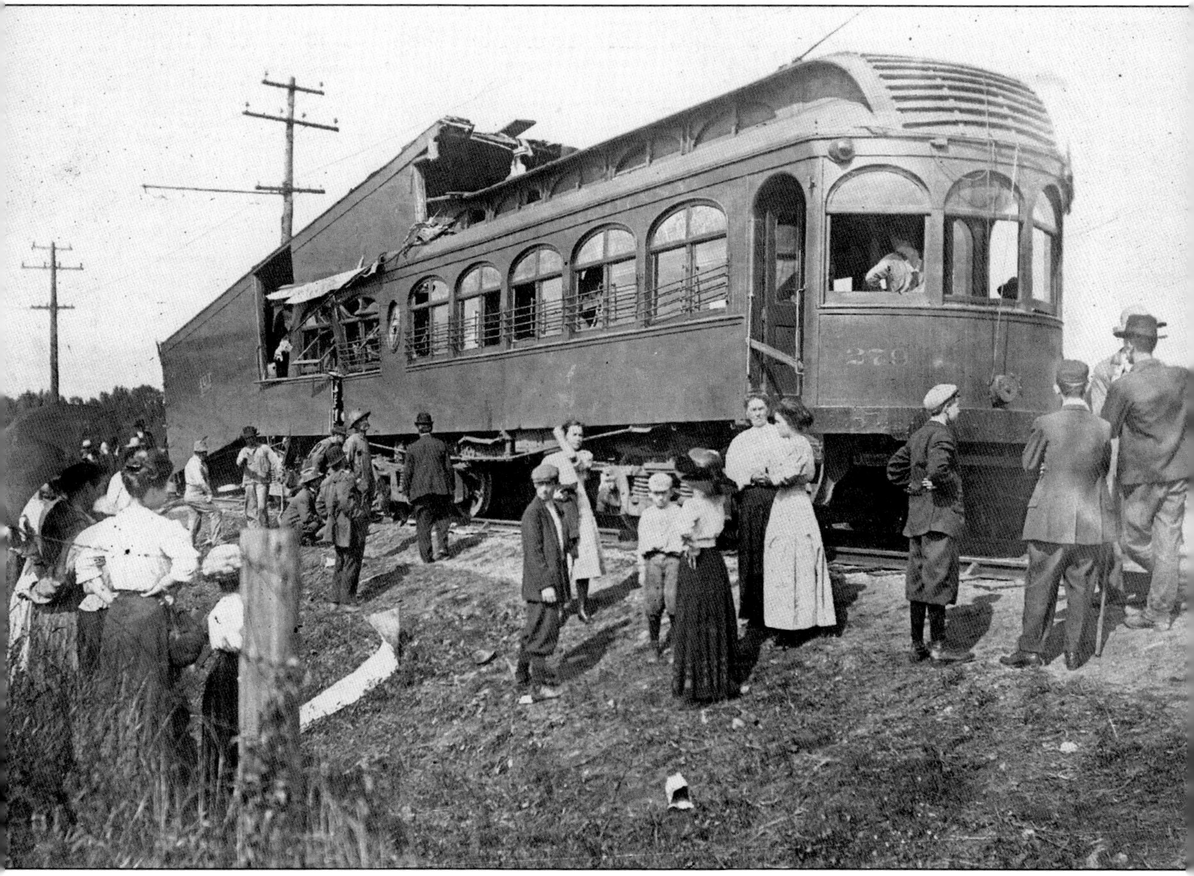

Six people died and 12 were injured when a southbound freight train collided with the northbound Indiana Union Traction Company's interurban at noon, Saturday, September 24, 1910, near Jackson Station, two miles north of Tipton. The crash occurred after the freight train failed to move onto the sidetrack that would have allowed the interurban to pass safely. Compounding the mistake was a clump of trees that obscured the cars as they approached the curve, where the fast-moving freight train plowed through the front of the limited. It was reported that the limited's motorman also was speeding to make up time after leaving Tipton 10 minutes late. News of the wreck spread fast by phone, and before the doctors could reach the accident scene, farmers from miles around were already tending to the victims. Among the casualties was a young doctor from Brooklyn, New York, on his way to be married that night in Kokomo. No one from Tipton was killed, but the conductor, B.M. Maines, and passenger Vincent Van Briggle, both of Tipton, were hurt. (Indiana Historical Society archives.)

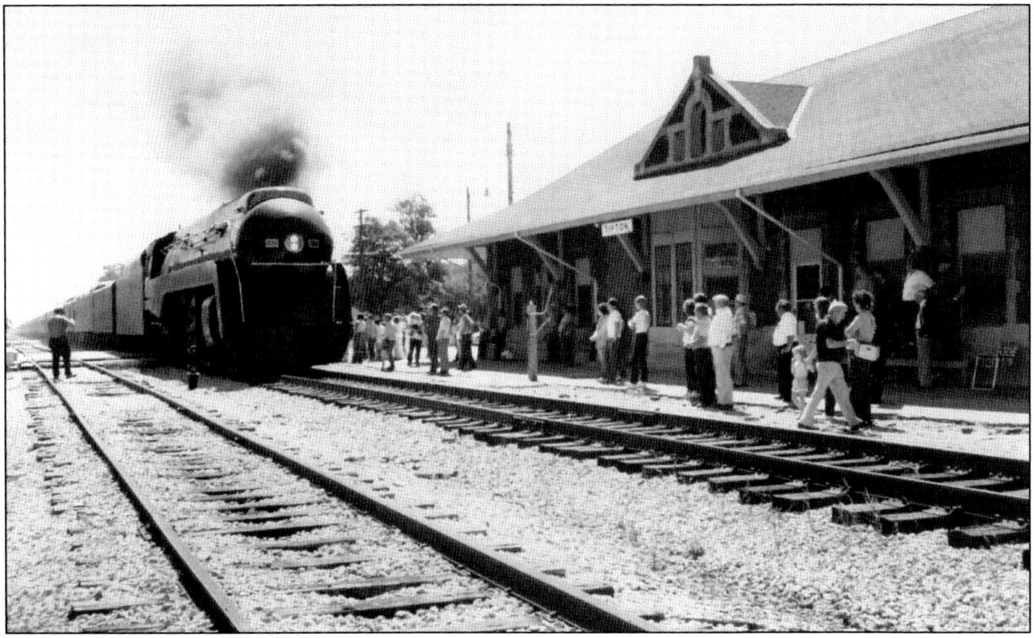

Norfolk & Western Railway's J Class steam engine made a stop in Tipton during the summer of 1982, during a special excursion run. The vintage engine was a 1950 product of the railroad's own Roanoke, Virginia, shop. Between 1838 and 1982, the Norfolk & Western Railway was formed by scores of railroad mergers, including the Nickel Plate, which served Tipton for decades. The N&W was the last major American railroad to convert from steam to diesel.

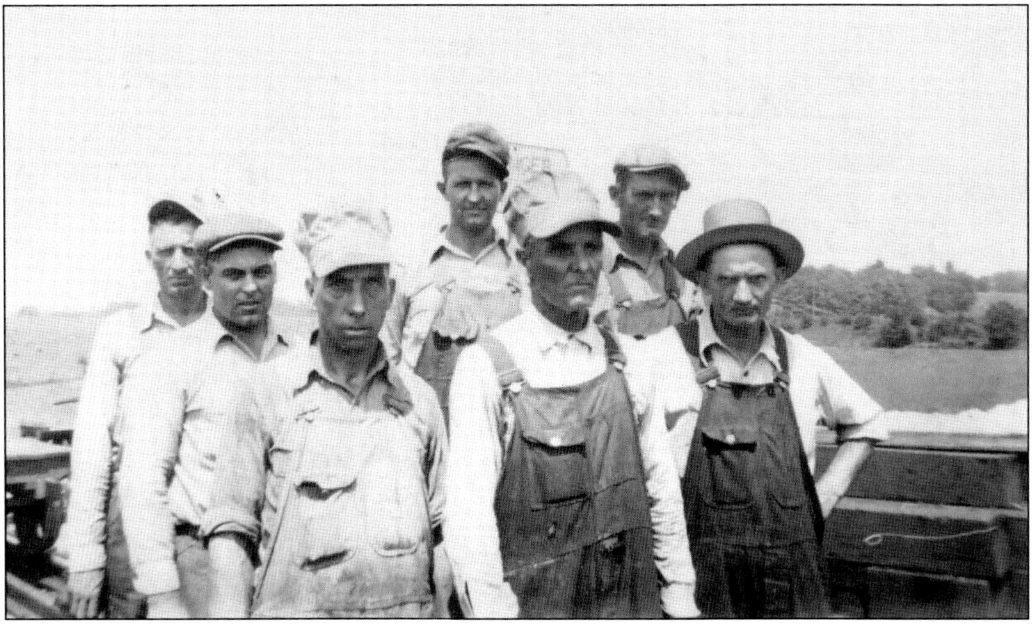

Behind every great railroad is a great maintenance crew. This Nickel Plate Railroad bridge and building gang from Tipton traveled statewide to keep the facilities in good repair. Pictured around 1935, the men are, from left to right, unidentified, Charles Tidler, ? Waugh, Milton Stansberry, ? Perkins, Bob Katness, and Bill Katness. (Bill Tidler.)

Three

Business and Industry

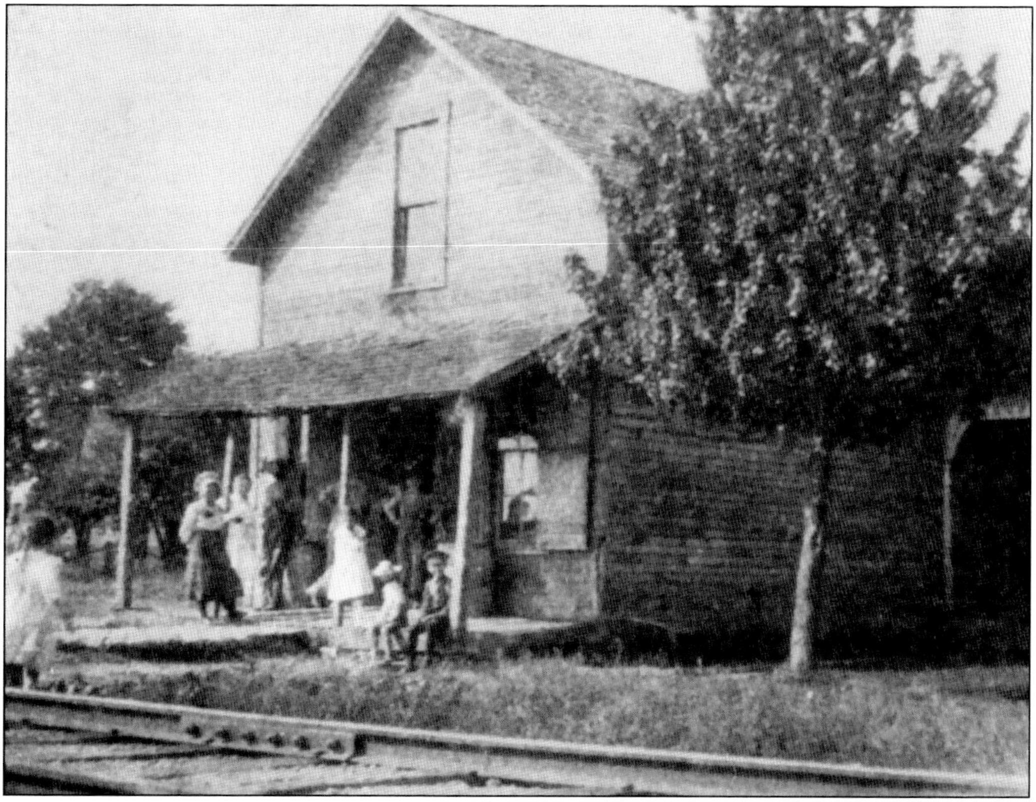

Railroads brought many businesses to Tipton County. One of them was this general store operated by Charles Wilson Fettig in Nevada around 1900. A note on the photograph identifies one of the boys as Berl Barlow, the girl leaning against the porch post as Hazel Fettig, and the girl crossing the tracks as Hazel's sister Hattie. The note also says, "The tree grew up and was cut down, but the stump is there yet." (Library archives.)

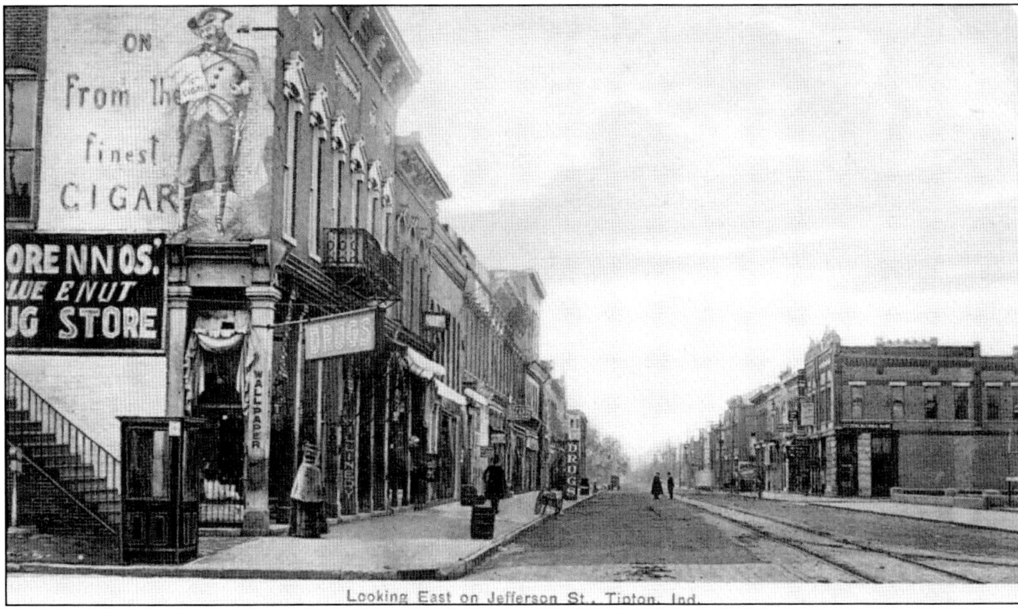

Both Tipton street scenes—above around 1898 and below some 45 years later—depict an eastward look down Jefferson Street. Above, facing an unpaved street with a strip of interurban tracks down the middle is the Blue Front Drug Store to the left. To the right is Citizens Bank. Below, Farmers Loan & Trust, on the left, and Foster's Jewelry, on the right, were common landmarks of their time. Today's downtown area appears much different, with many of the buildings either modernized or demolished. (Above, library archives; below, Alice Ricketts.)

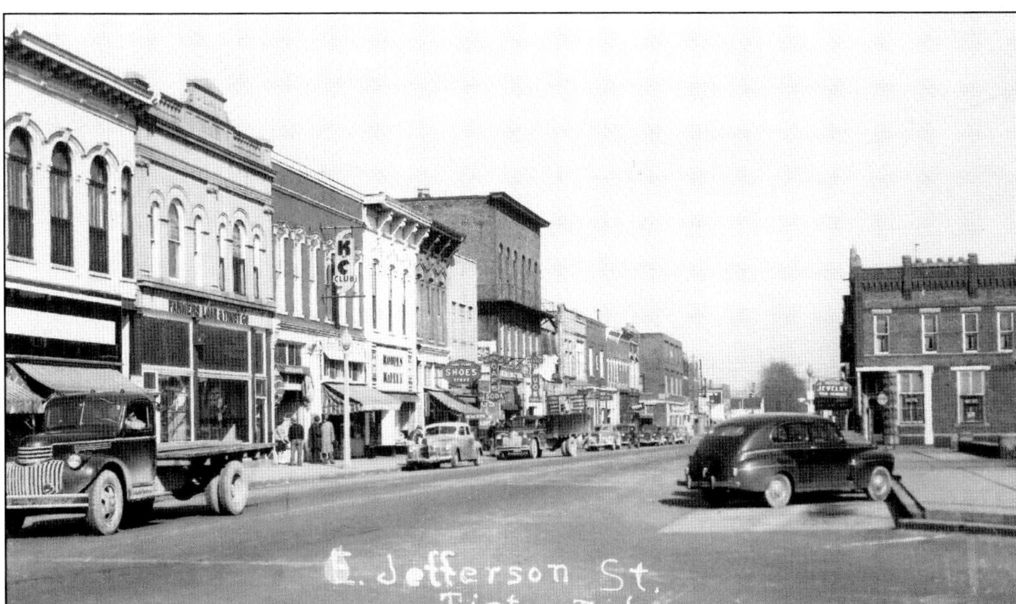

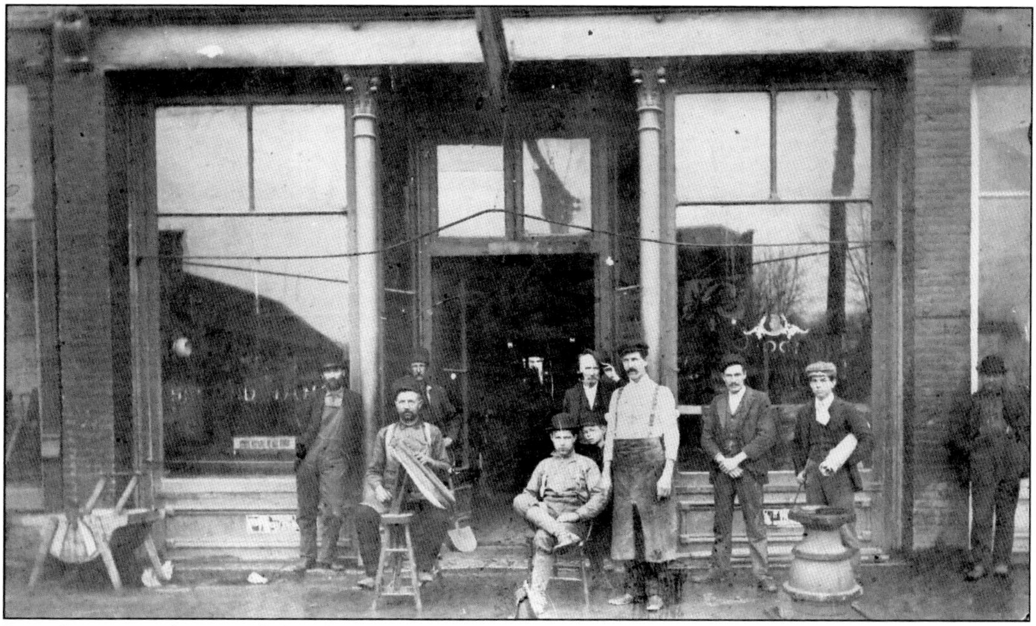

Joseph Coppock owned this harness and stove repair business in the Kleyla Building on the southeast corner of Jefferson and Independence Streets. Seated beside him is his elder son, Arba. Peeking from behind is younger son Ora. Also shown in this 1895 photograph are, from left to right, Henry Coppock, S. Meeker, an unidentified gentleman, Frank Fippen, Henry Holmes, and James Smith. (David Cox.)

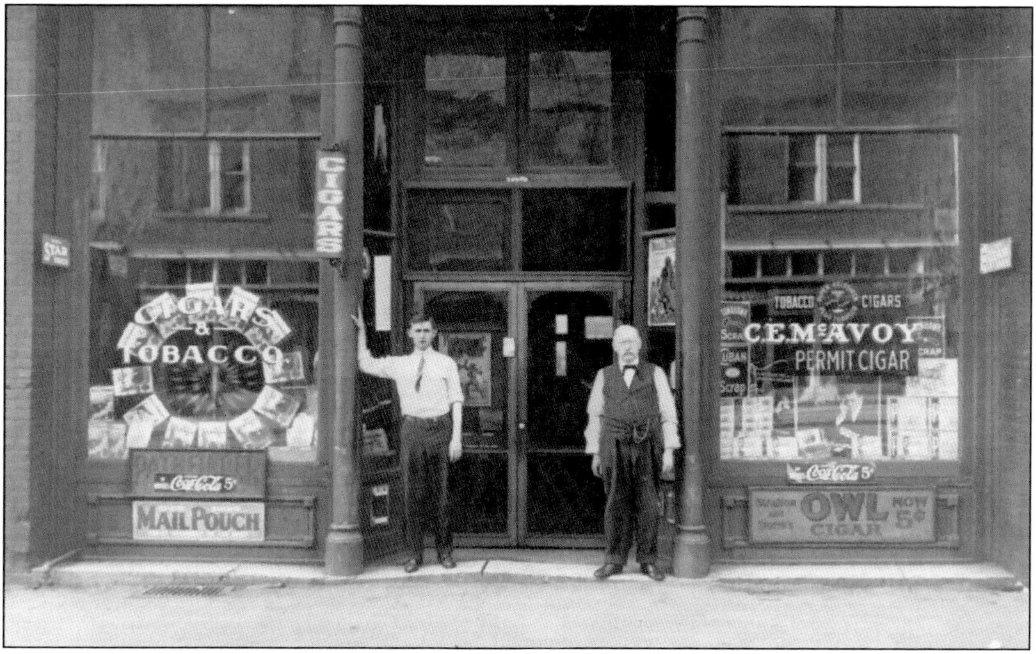

The C.E. McAvoy Cigar Store also occupied a storefront in the Kleyla Building. The men in this undated photograph are unidentified, but McAvoy is likely on the right. According to the July 31, 1911, edition of *Tipton Daily Tribune*, the cigar store was also the site of a blind tiger, more commonly known today as a speakeasy. (Library archives.)

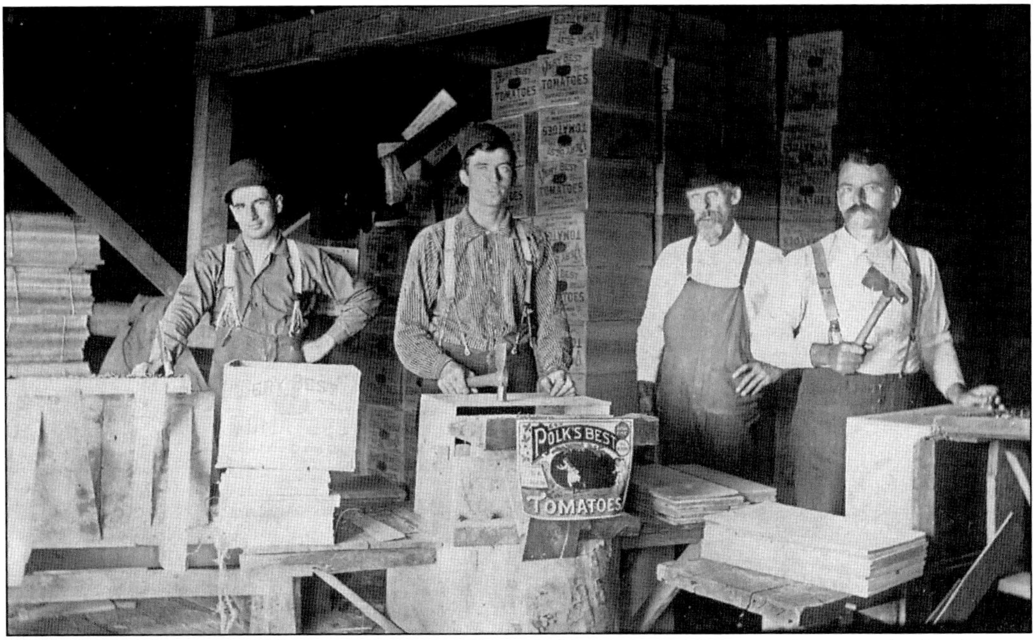

This undated photograph was taken at the Sharpsville Canning Factory. At its peak, the factory operated round the clock, producing up to 35,000 cans of locally grown tomatoes each day and employing around 200 workers. Pictured are box makers, from left to right, Harvey Hutto, unidentified, Peter Dewitt, and Miles Hutto. (Virginia Chambers.)

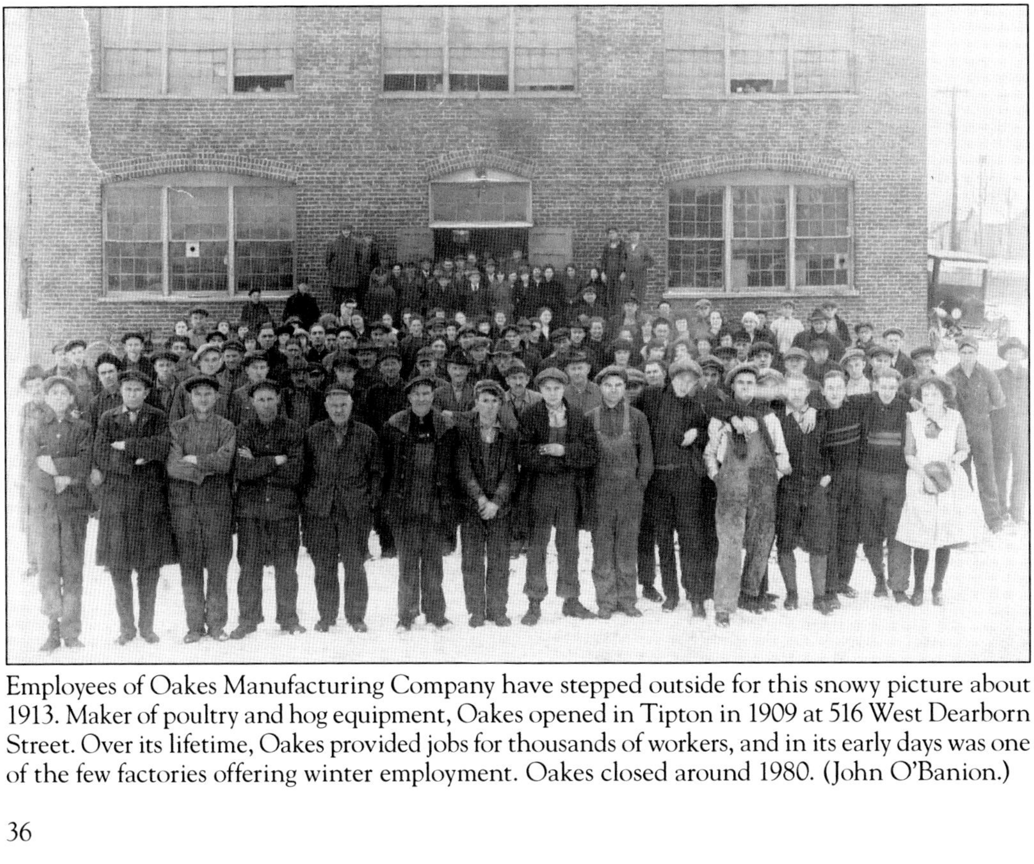

Employees of Oakes Manufacturing Company have stepped outside for this snowy picture about 1913. Maker of poultry and hog equipment, Oakes opened in Tipton in 1909 at 516 West Dearborn Street. Over its lifetime, Oakes provided jobs for thousands of workers, and in its early days was one of the few factories offering winter employment. Oakes closed around 1980. (John O'Banion.)

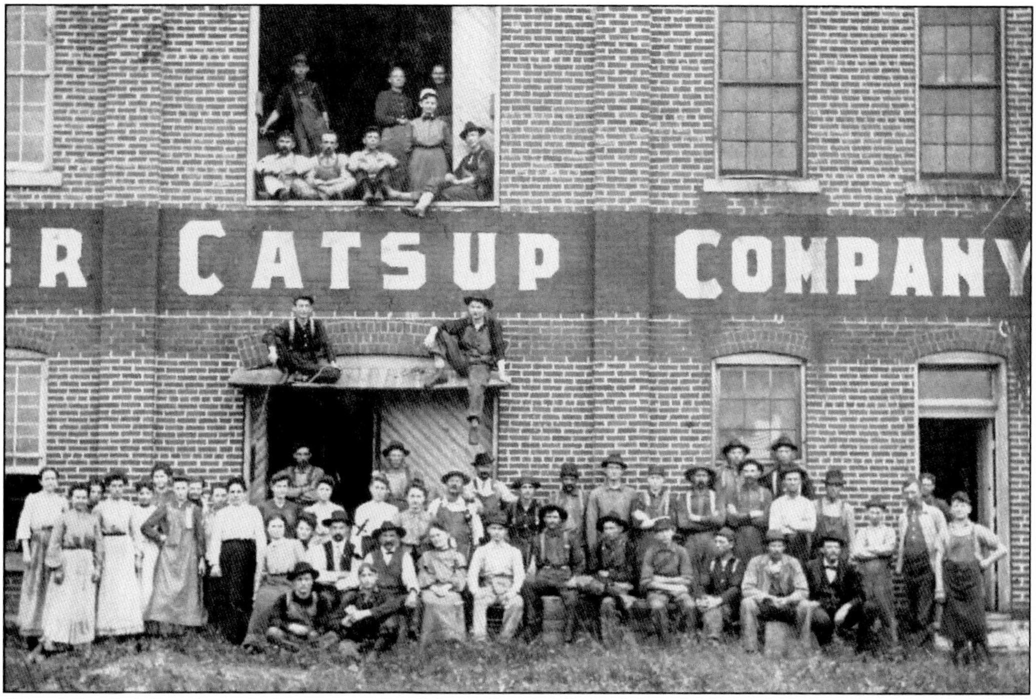

Here, the Snider Catsup Company workforce has gathered for a picture. The company opened in Tipton around 1902, occupying what would later house Perfect Circle. For a time, Snider operated day and night, shipping 1,800 cases of its catsup daily nationally and internationally. The factory shut down in 1921, moving most of the machinery to its Marion facility. It had been one of several canning factories operating in Tipton County. (Library archives.)

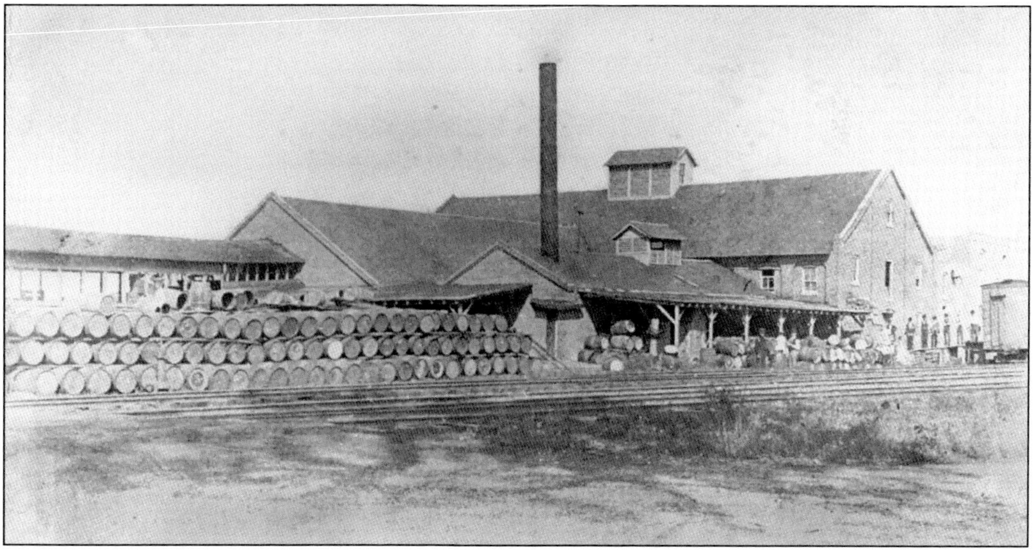

The Fame Canning Factory, operating on Tipton's north side by the railroad tracks, was built by N.S. Martz in 1893 of bricks salvaged from the county's second courthouse. The business was bought and sold three times before 1928, when Stokley's purchased it. It became a Tipton mainstay, filling the air each fall with the delicious scent of simmering tomatoes. Stokley's closed in 1984. (John O'Banion.)

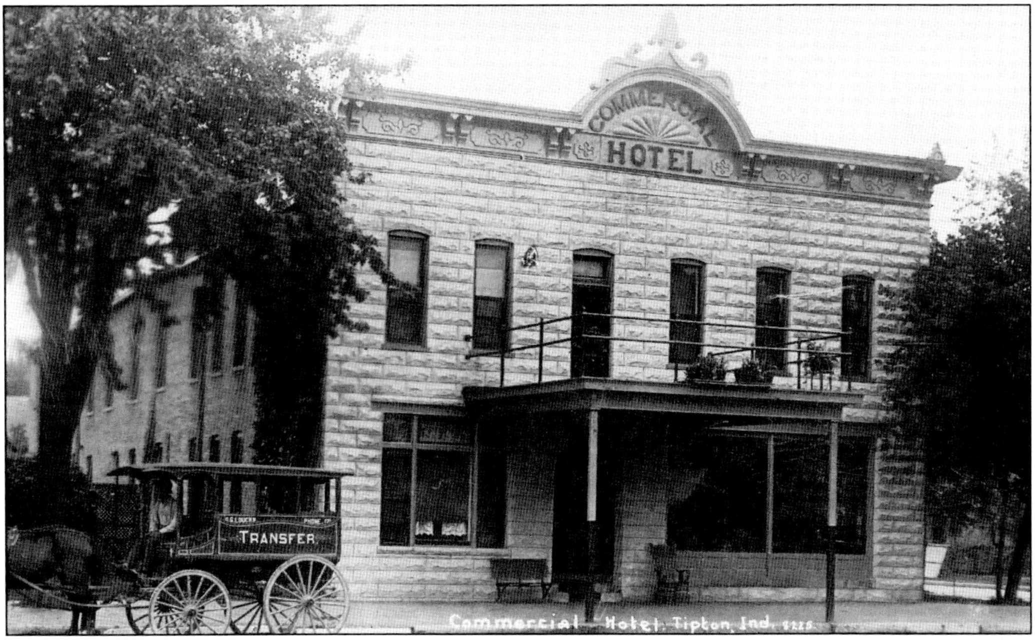

The Commercial Hotel, built in 1873, was long considered Tipton's finest and one of Indiana's best, with 30 rooms, an office, parlor, sample rooms for traveling salesmen, and a dining room. Its guests included William Jennings Bryan (1896), Franklin D. Roosevelt (1920), and several Indiana governors. Tipton's Fraternal Order of the Moose turned the building into its lodge home in 1937. It was destroyed by fire in 1992. (Alice Ricketts.)

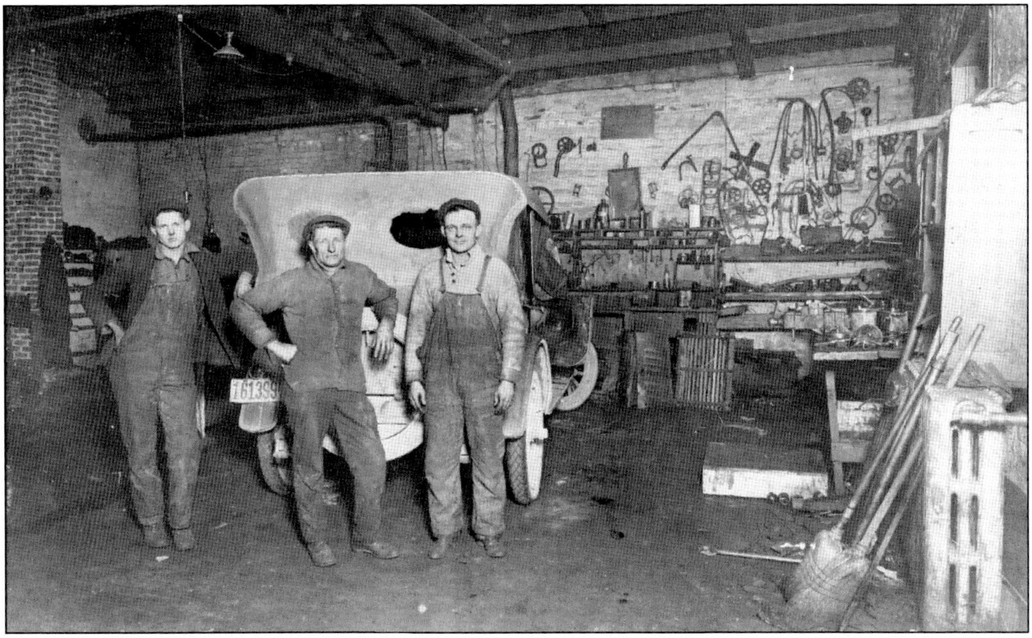

Pictured are, from left to right, Ray Mitchell, Tom Shope, and Henry Comer about 1925. The trio worked at the Callahan Motors garage, located in the brick building at 114 Madison Street, next door to the Elks Lodge. Francis Callahan owned and operated the dealership until he died in 1968. (Rosemary Comer.)

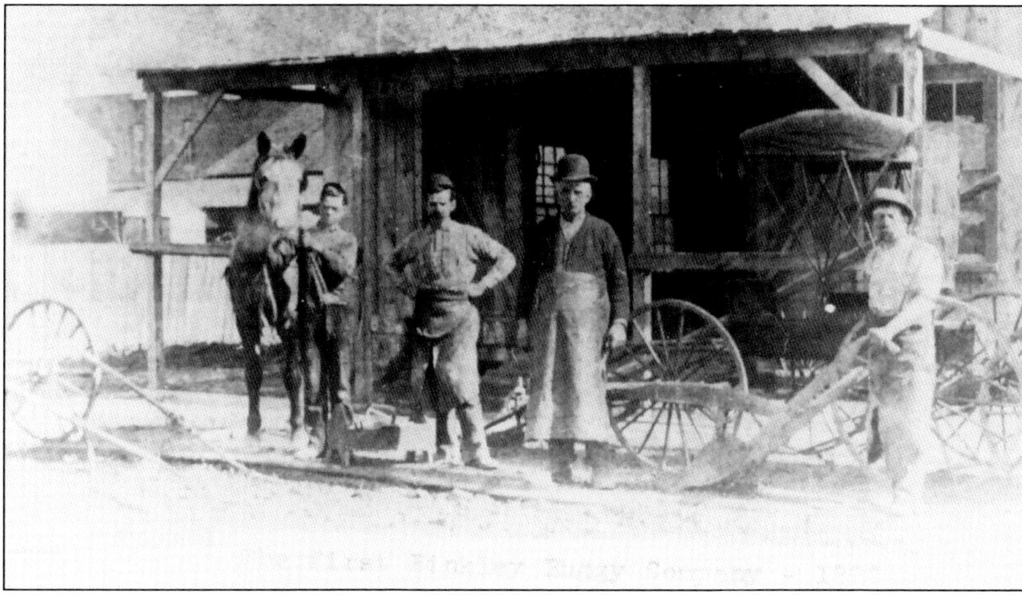

Henry Binkley arrived in Tipton in 1885 and opened a vehicle repair shop on the southeast corner of Madison and Court Streets (above). In 1891, he formed a partnership with his son Harry. As the business expanded, they relocated to a large building in the 100 block of South West Street (below). Incorporating in 1903 as Binkley Buggy Company, the Binkleys took another partner, Charles Grishaw. Together, they built a reputation as one of Indiana's finest and most sought-after carriage makers, filling more than 1,000 orders annually. In turn, Binkley became one of Tipton's largest employers, supporting a workforce of 35 with a monthly payroll that exceeded $2,000. The company permanently closed September 1, 1919. (Both, library archives.)

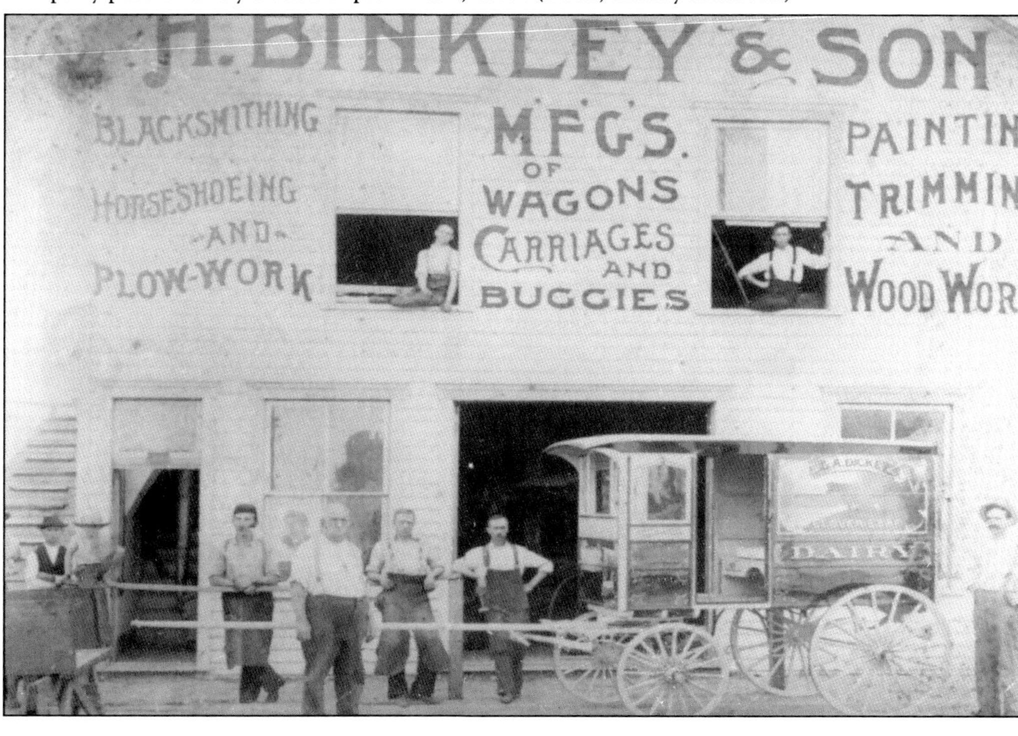

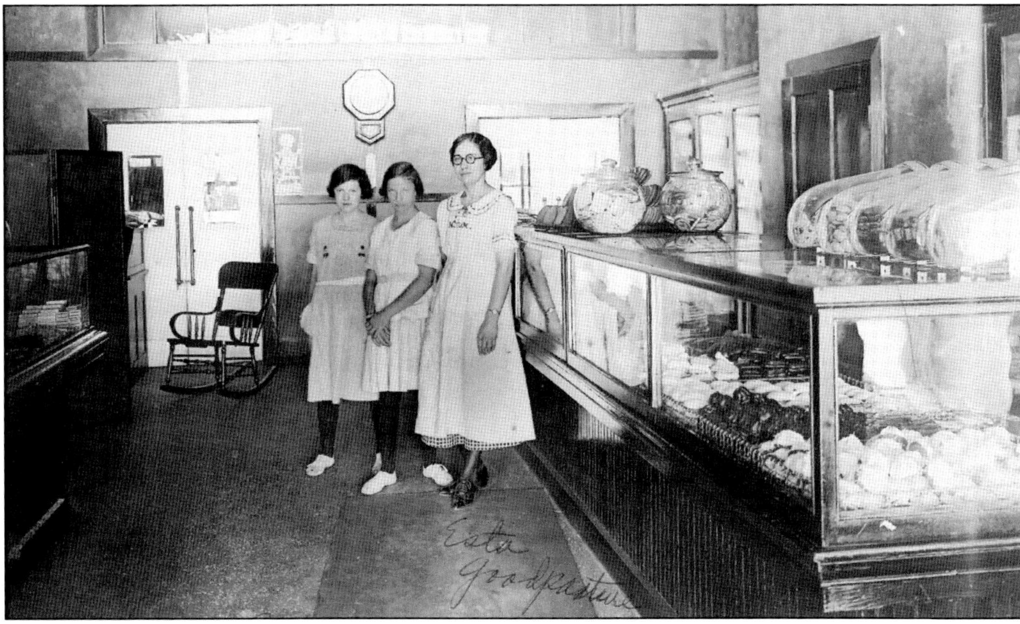

Esta Jane Goodpasture, right, and friends stand inside the Haas Bakery, located on Tipton's South Main Street, around 1915. Owner Fred Haas earned praise for his bread, rolls, pies, and cakes, some of which can be seen in the display case. Haas sold the bakery in 1922 and moved to Los Angeles, California, where he entered real estate.

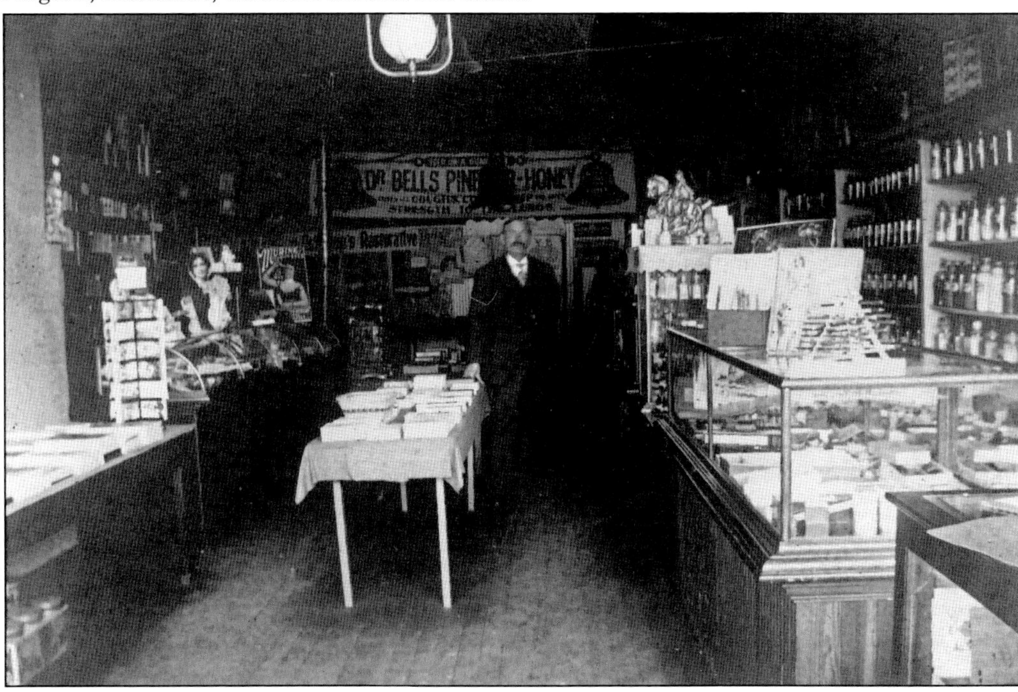

Elison Cooperider is shown in his Kempton drugstore, around 1915. Cooperider operated his business for some 20 years before he and his wife moved to Kent, Indiana, in 1917. A native of Jefferson County, in which the town of Kent is located, Cooperider established and operated another drugstore there for many years.

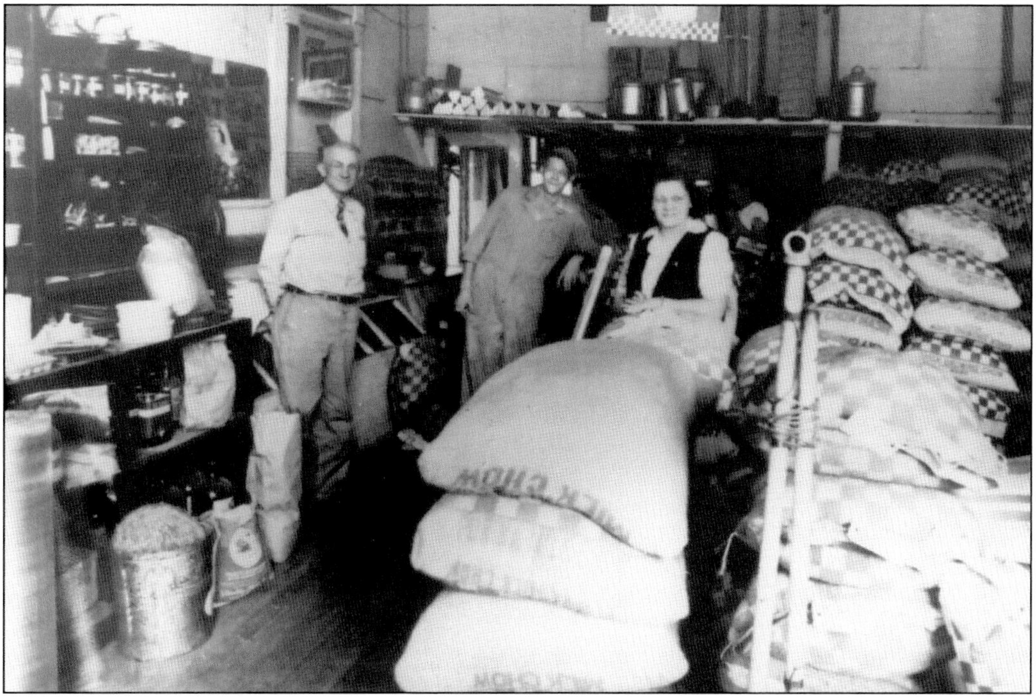

Roy Girard, left, poses with two unidentified employees at his Tipton Hatchery on Court Street, about 1948. The business was equipped with two electric hatchers, each with a capacity of 47,000 eggs. Girard enhanced production with a moisture device he invented for the hatchers. At its peak, the business averaged 2,000 chicks daily. Girard also provided area farmers with eggs, feed, and equipment. (Library archives.)

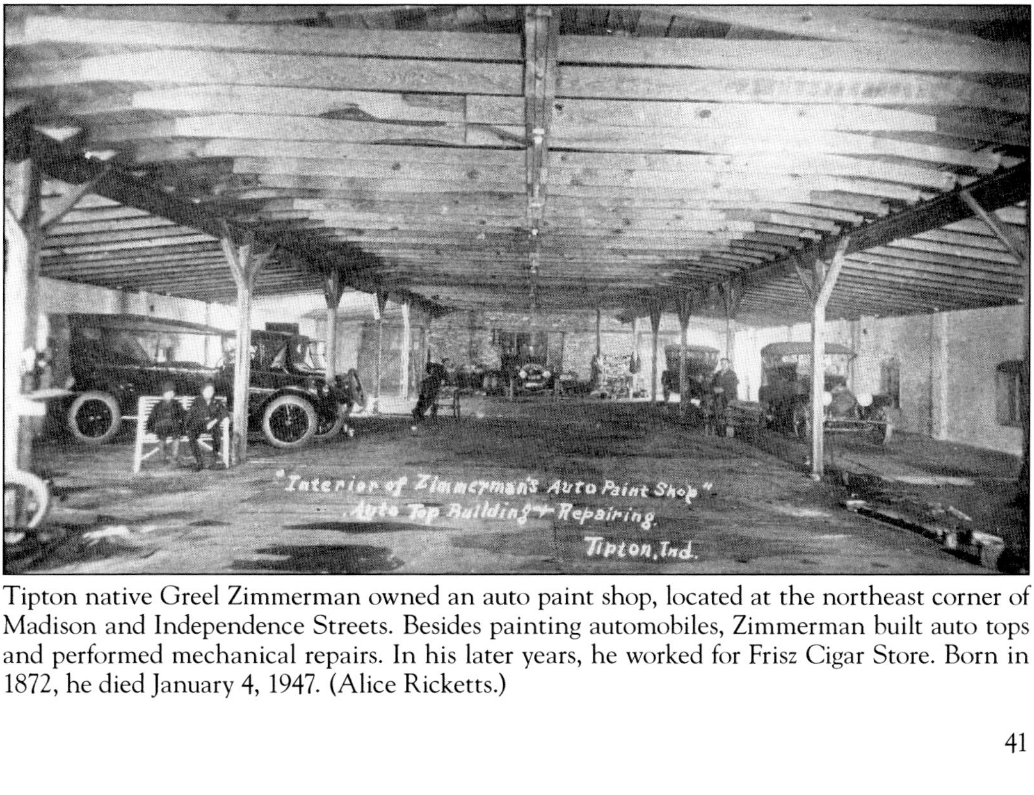

Tipton native Greel Zimmerman owned an auto paint shop, located at the northeast corner of Madison and Independence Streets. Besides painting automobiles, Zimmerman built auto tops and performed mechanical repairs. In his later years, he worked for Frisz Cigar Store. Born in 1872, he died January 4, 1947. (Alice Ricketts.)

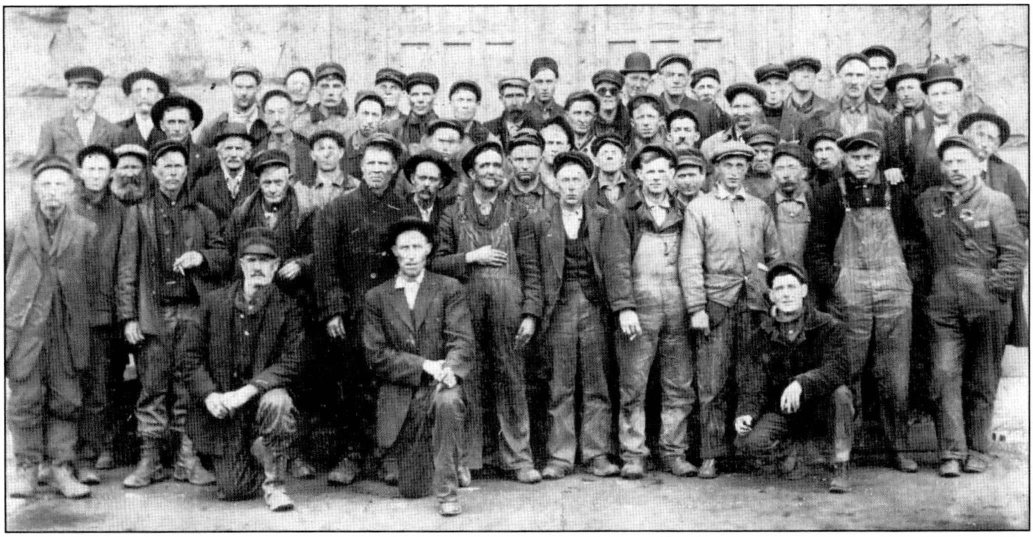

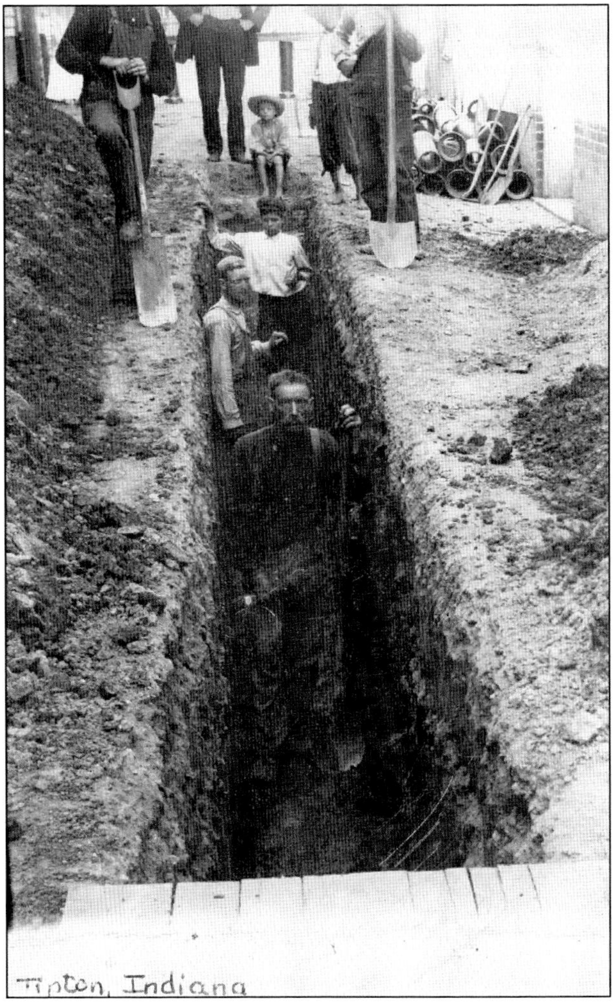

Above, Tipton's Elmer L. "Montie" Harvey is among these men gathered at the back door of the Tipton Courthouse, around 1938, after landing employment with the Works Progress Administration (WPA). At left, a WPA crew digs water and sewer lines in Tipton. The WPA was a federal relief measure established in 1935 by an executive order of Pres. Franklin Roosevelt. The program provided paying jobs to more than 2 million unemployed people during the Depression years, stimulated the economy, and launched reforms that states had been unable to fund. WPA was responsible for a variety of enhancement projects, including highways and building construction, slum cleanup, reforestation, and rural rehabilitation. In Tipton, WPA projects included the golf course, swimming pool, fire station improvements, and 300 miles of roads, city streets, sewers, and sidewalks. (Above, Joan Wray; left, Alice Ricketts.)

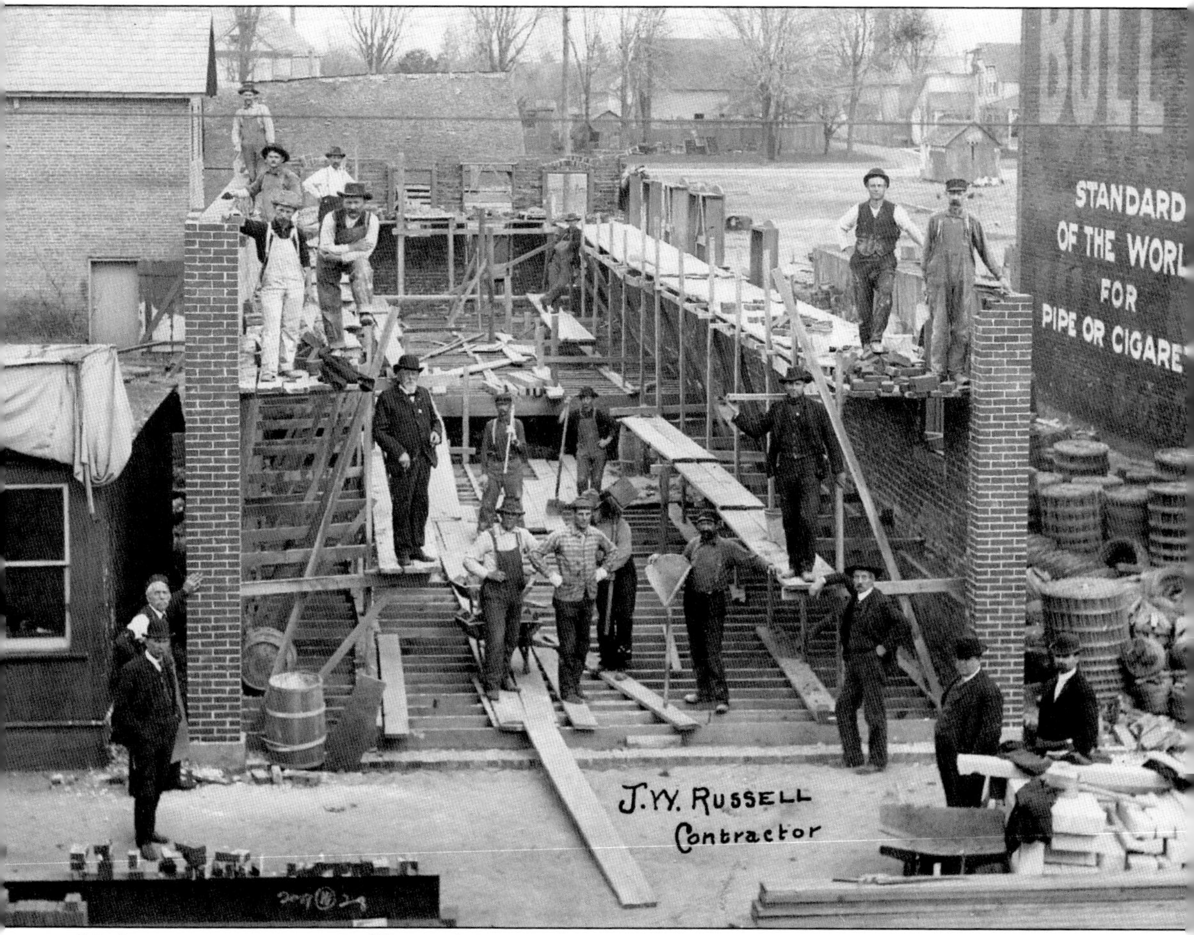

Under construction is Waffler and Bates restaurant, owned by Fred Waffler and Al Bates, at 31 East Jefferson Street, around 1900. The workmen pose on the scaffolding. Among them is Tipton's revered Civil War veteran, Capt. Thomas Paul, the bearded man standing on the lower plank on the left. On the left in the work apron is J.H. Van, pioneer shoe and harness man of Tipton. The contractor, James W. Russell, was one of Tipton County's earliest residents, his family having moved to the county in 1854, when he was still an infant. Often referred to as a "pioneer artisan," he started his carpentry and contracting business in Goldsmith in 1881. Russell was a Spanish-American War veteran, serving with Company I, 160th Indiana Volunteer Regiment. He died in July 1936 at the age of 82, outlived by the buildings he constructed. The Waffler and Bates Building was flanked by U R Next Barbershop to its west and J.C. Lindsay Drug Store on its east. (Library archives.)

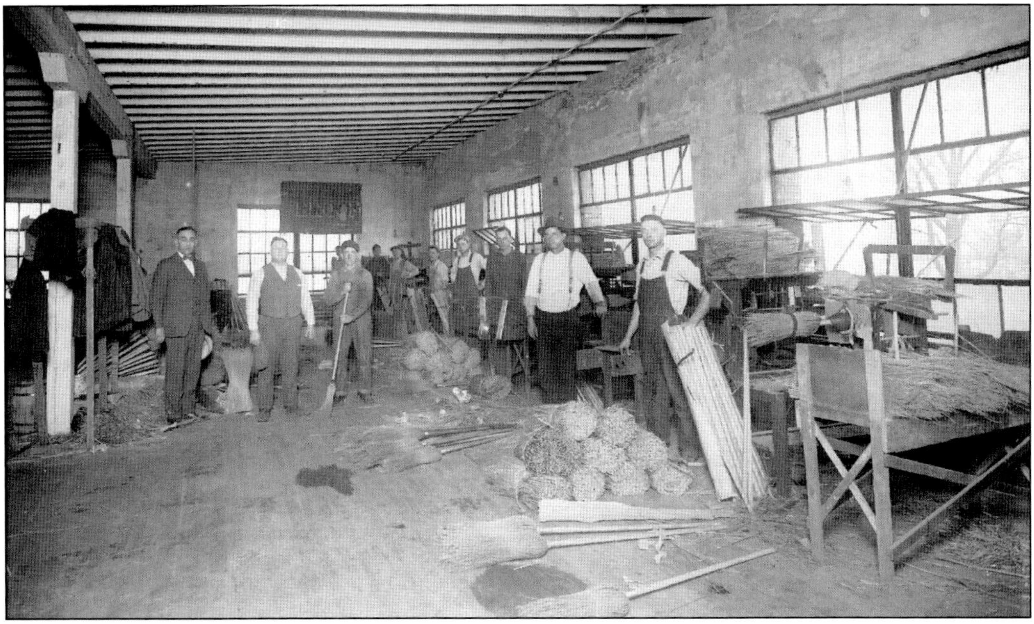

J.J. McIntosh and Sons broom factory was a Tipton mainstay for three generations, founded in 1888 on a farm in Madison County, where McIntosh raised broomcorn. After selling a wagonload of brooms to Leeson's of Elwood in 1897, he moved his operation to a barn on Tipton's Poplar Street and later to larger quarters on Ash Street. The company moved again around 1915 to a new brick factory on East Street, pictured above, where it remained until closing in 1963. J.J. died in 1921 in an accident at the factory while boarding his horse-drawn wagon. His sons, Guerney and Jesse, assumed the business. Guerney became sole owner in 1929 and eventually passed the company on to his son Charles. Below is J.J. in his wagon, around 1917. (Both, McIntosh family.)

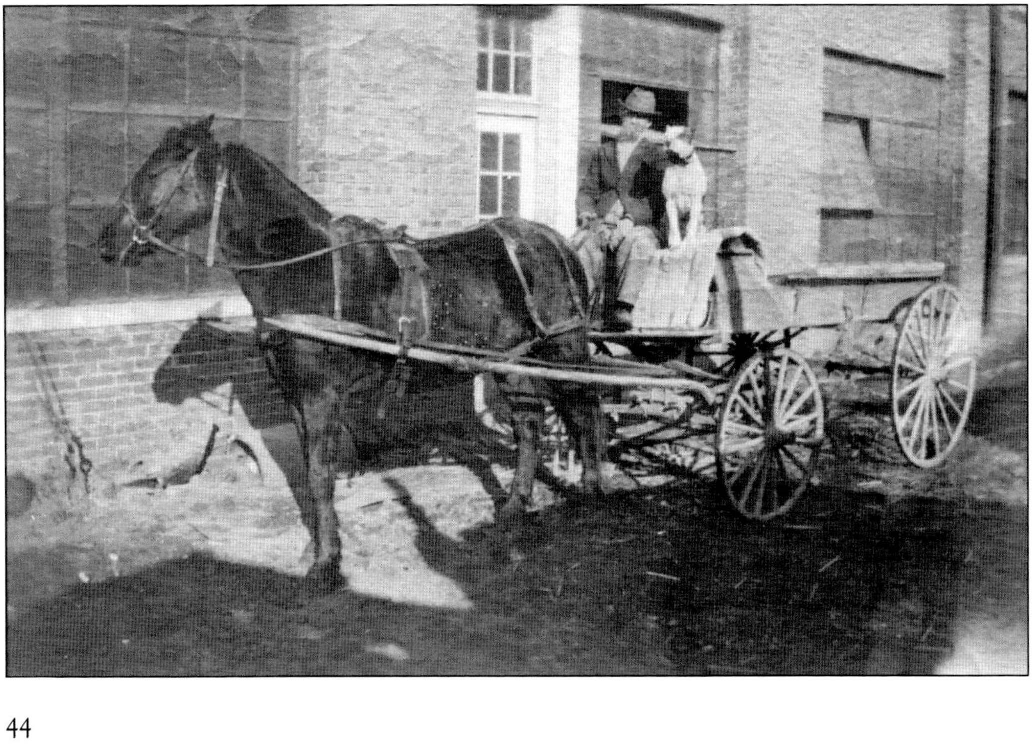

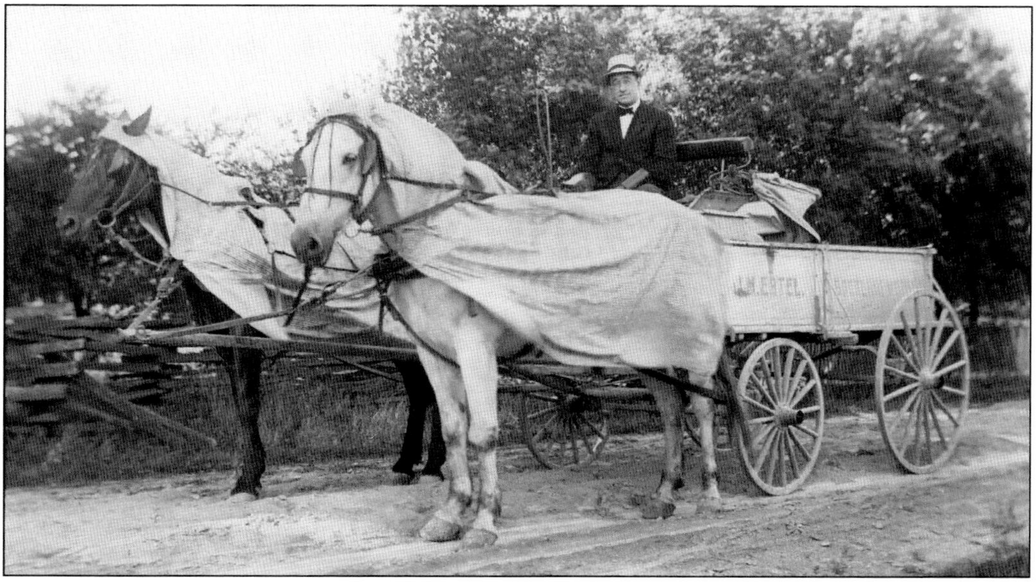

Ertel's Bottling Works, founded by John M. Ertel in 1914, was located on North East Street, next door to his home. Ertel's was later run by his son Ed, whose children Betty, Mark, Rita, Joan, and Jim helped with the production. Ertel sold lemon-, strawberry-, and sarsaparilla-flavored carbonated drinks, which he delivered daily within a 40-mile radius of Tipton. The beverages sold for 60¢ a case or 5¢ a bottle. John Ertel died July 31, 1945. The company closed in 1967. The undated photograph above shows Ed Ertel driving his horse-drawn delivery wagon. Below, Jim Ertel sits behind the wheel of the company's then new, modern delivery truck, about 1940. (Both, Gary Ertel.)

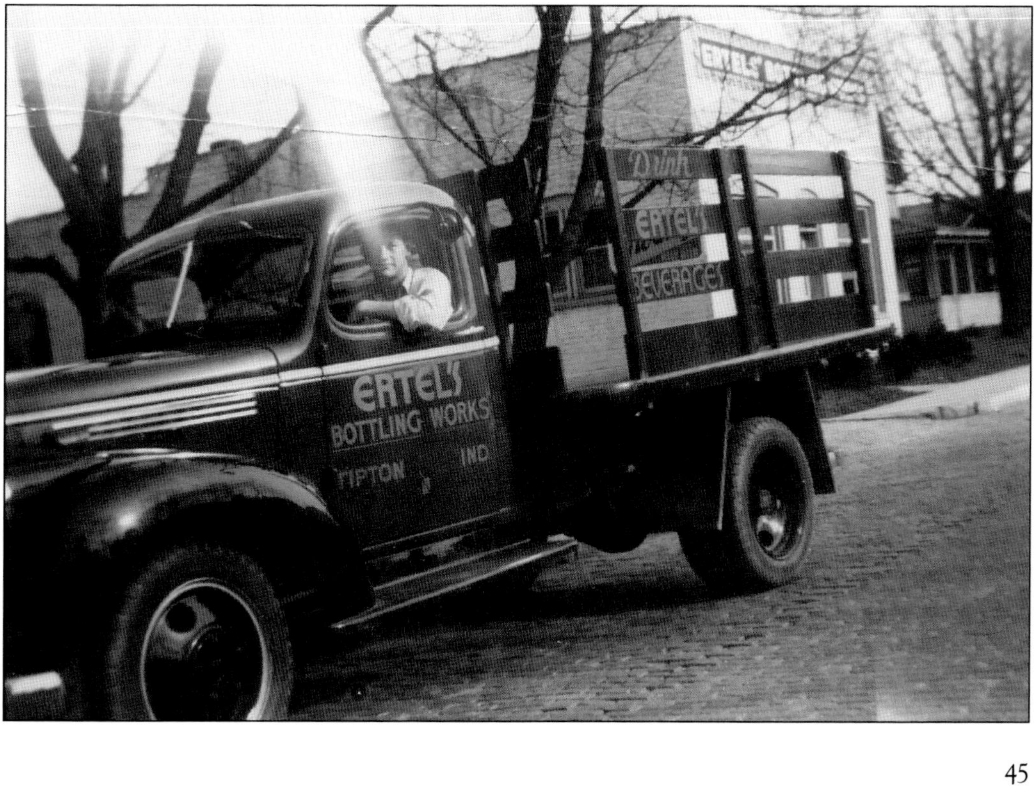

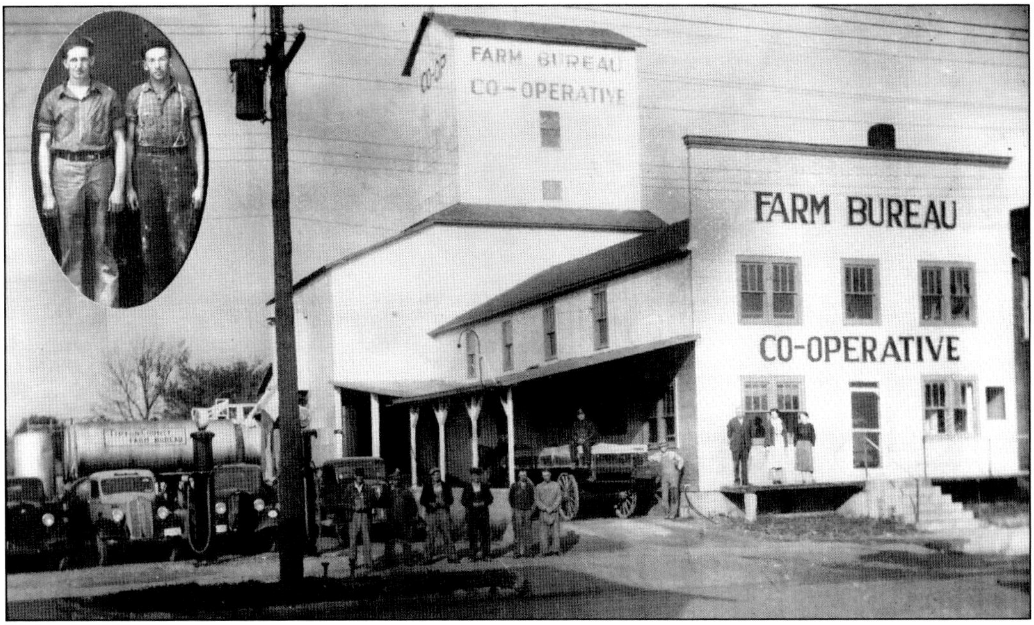

Farm Bureau Cooperative was located on North Main and Erie Streets at the railroad junction. Shown in this 1935 photograph are, from left to right, (standing along the street) Jess Cochran, Paul Grime, Roy Moody, and Ralph Amsbury; (posing next to the wagon) H. Cole and Vern Steven; (office staff on the porch) Forest Griesel, Mildred Bergman, and Chrystal Hendricks; (inset) Elmer Ziegler and John Mattingly. (Ken Ziegler.)

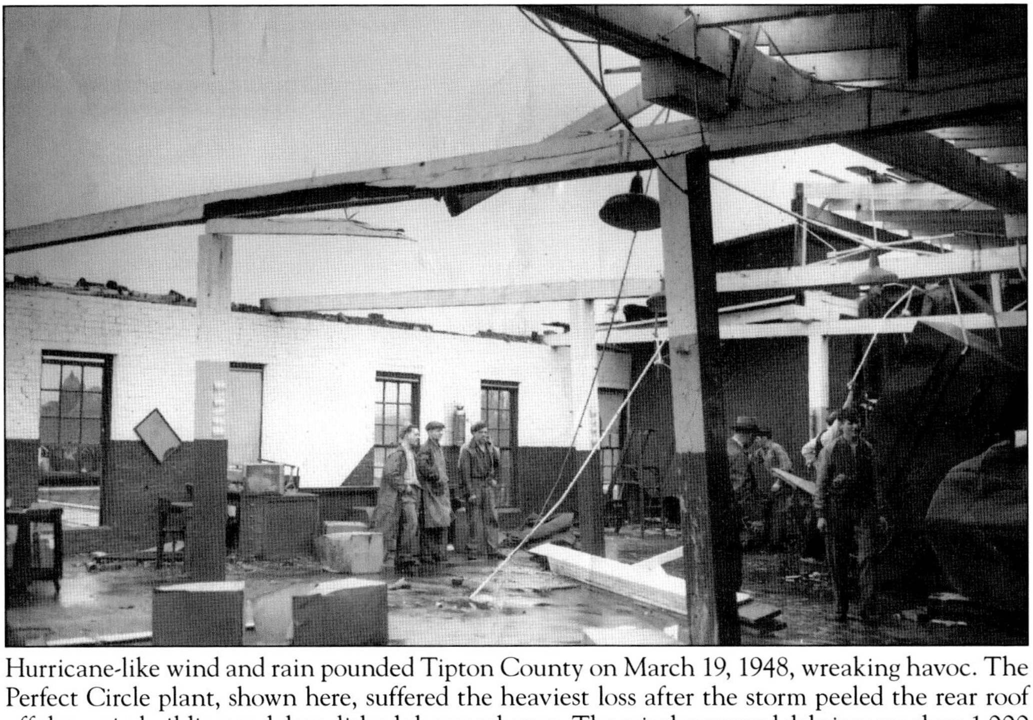

Hurricane-like wind and rain pounded Tipton County on March 19, 1948, wreaking havoc. The Perfect Circle plant, shown here, suffered the heaviest loss after the storm peeled the rear roof off the main building and demolished the warehouse. The wind scattered debris more than 1,000 feet. No injuries were reported. (Joann Boes.)

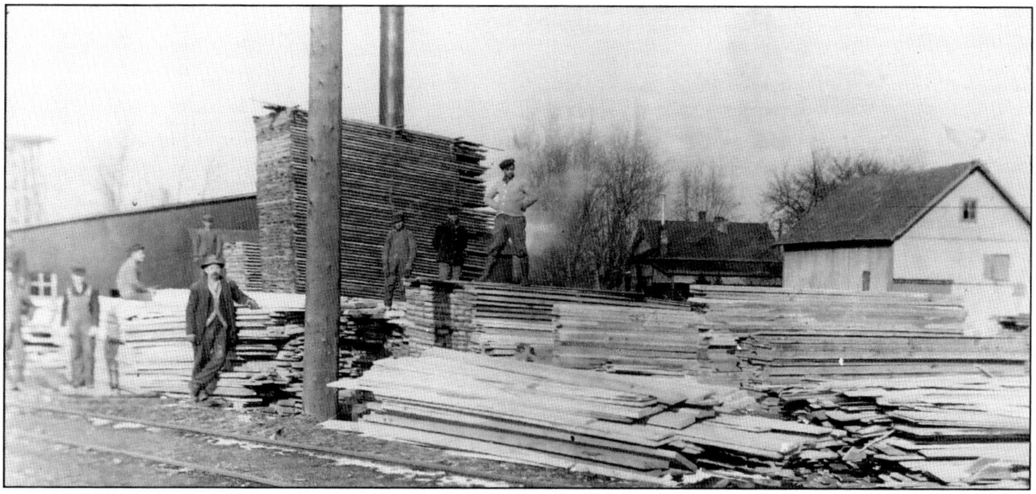

Workers pause at the F.J. Fralich Lumber Company, located along the railroad tracks at East Jefferson Street. The company was established in 1887 by F.J. Fralich and sold to S.R. Cornish in 1914. J.P. Smith of Goldsmith later acquired it. It changed hands a few more times until, in 1938, it became Tipton Lumber Company. It remained that until 1990. The building was demolished in 2001. (Alice Ricketts.)

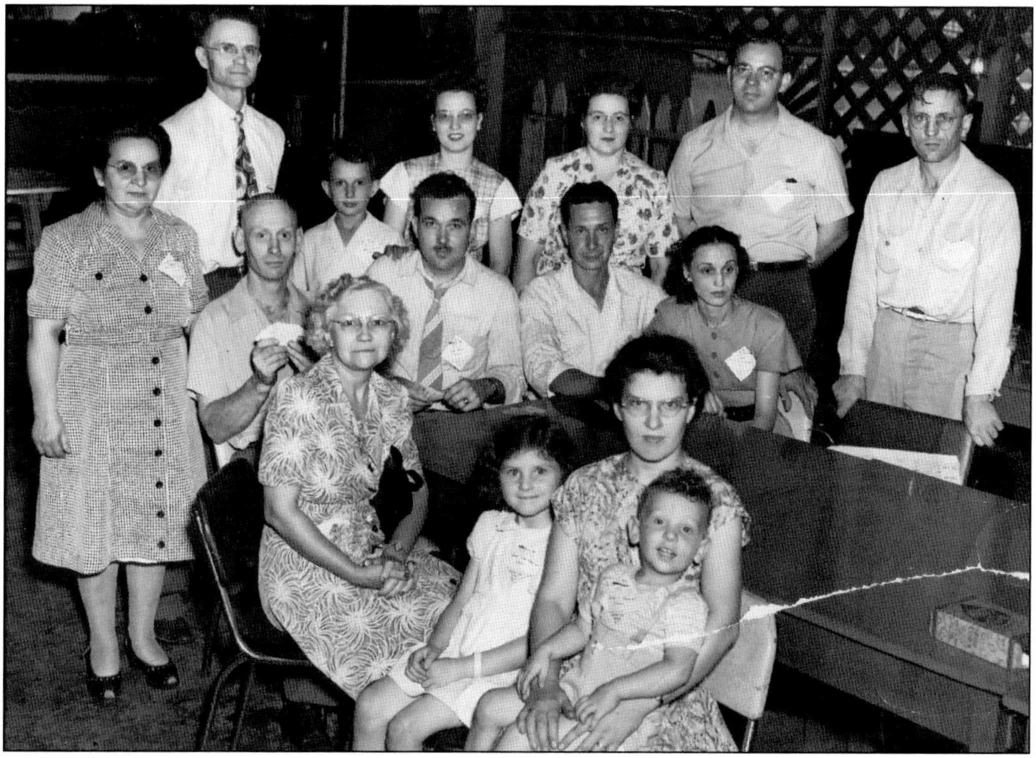

Employees of Tipton Lumber Company around 1948 enjoyed a company party at Riverside Amusement Park, Indianapolis. Tipton Lumber was located where The Medicine Shop stands today. Identified are, from left to right, (seated in front row) unidentified, Janet Raquet (Driver), Marjorie Dickover Raquet, and Terry Raquet; (standing) Naomi Stoops, George Stoops, Jerry Stoops, Thelma Roe, Bernice Lee, Harold Lee, and Harold Raquet. (Janet Driver.)

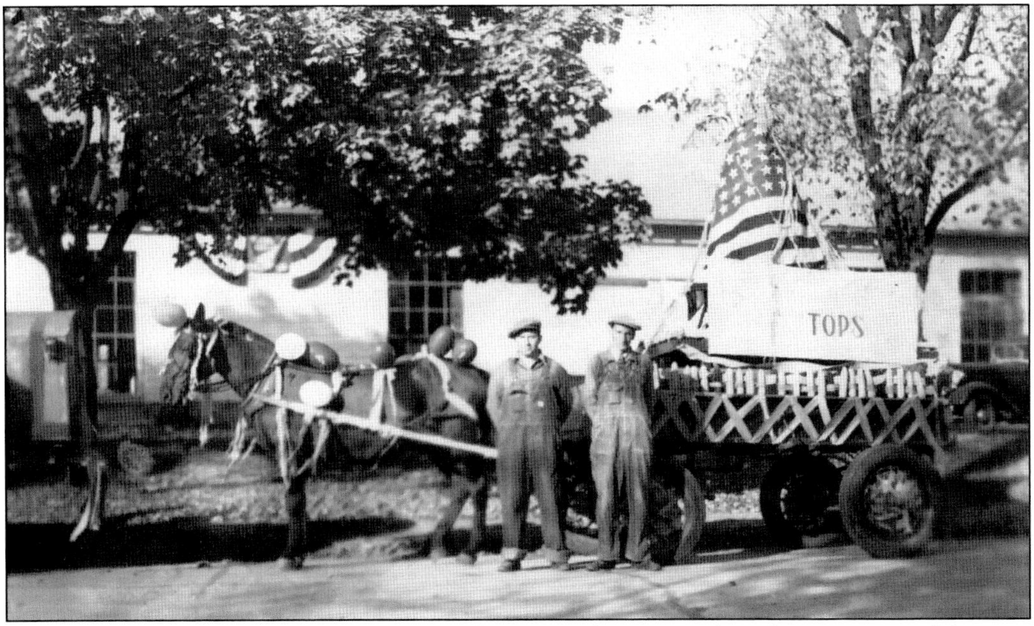

Ralph and Virgil Shupperd operated Shupperd Union Delivery, traveling the Tipton area delivering orders to the customers of various grocers for some 40 years. They closed their business in the early 1950s. Here, their wagon is decorated for a Fourth of July parade around 1935. (Evelyn Brooks and Delores Jones, Virgil's daughters.)

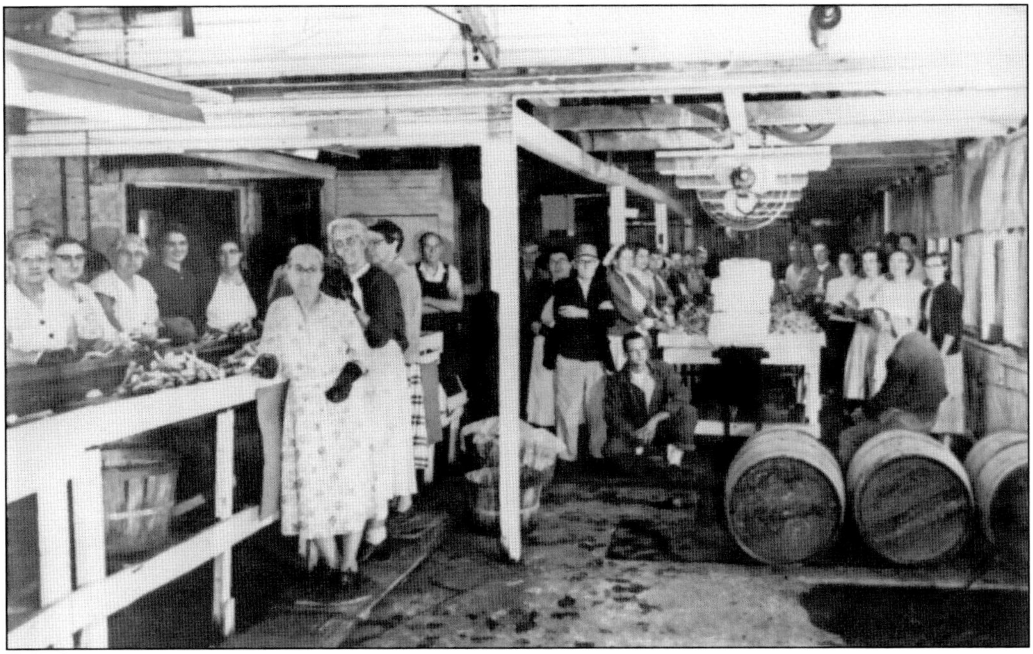

Pepper packers pause for a picture at the Jacqua Packing Company, located at 439 Maple Street, about 1950. Identified is Ocie Manlove, the second woman standing left of center in the dark-colored sweater. The company opened its Tipton-based operation in 1942, providing employment for many local people and purchasing crops from area growers. Jacqua's food products were sold in several states. The company closed around 1956. (Library archive.)

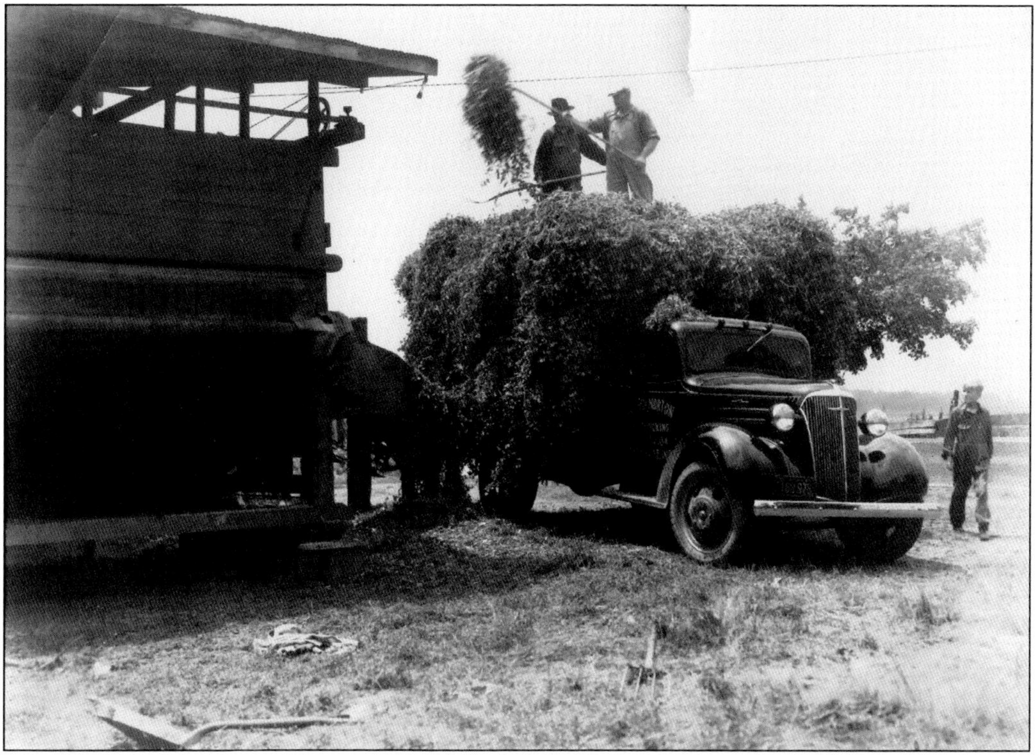

This photograph, presumed snapped outside the Sharpsville Canning Factory, shows Thomas Paul Pratt, son of Thomas B. and Nellie E. Pratt (see page 64), wielding a pitchfork full of peas. The lettering on the truck reads: "Willard Horton, Gen. Trucking, Phone 3-184, Sharpsville, Ind." The photograph is undated, but the year on the Indiana license plate is 1937. Others shown in the photograph are not identified. (Joan Wray.)

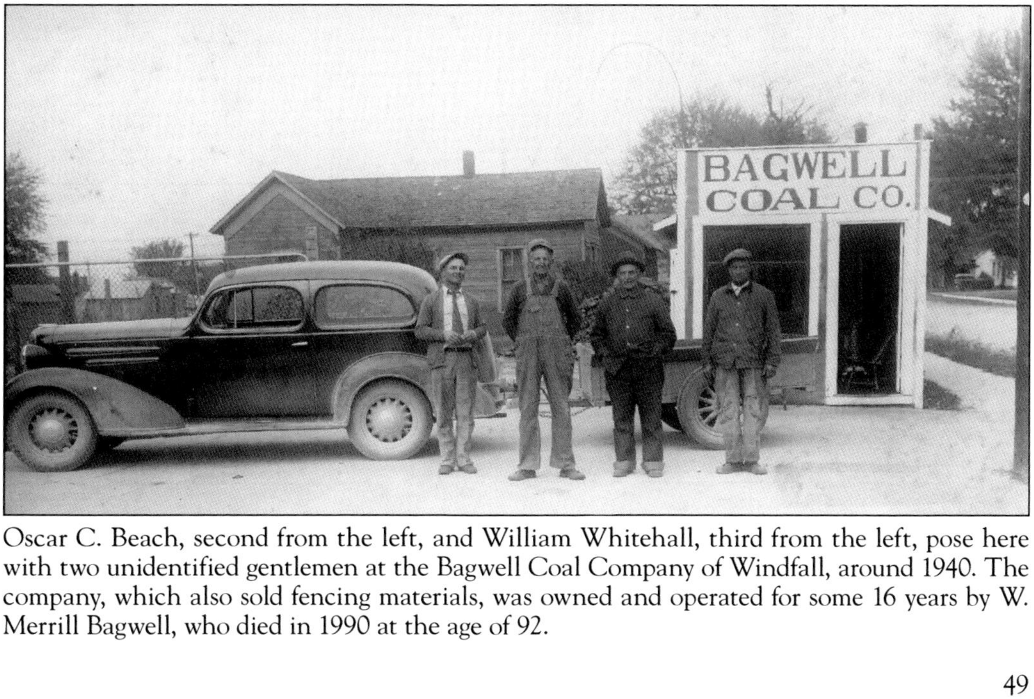

Oscar C. Beach, second from the left, and William Whitehall, third from the left, pose here with two unidentified gentlemen at the Bagwell Coal Company of Windfall, around 1940. The company, which also sold fencing materials, was owned and operated for some 16 years by W. Merrill Bagwell, who died in 1990 at the age of 92.

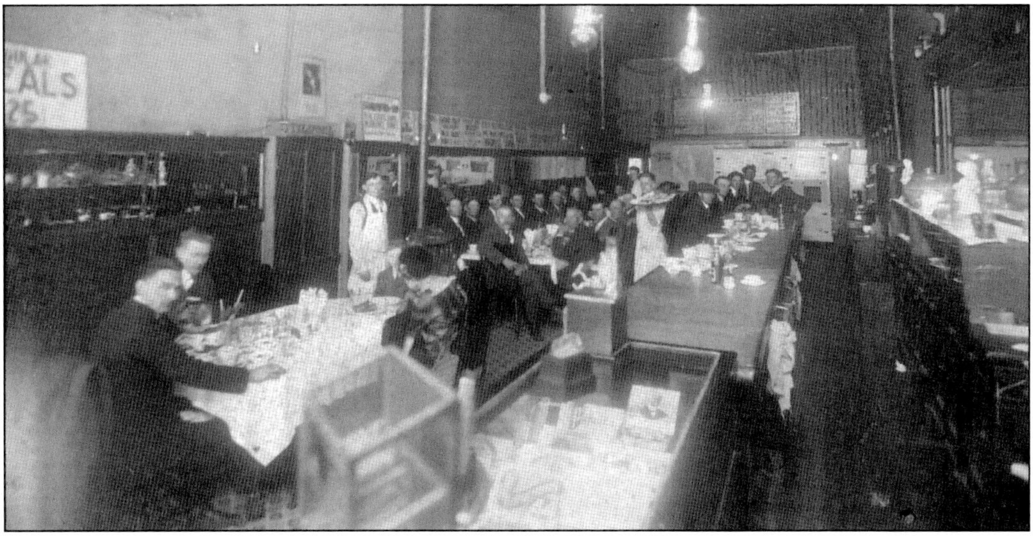

Below, Gilbert Hooten (right) stands outside his Court Street business, Hoot's Restaurant, with an unidentified cook. The photograph above, dated December 3, 1915, shows Hooten inside the busy eatery. One can almost hear the dishes clanking and smell the coffee. Hoot's served an array of sandwiches with tea or milk for 15¢. It also served dinners—roast beef or pork with potatoes and gravy—for 15¢ and with bread and butter for a quarter. Oysters apparently were in demand at Hoot's, where oyster stew was 20¢ and a half-dozen fried or raw cost 10¢. Hooten, a Tipton County native, owned restaurants in Tipton and Atlanta several years but gave them up to become a conductor for the Nickel Plate Railroad, from which he retired. Born in 1888, he died in 1959. (Both, Deb and Ray Tharp.)

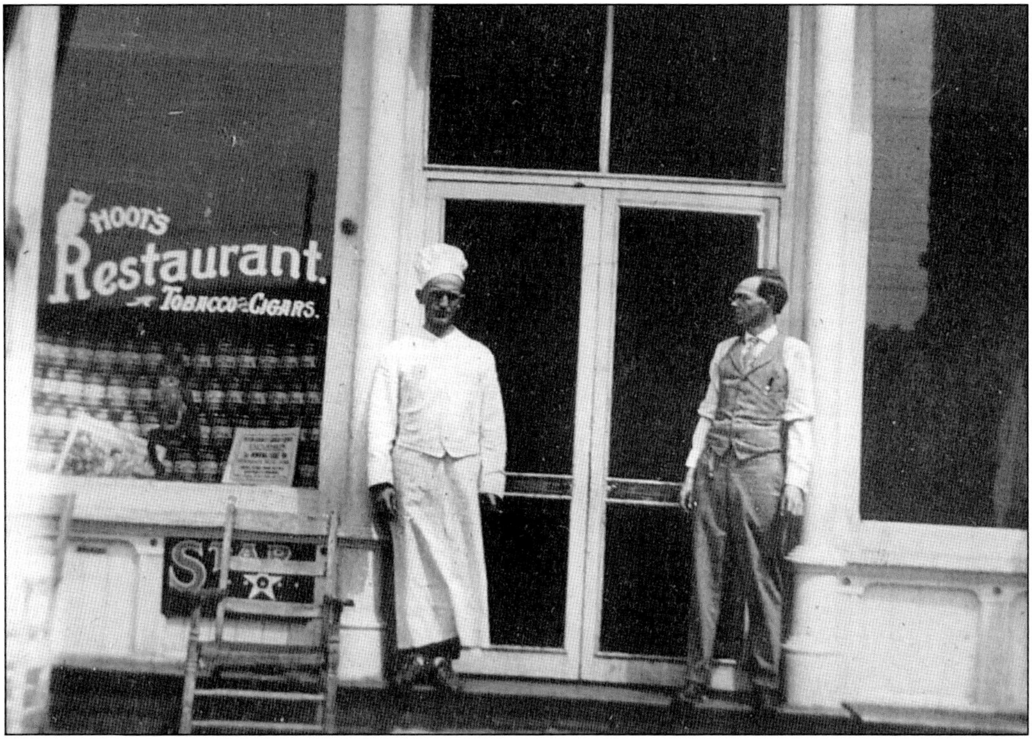

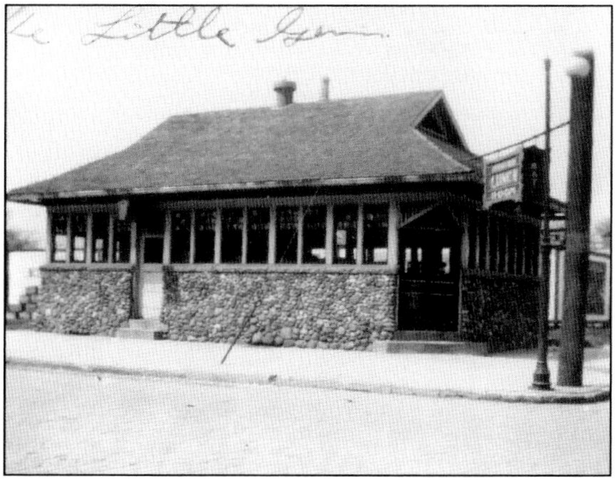

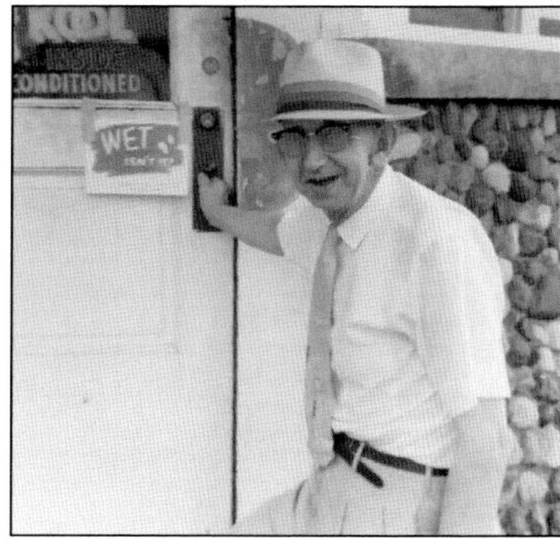

In 1910, Charlie Bates built the Little Gem on the corner of Main and Madison Streets, across from the interurban terminal. He operated the restaurant until 1920, when Guy Burokes took over for a couple years. Burokes sold it to Kirklin resident D.L. Campbell (below right), who moved his family—wife Mary Minnie, son Coe (below left), and daughter Olive—to Tipton. They all worked there, along with loyal employee, Carl Harvey (above). Throughout the Campbells' first 10 years, the Gem never closed. That changed during the war years, when it began closing at 7:30 p.m. In a 1966 *Tribune* article, Coe says his customers cannot get enough of the Gem's baked beans and brain sandwiches. The Little Gem closed permanently at the end of the business day on May 28, 1966. Since then, numerous businesses have resided there. (Above, Richard Harvey; below, library archives.)

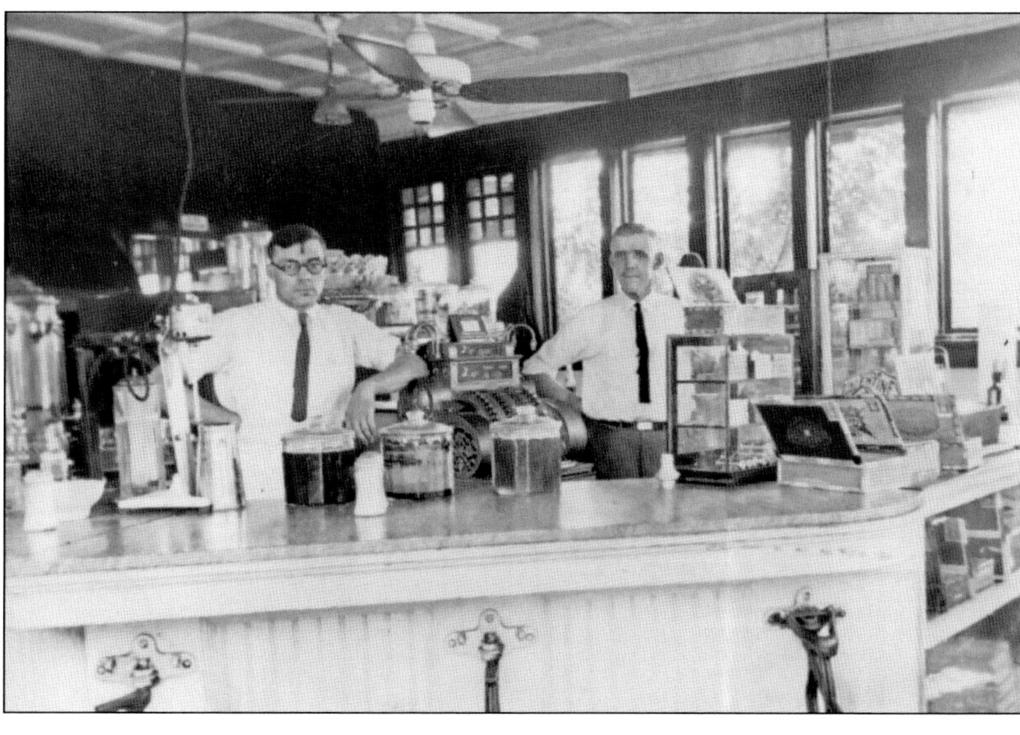

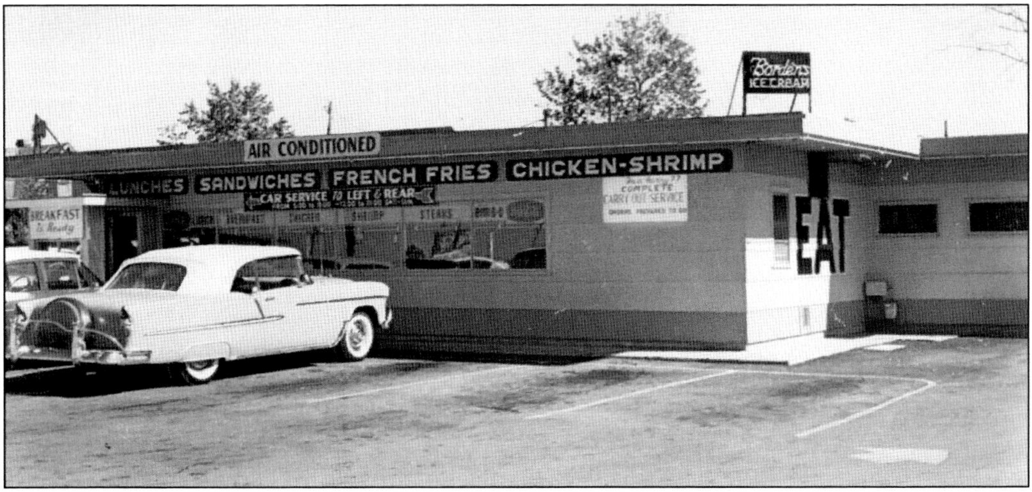

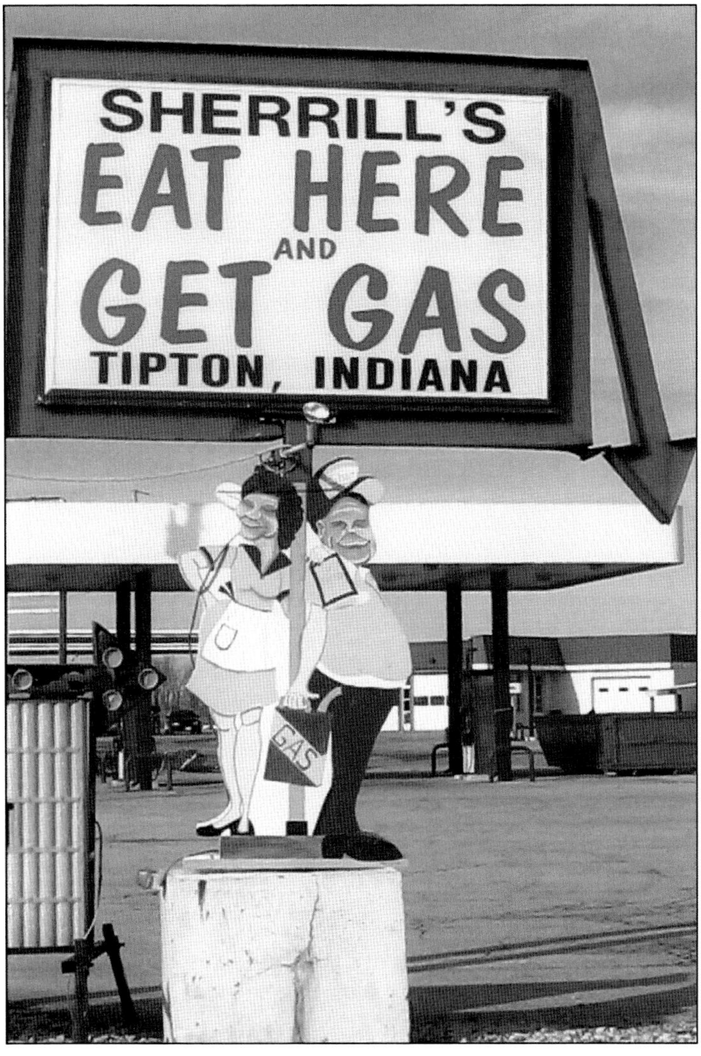

Roscoe and Mary Wiggins built Briggs Drive-in at the intersection of State Roads 28 and 31 in 1954. For 20 years, the restaurant was among the county's best loved. Praised for its home-style dinners, Briggs credited its meticulous cook, Gertrude, who whipped up every dish from scratch, even jelly. Mary's longtime involvement with the Indiana State Fair earned her connections with many celebrities, and there was no telling which of them might drop in at Briggs next. Among them were broadcaster Arthur Godfrey, race car driver A.J. Foyt, and the entire Notre Dame football team. The Wigginses sold the business in 1973 to the Sherrill family. Sherrill's popular "Eat Here and Get Gas" road sign (left) prompts smiles by diners and passersby. Operated by Debbie Sherrill, the restaurant is still a county favorite today. (Above, Alice Ricketts; left, author's collection.)

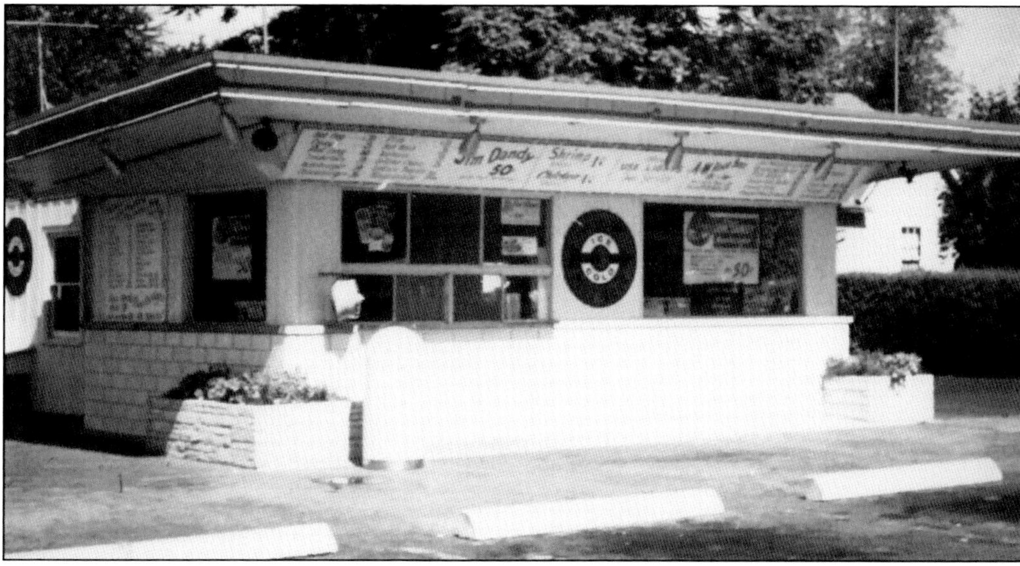

Two of Tipton's favorite eating places in the 1950s and 1960s were the A&W Root Beer stand (above), known for its hot dogs and frosty mugs of root beer; and the Polar Bear Frozen Custard (below), popular for its freezer-fresh vanilla and chocolate ice cream. Harry Reasner Jr. purchased the ice cream stand in 1950 and expanded his business venture in 1955 with the root beer stand. Both were seasonal and frequented by patrons of all ages. The establishments hired high school students to prepare and serve orders, the A&W offering curb service. The A&W became the Jim Dandy Restaurant in 1966. The Polar Bear transformed in 1981 to a traditional fast-food establishment, and in 1988, the Reasners converted it to a Dairy Queen. Both restaurants occupy their longtime locations and remain in the Reasner family today. (Both, Dave Reasner.)

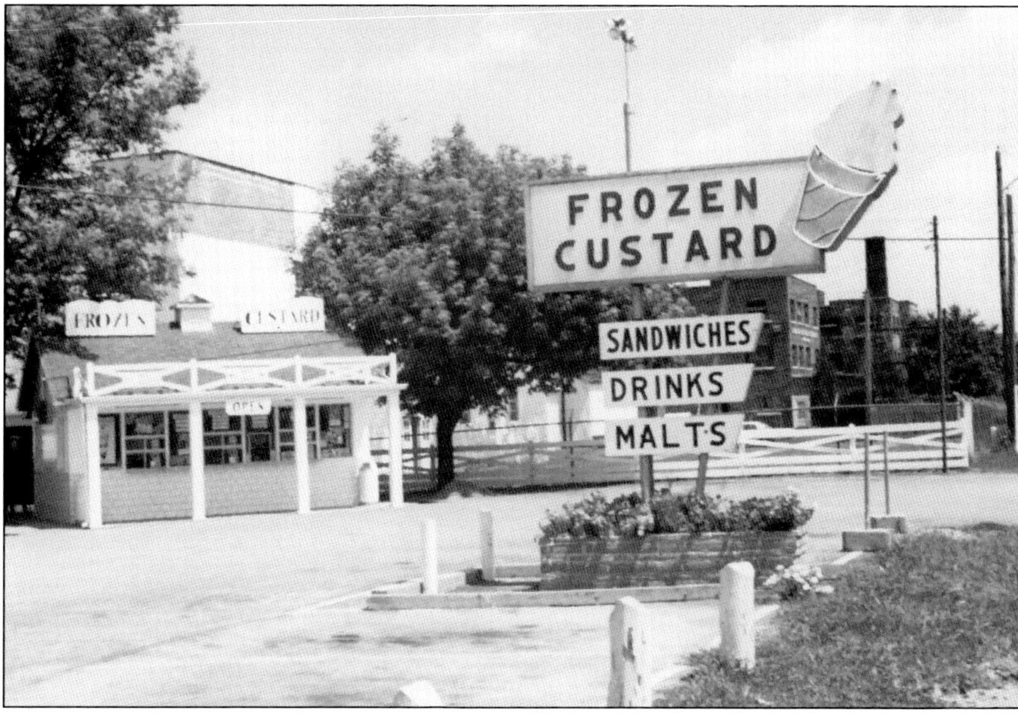

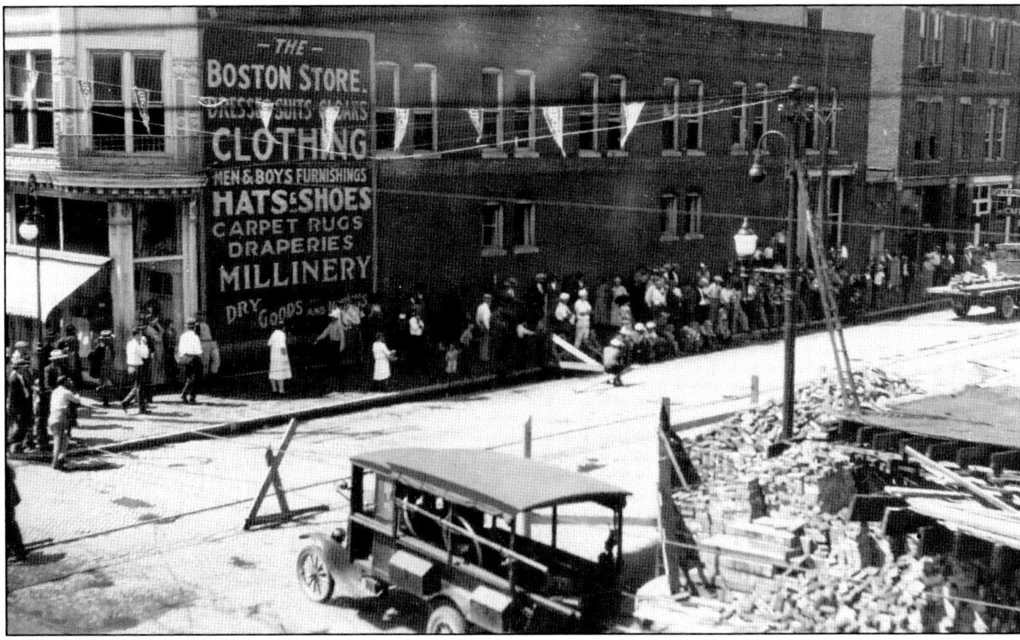

Citizens National Bank stood at the corner of Court and Jefferson Streets for decades. Above, buildings at the northwest corner of Main and Jefferson were razed in 1925, making room for a new Citizens Bank, which opened in September 1926. Unfortunately, it was destroyed January 6, 1930, by fire. Although the bank was gutted, its vault was left intact. The bank was rebuilt and reopened later that year. (Stephen Doi.)

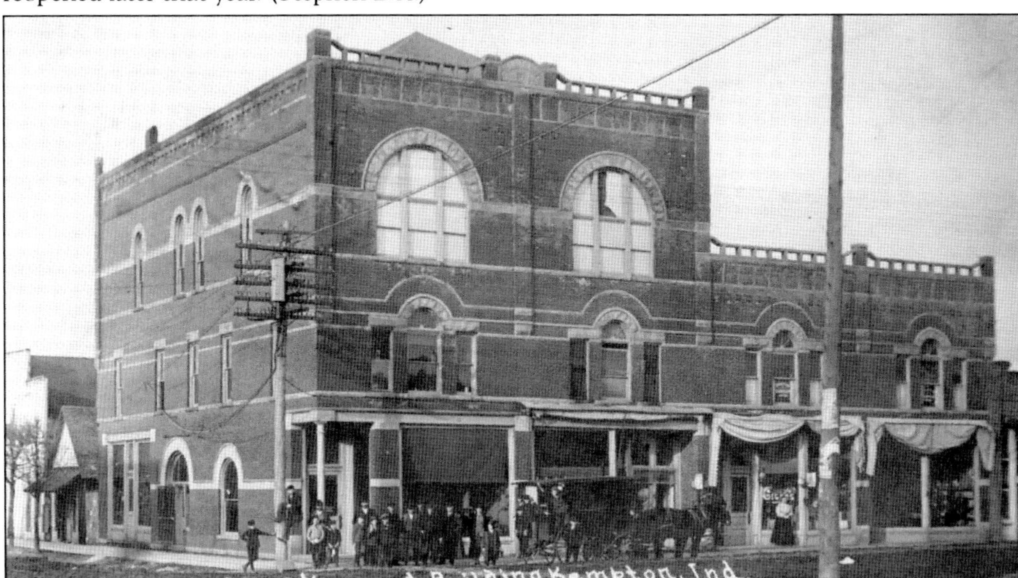

Over the years, Kempton's Vanvorst Building, shown here in 1909, housed the Kempton Bank, telephone and newspaper offices, a theater, and a ballroom. In September 1925, three robbers entered the bank but fled after alarms sounded. The armed bandits stole and hid Dr. W.F. Dunham's Ford as a backup getaway vehicle, but they did not need it. They escaped in their own car but were later nabbed in another county. (Alice Ricketts.)

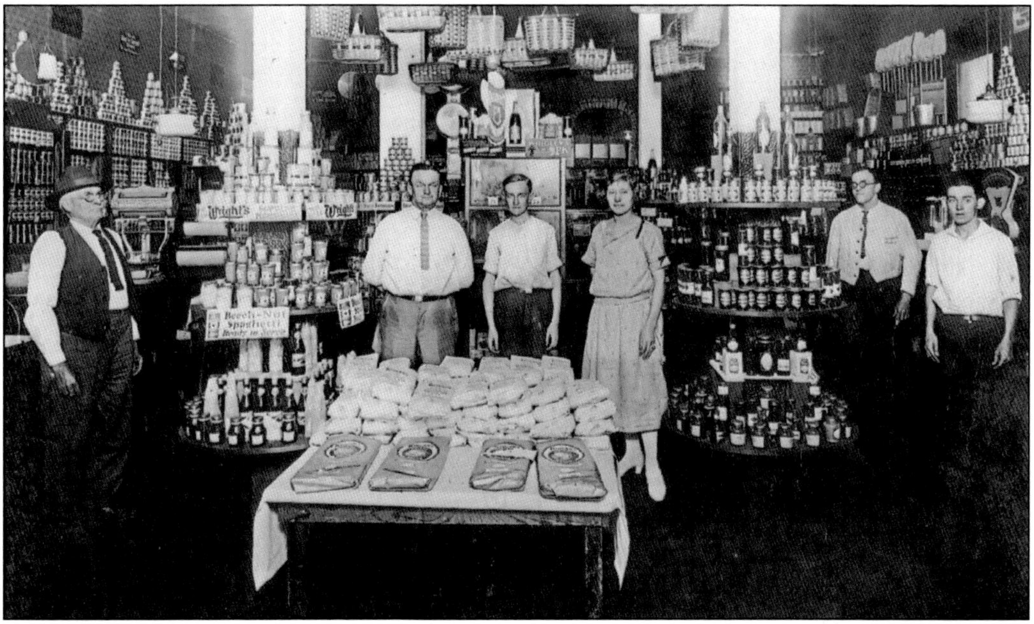

The Bargain Grocery was located at 20 South Main Street, Tipton. Shown in the center are store owner Rueben Lett, left; Rueben's son Ralph; and employee Esther Dunn. The man on the far left and the two on the right are unidentified. The photograph was taken in 1924. (Tom Lett.)

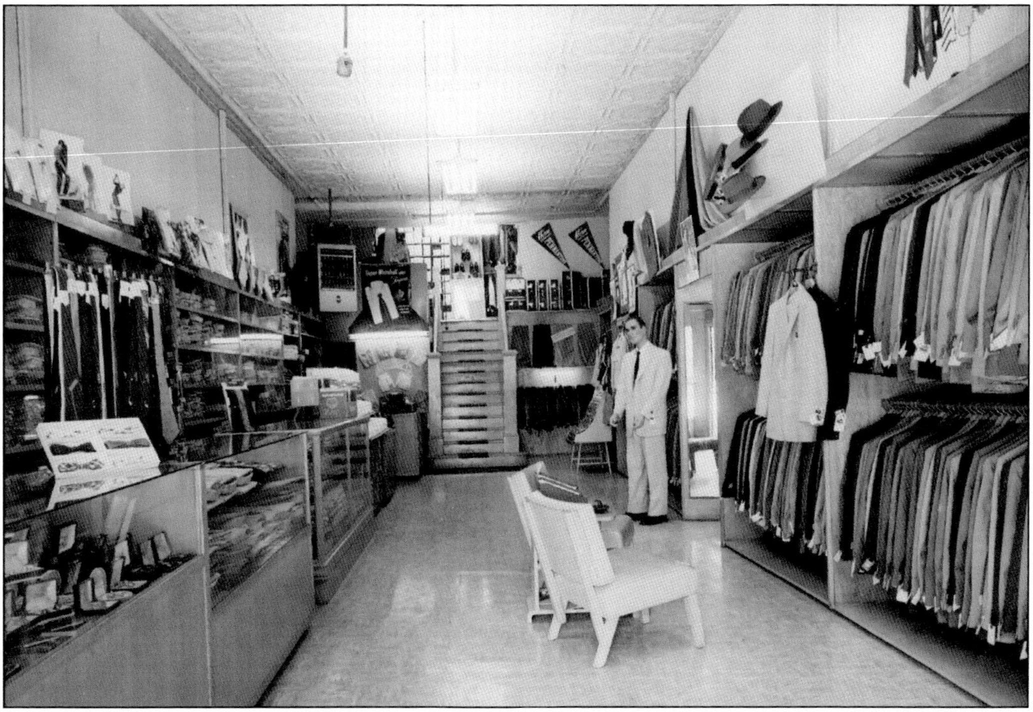

Lett's Men's Store, owned by Robert Lett, occupied a Jefferson Street storefront in the heart of downtown Tipton from the mid-1950s through the early 1960s. Before the lure of suburban shopping malls and big-box stores that began springing up in the 1960s, locally owned and operated men's and women's clothing stores such as Lett's flourished. (Tom Lett.)

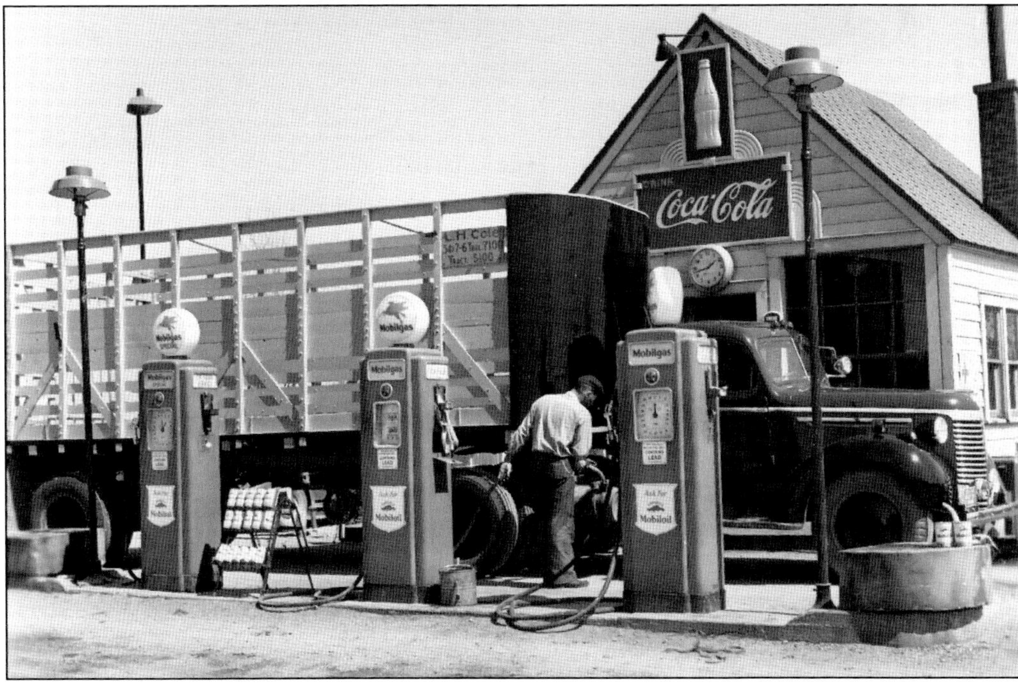

Oren Egler's Mobil gas station occupied the southeast corner of the intersection of 28 and 31, offering motorists 24-hour service. In this c. 1950 photograph, Scott Bilby is filling up Lloyd Cole's tractor-trailer. The July 29, 1952, *Tipton Tribune* reported that the state civil defense maintained an observation post at the station to keep a round-the-clock watch for Soviet aircraft. (Viola Jones.)

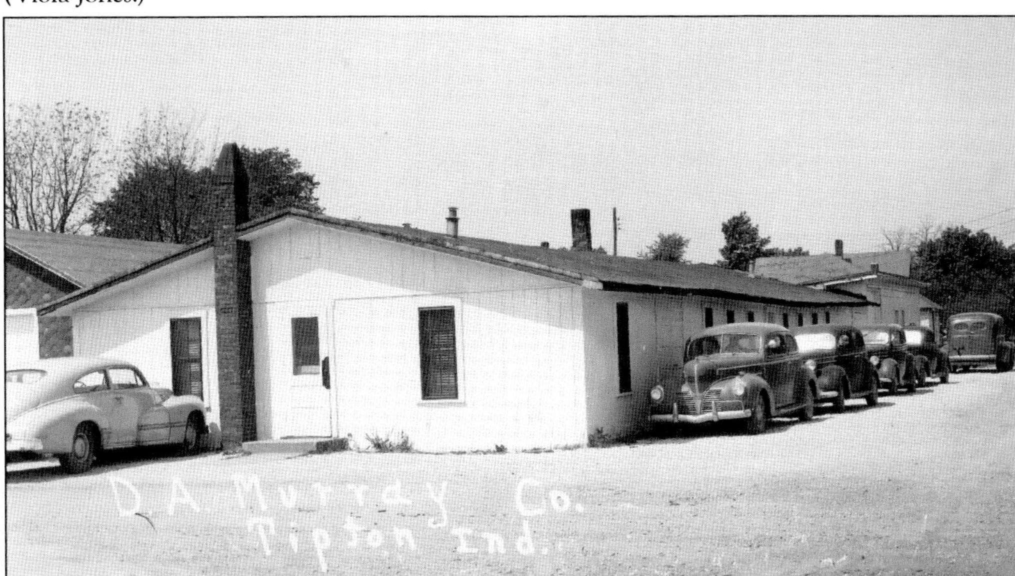

D.A. Murray founded the D.A. Murray Company (DAMCO) at 632 Mill Street around 1937. The company manufactured a variety of electrical cords and wiring devices, which were sold throughout the United States. Born in Elwood in 1898, Murray lived in Tipton most of his life. He died in 1964. DAMCO merged with Anixter Brothers Inc. four years later. (Alice Ricketts.)

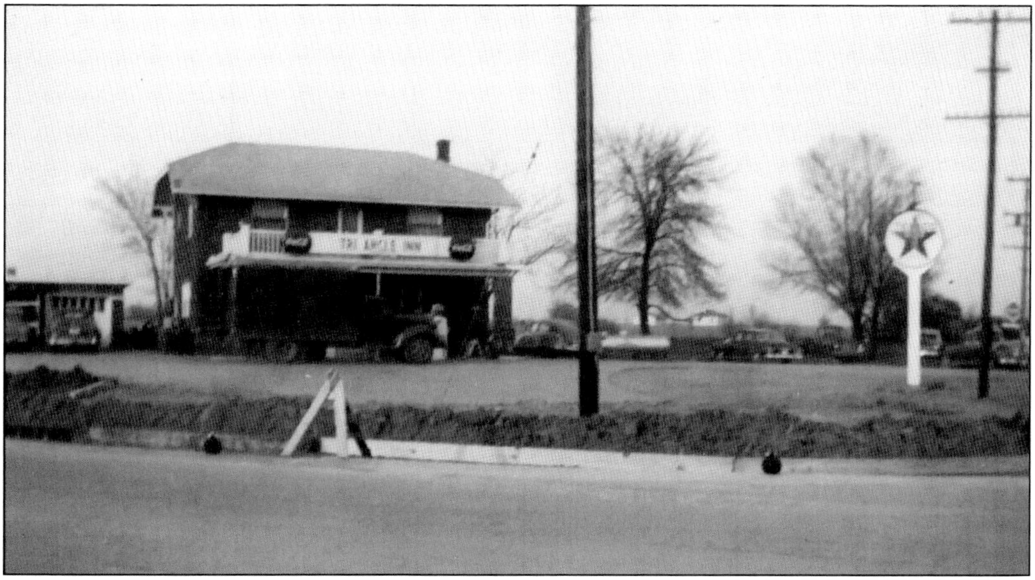

The Triangle Inn—a combination Texaco service station, grocery store, and restaurant—served motorists on the northeast corner of the busy intersection of State Roads 28 and 31 about five miles west of Tipton. Under the ownership of Gene Baranowski, the Triangle Inn remained in business until the mid-1950s. (Gene Baranowski.)

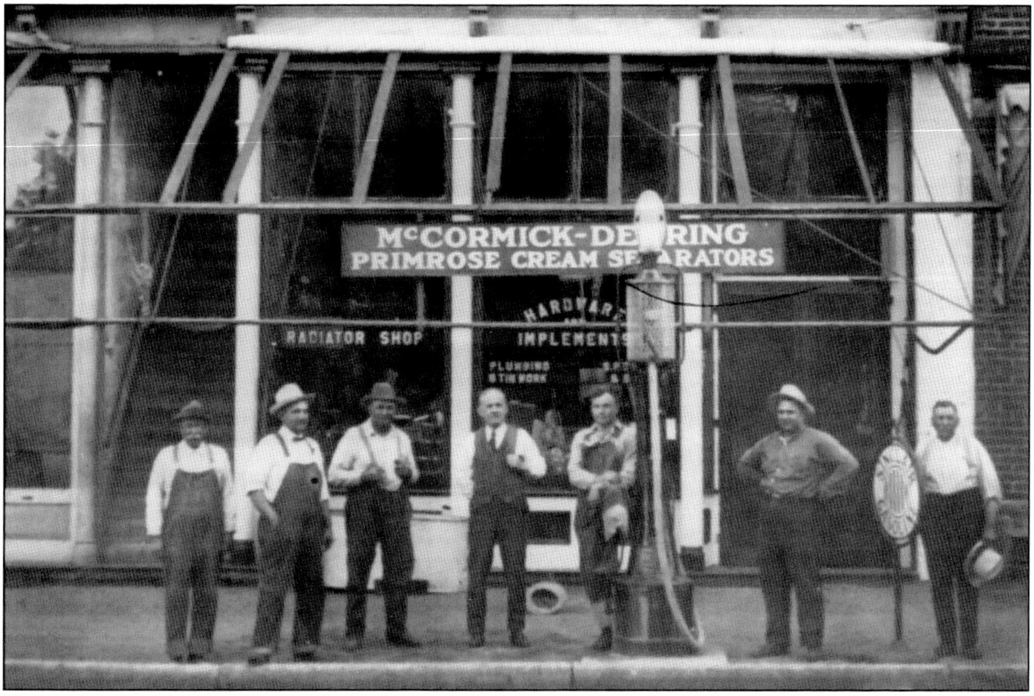

Seven unidentified gentlemen stand before S.P. Bryan and Sons in Windfall, around 1930. The store, owned by Simon P. Bryan, sold hardware, International Harvester and McCormick-Deering farm implements, and Sinclair gasoline. Bryan was born in Clinton County in 1858 and married Nettie Ramsey, also of Clinton County, in 1880. They had four sons and moved to Windfall around 1920. Bryan died in 1939. (Library archives.)

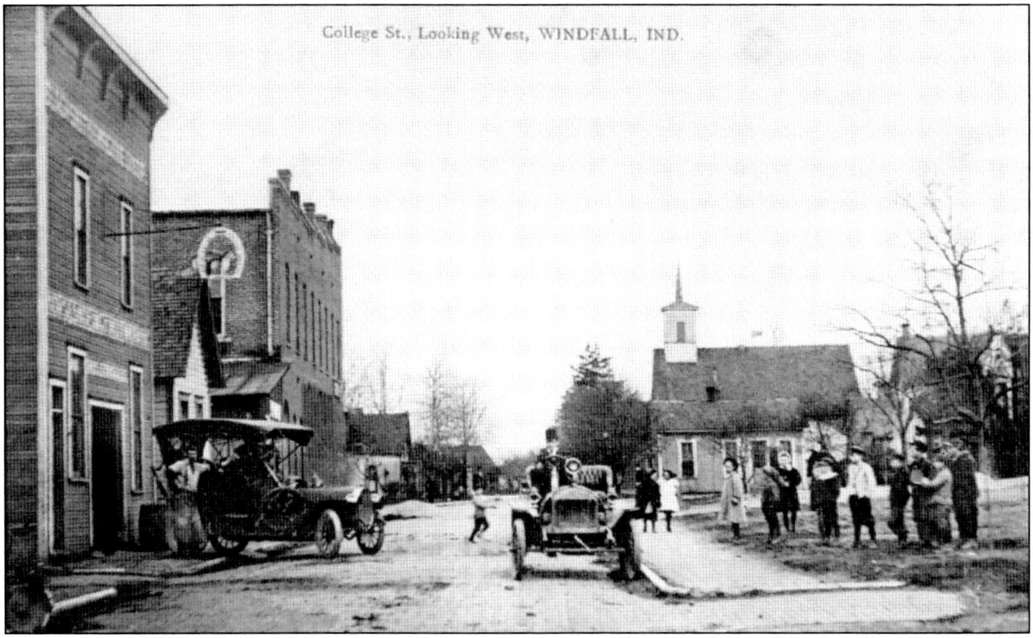

Looking west down Windfall's College Street, this photograph provides a glimpse of daily life there around 1910. A young boy scampers across the wet street to join a line of children, perhaps awaiting rides after school. Two gentlemen—one behind the wheel of his roadster and the other standing next to his Model T—gaze at the photographer. Nearby is the Methodist Episcopal Church, then one of three churches in Windfall. (Alice Ricketts.)

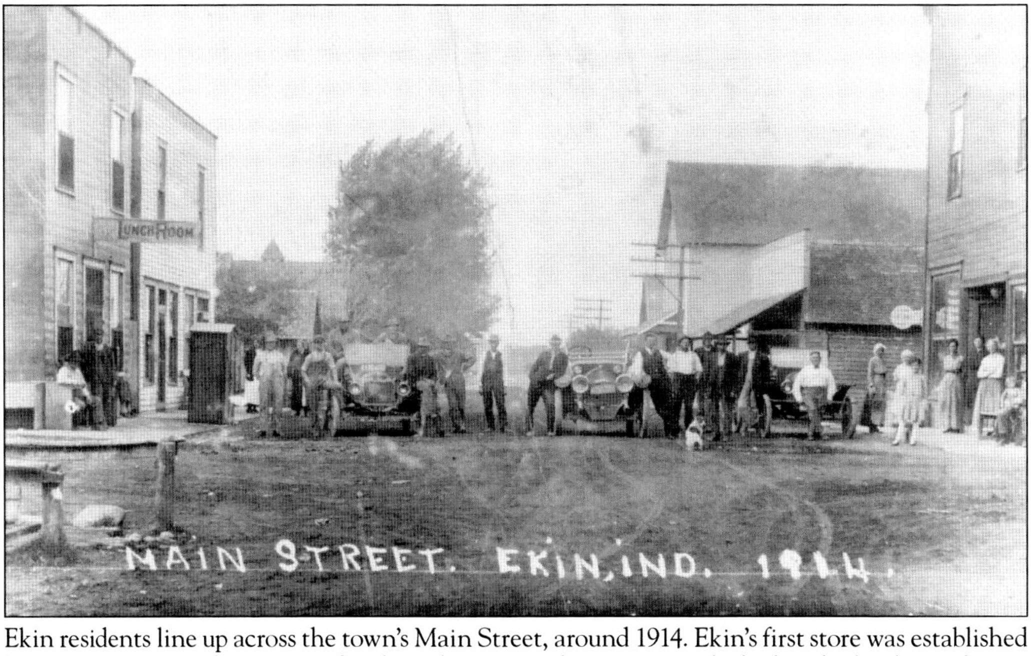

Ekin residents line up across the town's Main Street, around 1914. Ekin's first store was established by James McKee and was in use for about five years. Ekin's roots are linked to the lumber industry; hundreds of acres of unbroken forests existed as late as 1880. In 1883, the town contained two general stores, two millinery shops, a sawmill, and a blacksmith. (Penny Manier.)

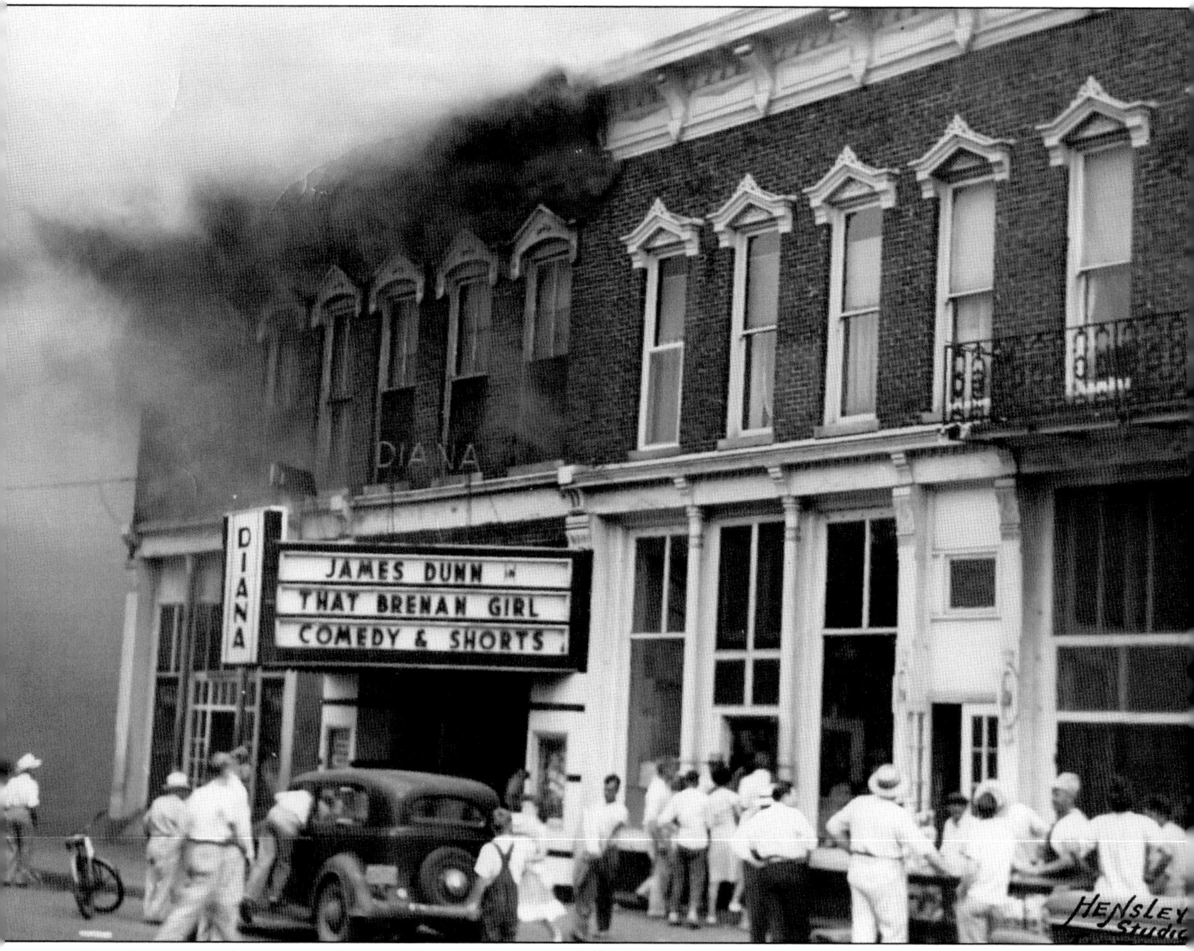

Smoke pours from the Diana Theater's second floor during an August 20, 1947, fire, hindering firemen in their battle against the flames. Witnesses agreed that the fire seemed to explode, shooting smoke through the front door and halfway across the street. Upon the firemen's arrival, they found an inferno at the rear of the auditorium, and smoke was so dense, they could not fight the fire inside. The roof, second floor, and much of the east wall collapsed, injuring one of the firefighters and forcing the rest of them to battle the blaze from a nearby rooftop. After about two hours, the crews finally managed to extinguish the fire. The incident left the building's front intact, but fire, smoke, and water took their toll inside. The Diana was a total loss. Theater owner Nick Paikos vowed he would rebuild. (Jim Paikos.)

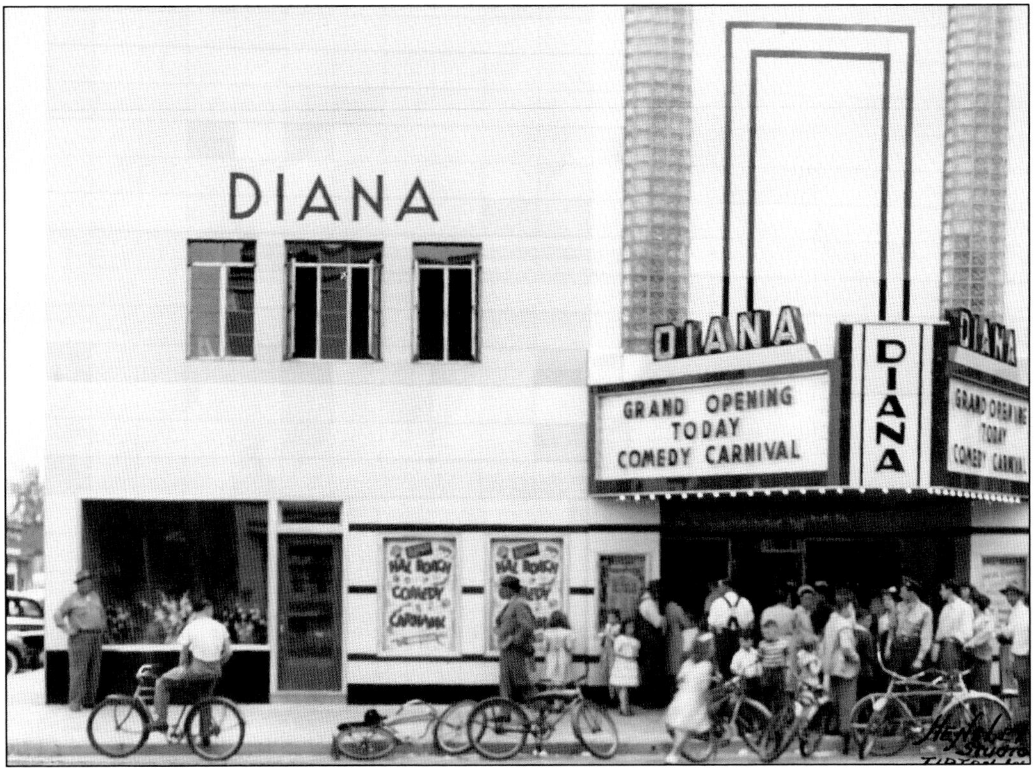

Baskets of congratulatory flowers, two and three rows deep, decorated the lobby of the Diana Theater on Sunday, April 25, 1948, the day Nick Paikos first opened the doors to his rebuilt, modernized movie house (above). The day before, the Paikos family worked steadily from dawn to dark to ensure that every detail would be ready for the grand reopening, and they succeeded. Theatergoers packed the Diana's rebuilt, newly air-conditioned auditorium (below). Paikos, who immigrated to the United States from Greece at the age of 14, took over the Diana in 1926. During the next 54 years, he consistently greeted his patrons with a handshake and a warm smile. Paikos died August 26, 1980, at the age of 78. A large portrait of him has graced the lobby ever since. His son Jim carries on his father's legacy. (Both, Jim Paikos.)

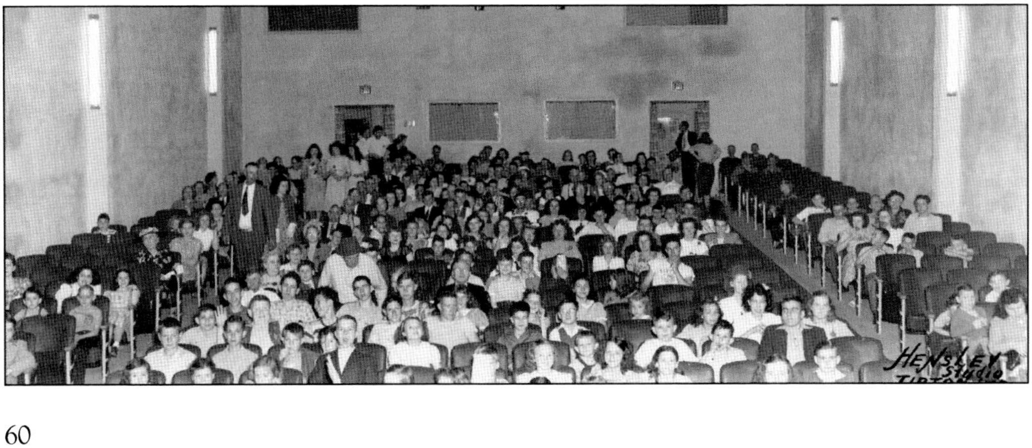

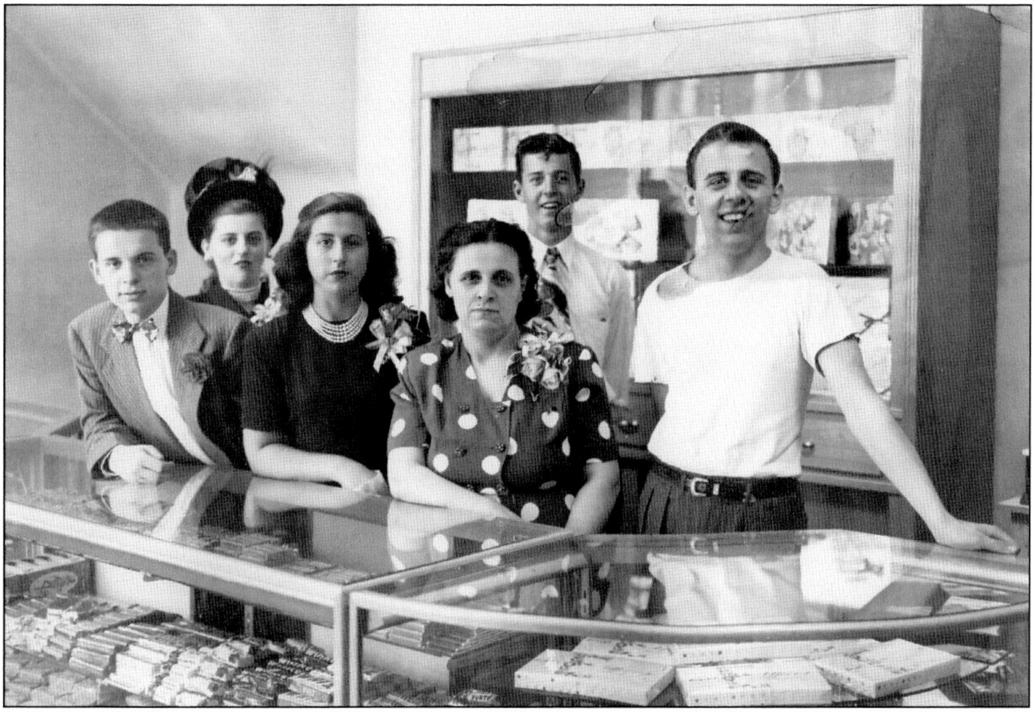

Running the Diana Theater was a family affair for the Paikoses, especially on the day of the Diana's grand reopening. Above, tending to the new sweet shop are, from left to right, Jim Paikos, Georgia Stevins, Sara H. Spensos, Sophia Paikos, Art Smeltser, and Larry Paikos. Shown at right, the ever-congenial Nick Paikos welcomes an estimated 1,500 theatergoers with his signature smile. For the special event, Paikos treated the eager, returning movie patrons to a Hal Roach comedy carnival. In its April 26, 1948, report of the reopening, the *Tipton Tribune* quotes Paikos, who said, "Tipton is a wonderful town. The people have been mighty good to me." The feeling was mutual. (Both, Jim Paikos.)

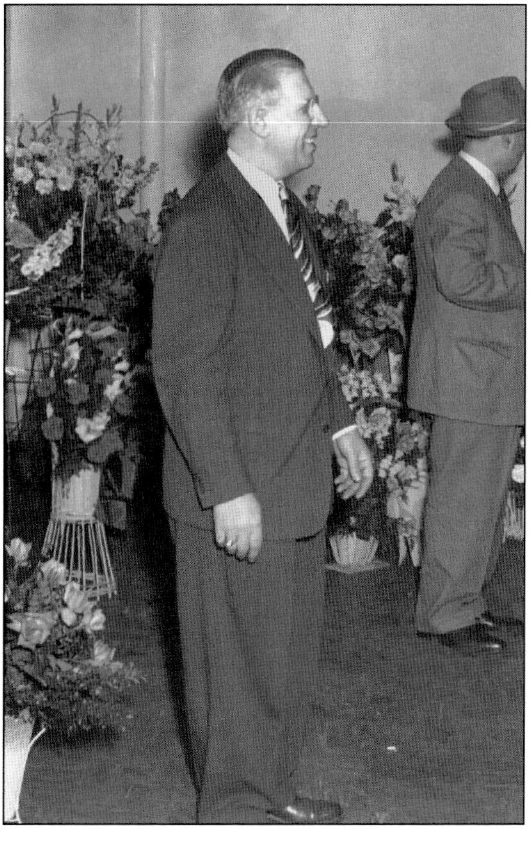

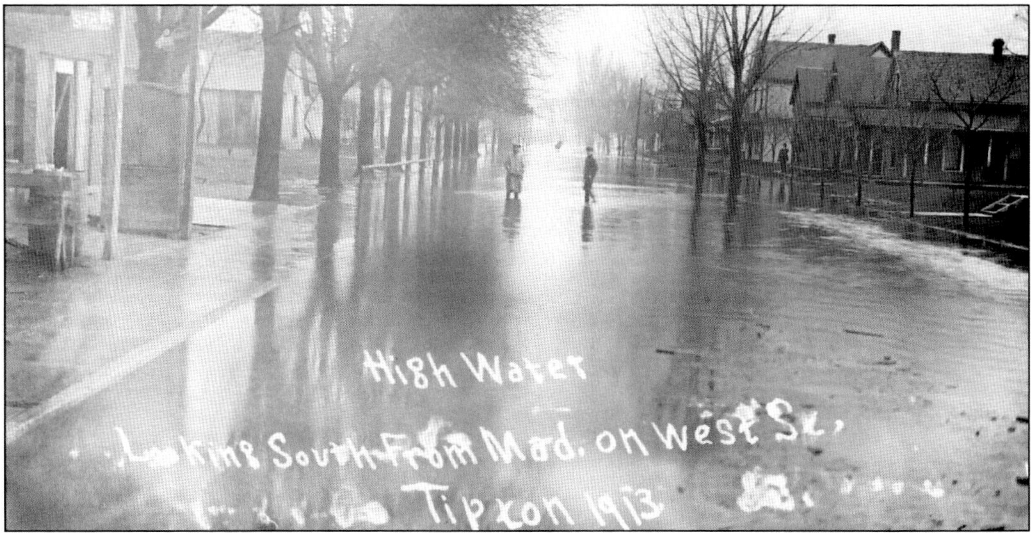

Friday, March 21, 1913, across the Midwest, the rain started with fierce winds that blew down trees and peeled off roofs. Saturday, it was still pouring, and by Sunday, it was coming down in torrents, accompanied by heavy hail and lightning. By Monday, the nonstop storm had flooded several states. In Tipton, Cicero and Buck Creeks burst their banks, spilling water north, south, east, and west, forcing residents to hustle for higher ground with whatever belongings they could manage in tow. Trains stopped running. People took shelter. Not since 1896 had Tipton seen such a deluge. Finally, Tuesday, the rain stopped and the floodwaters started to recede. Hundreds flocked to the courthouse tower to marvel at the flooded countryside. According to the *Tribune*, the view was "very good." (Above, library archives; below, Alice Ricketts.)

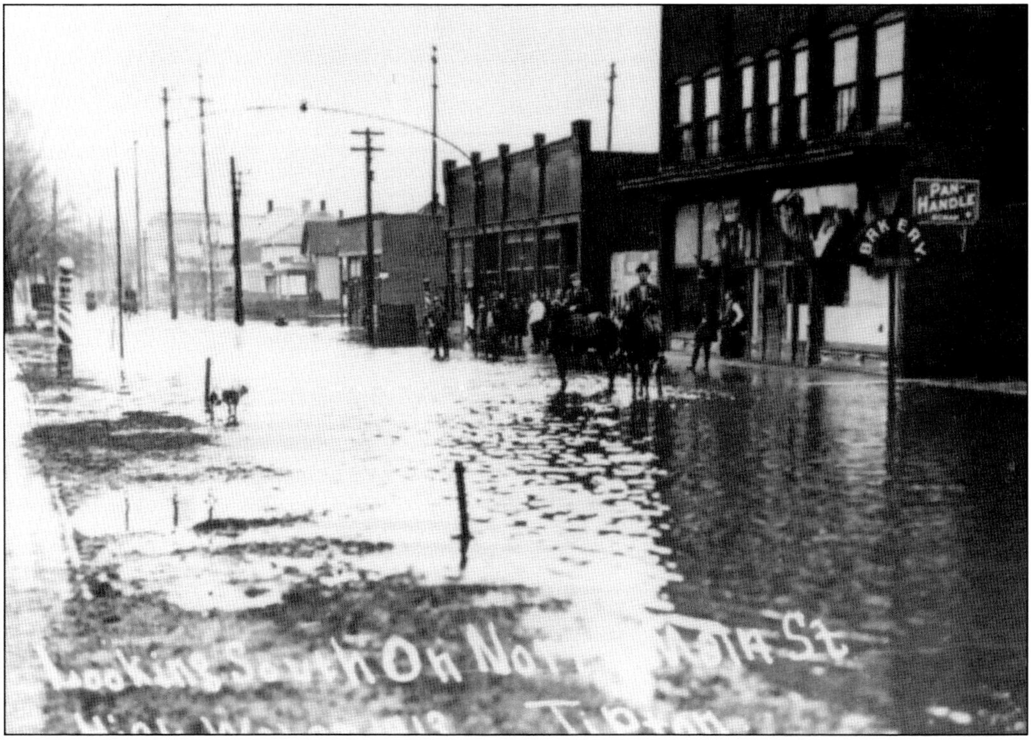

Four

AGRICULTURE

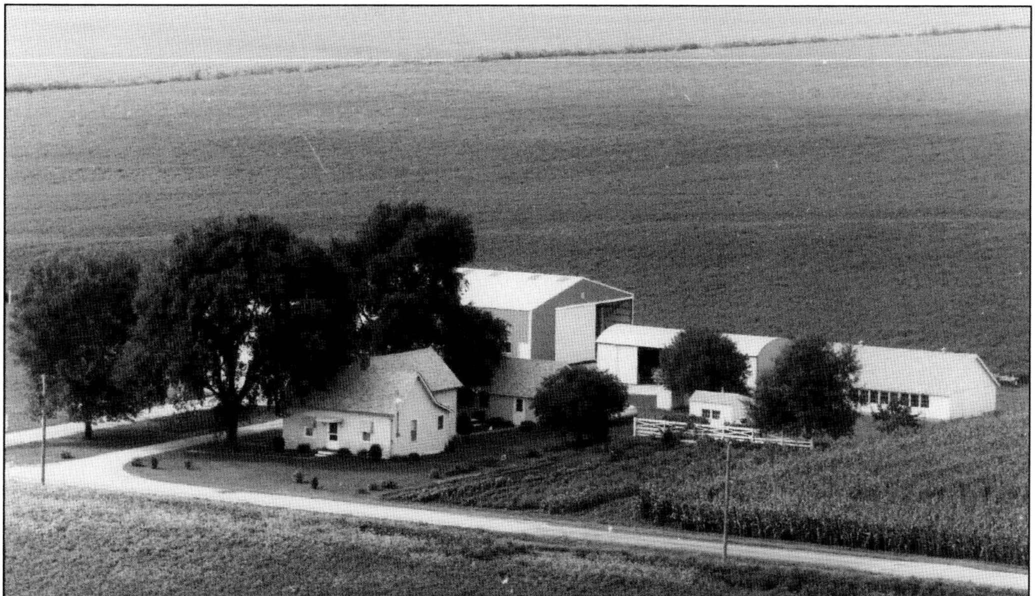

The farm shown in this aerial photograph is located near Hobbs. At the time the photograph was taken, the farm belonged to Sarah and Lloyd "Doc" Brinson, who lived there all their married lives and raised corn and soybeans, hogs, cattle, and chickens. Sarah had grown up on the farm, which had been in her family many years prior to the Brinsons' marriage. Sarah passed away in 1997; Lloyd died in 2002. (Heather Magee.)

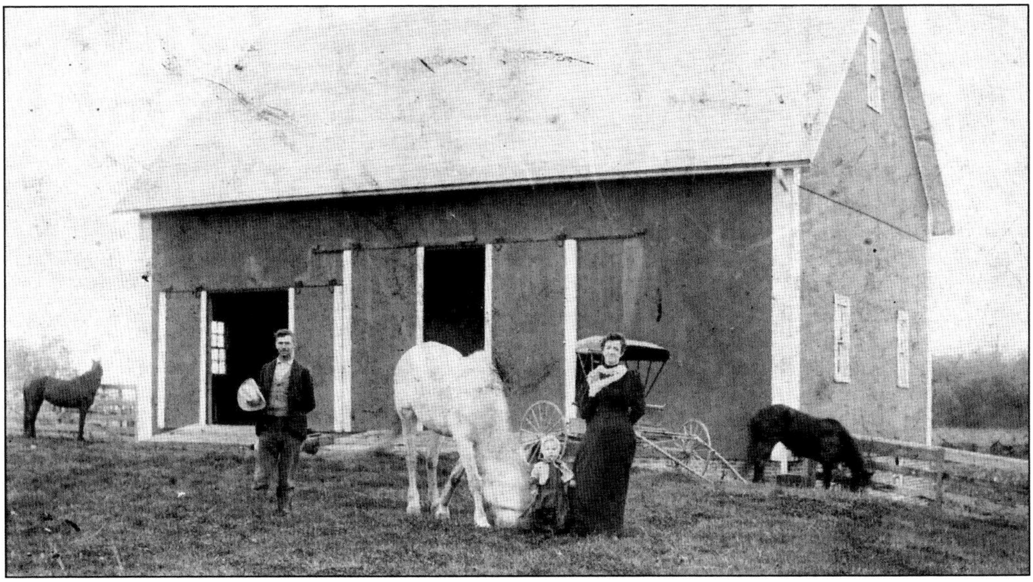

Thomas B. and Nellie E. Pratt pose with their daughter Agnes Geneva "Peg" on their farm, located southeast of Tipton, around 1907. The Pratts married in 1893 and were farmers until 1939, when they moved to Tipton. Thomas was born in rural Sharpsville in 1874 and died in 1950. Nellie was born near Brooksburg in 1875 and died in 1961. (Joan Wray.)

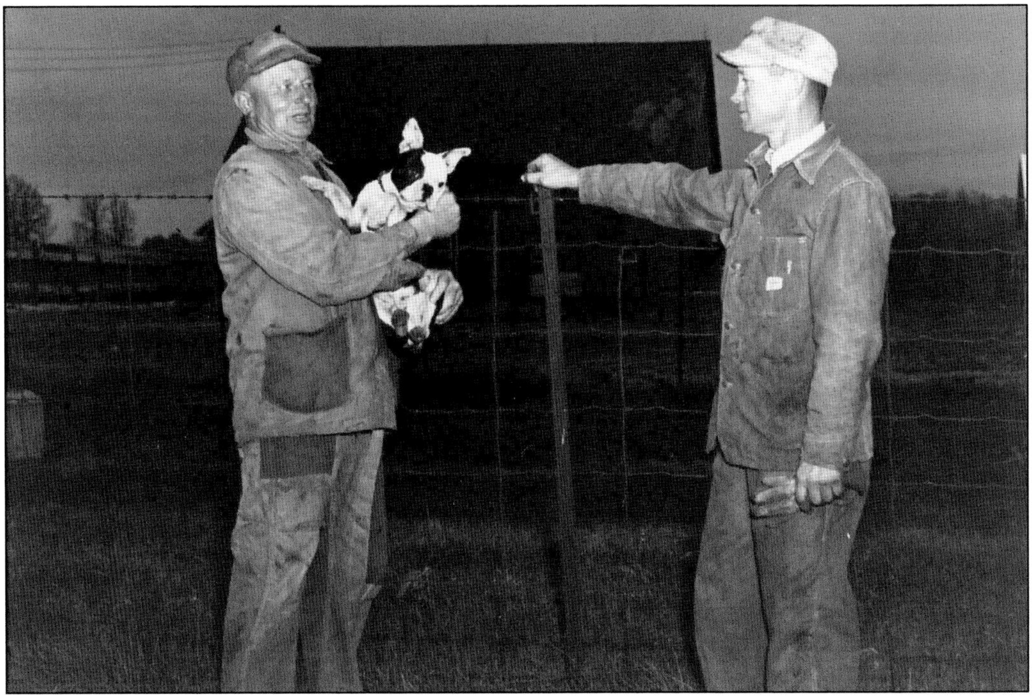

Tipton County farmer Theodore Funke, left, with son, Joe, gained distinction with his unique white corn, grown from a seed that had been in the Funke family for more than 100 years when it was brought to this country in 1884 by his German-born father, John T. He had obtained it from his grandfather. The hearty, fast-growing corn became known as "Funke's 90-Day White." (Catherine and William Funke.)

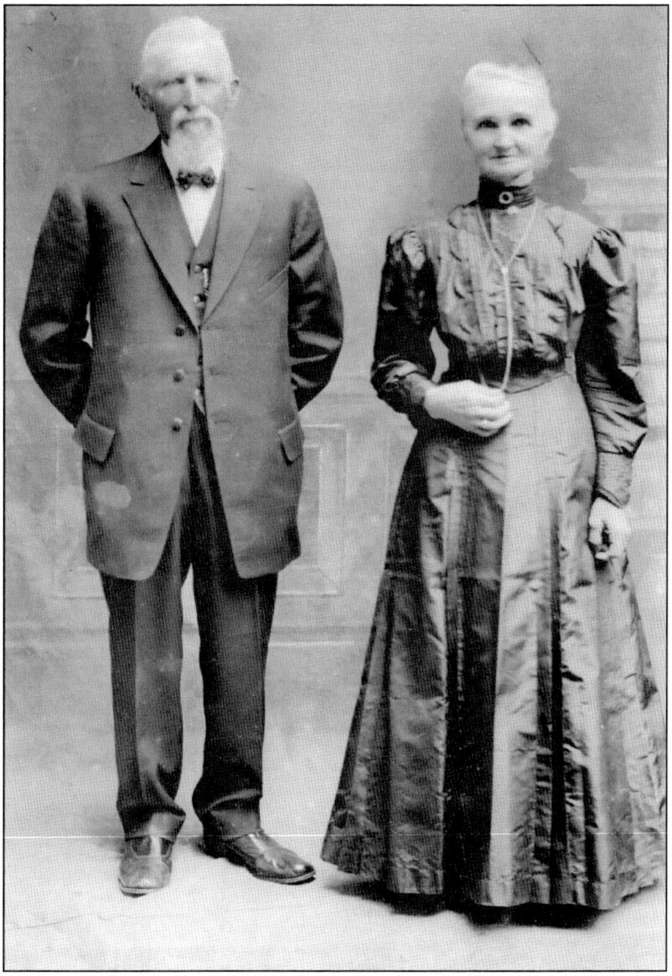

John and Josephine Funke married in Franklin County April 18, 1861. They relocated to Tipton County in 1887, settling on farmland three miles east of Tipton. An April 18, 1921, *Tribune* article states that the Funkes "spent their best years developing and making the land one of the finest farms in the county." John died at home in 1923. Josephine died in 1928, also at home. (Catherine and William Funke.)

Before the invention of modern combines, threshing was a laborious, all-day event requiring help of many farmhands. The photograph shows threshing at the Funke farm around 1940. Friends and family met there for the day, and the menfolk worked the fields while the wives remained at the house cooking up a huge meal. Threshing is the process of separating the chaff from the gain. (Catherine and William Funke.)

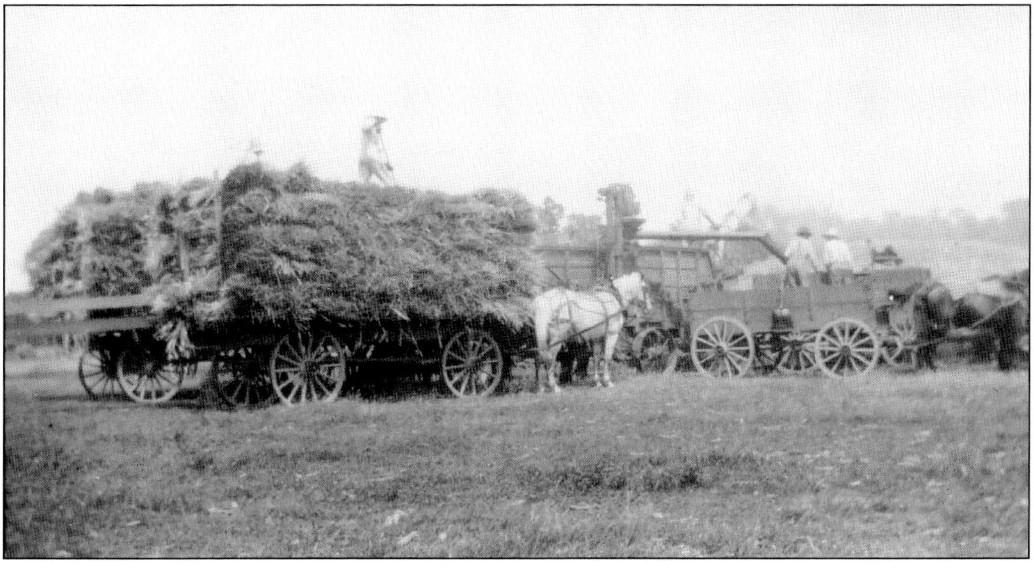

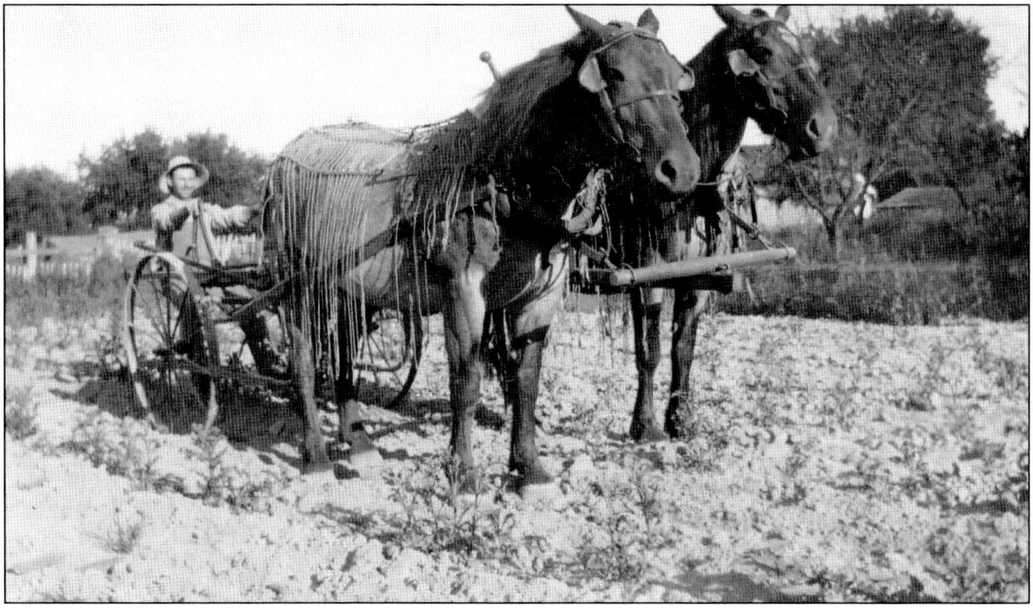

In this c. 1920 photograph, Tipton County farmer Willard Smith drives a two-horse plow on his land located on County Road 400 South near Kempton. Smith equipped the horses with corded horse-fly nets, designed to scare away flies and spare the horses from their bites. Smith died April 1, 1931, at the age of 45. (Viola Jones.)

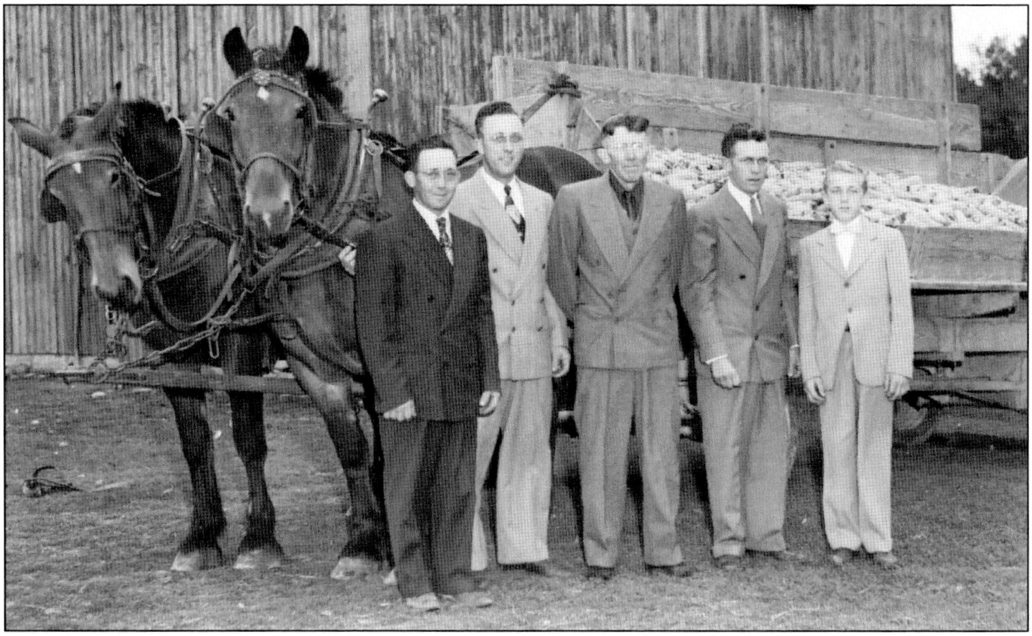

Francis Valentine Dane (center) and his four sons, from left to right, Joseph, Henry, Bernie, and Clem, have decided to have their picture taken one Sunday, likely in the fall of 1948, after church at the family farm southeast of Tipton. Francis was a farmer, who, with the help of his sons, raised soybeans, tomatoes, wheat, and corn, as evidenced by the wagon full of corn. (Heather Magee.)

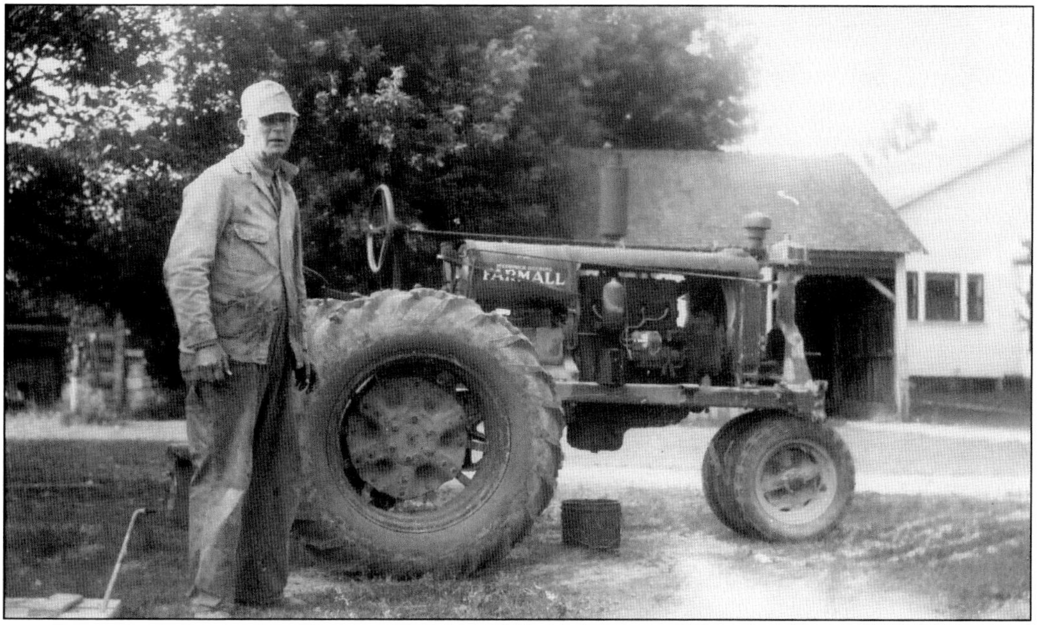

James Mont Hawkins pauses from the work he's doing on his Farmall tractor at his Sharpsville farm around 1942. Hawkins and his wife, Belle, were lifelong Tipton County residents. He raised cattle and crops two miles east of Sharpsville on the farm his father, Jonas, had built in 1894. (Gae Matchette.)

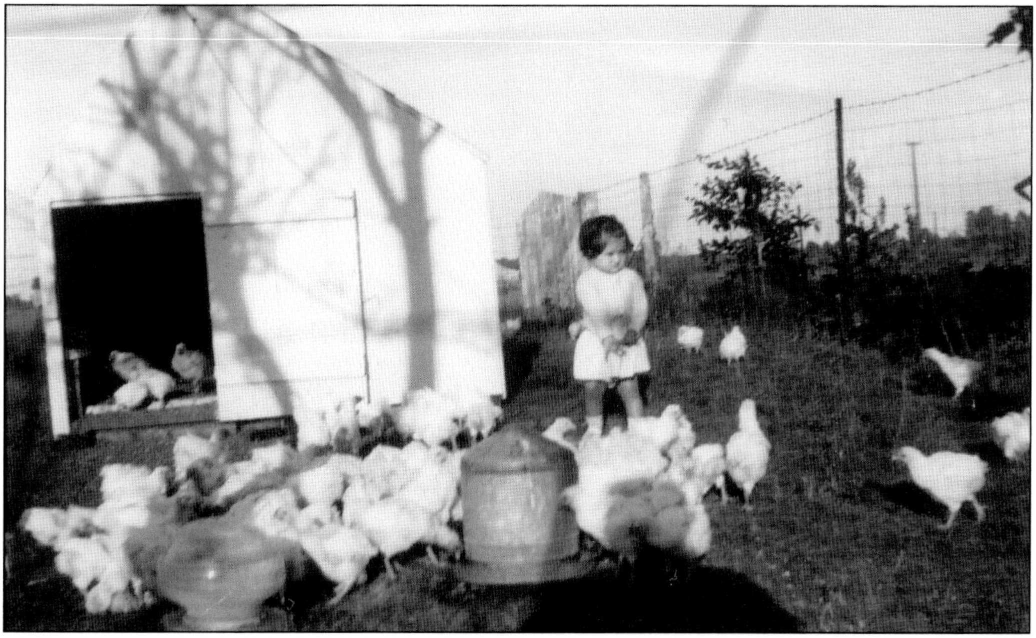

Little Ann Durr scatters feed for a flock of chickens during one of her frequent visits to the farm belonging to her aunt and uncle, Sarah and Lloyd Brinson. The photograph, likely taken in 1953, shows Ann performing one of the chores she enjoyed each time she took a trip to the "country." (Heather Magee.)

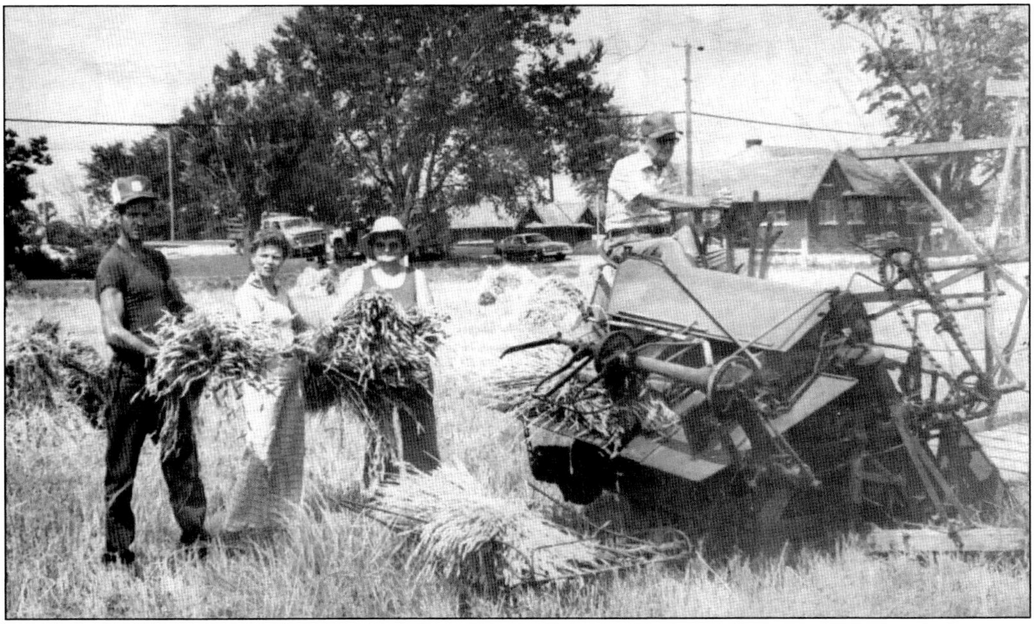

Shocking wheat was a family affair in the summer of 1958 for the Zieglers. From left to right, they are Ken; his sister, Mildred; their mother, Ann; and their father, Elmer, who is driving the binder. The Ziegler farm is located near the junction of State Roads 213 and 28. (Ken Ziegler.)

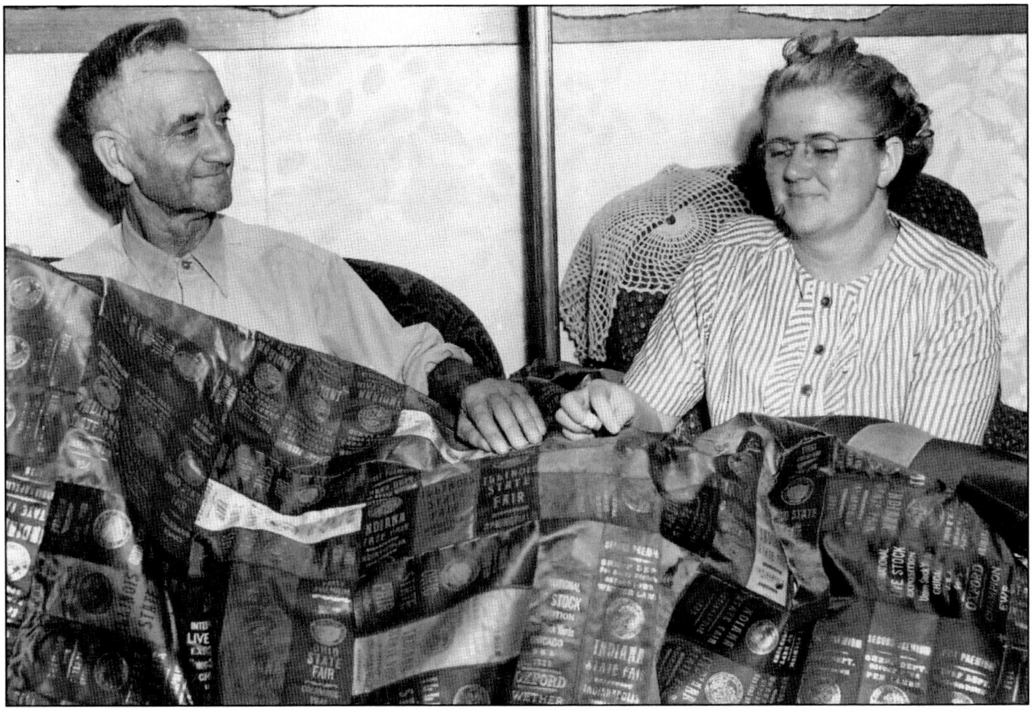

Ozy "Ote" Quakenbush of Sharpsville and his daughter Maxine Nash display the quilt that was handcrafted for him by his mother-in-law, Lula Ramseyer. The quilt is made of the ribbons he won at the Indiana, Illinois, and Ohio state fairs and other shows for his Oxford sheep. This photograph was taken in 1944, a short time before his death. (Madonna Alderson.)

Five

FAITH AND COMMUNITY

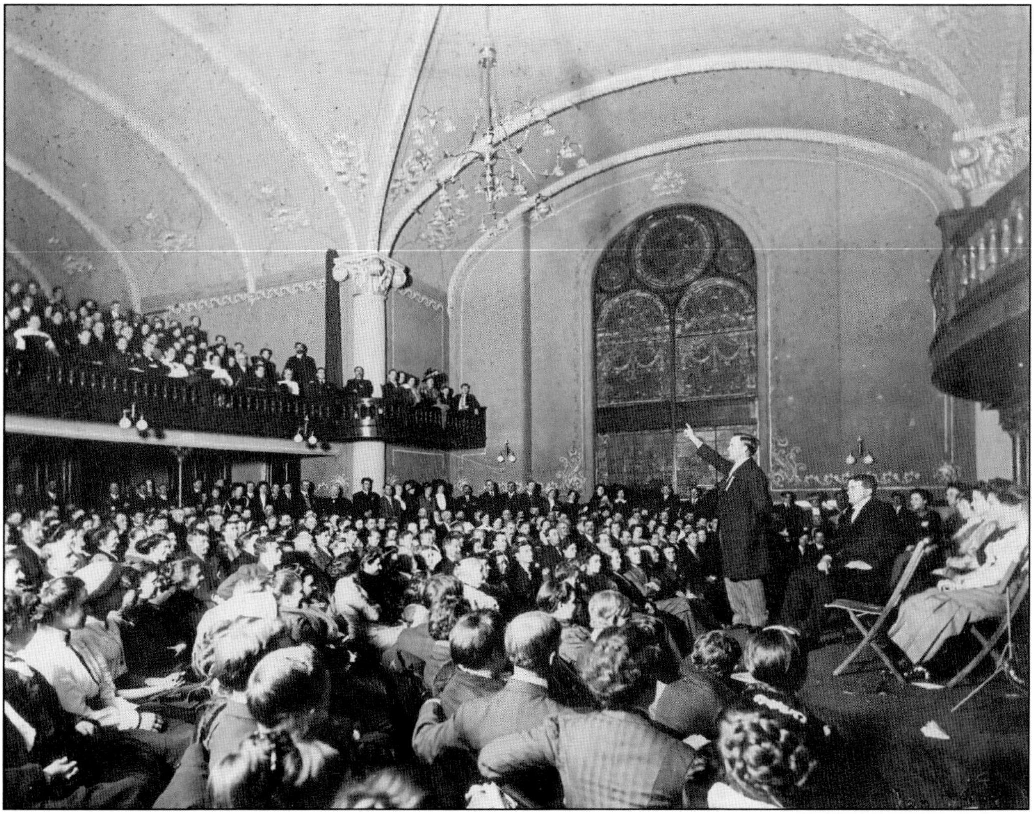

A rousing sermon in the sanctuary of West Street Christian Church captures the congregation's interest. The event, part of a revival series at the church in January 1912, was headed by Evangelist Snively, a popular preacher who spoke at churches throughout the United States. Attendance reportedly exceeded that of any previous such event and resulted in numerous new members and many donations. (Janet Driver.)

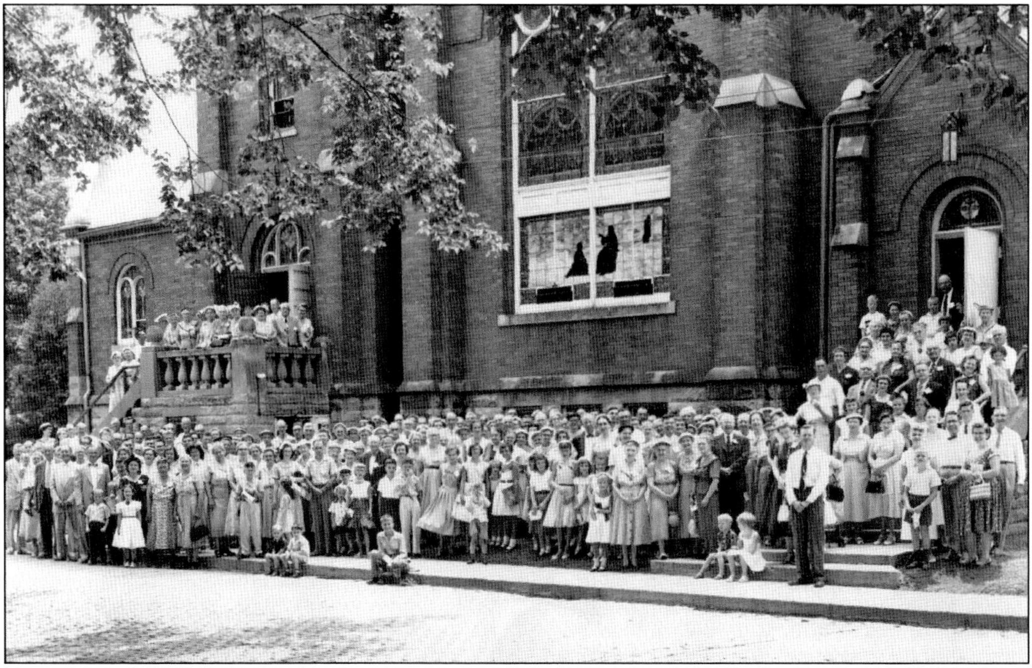

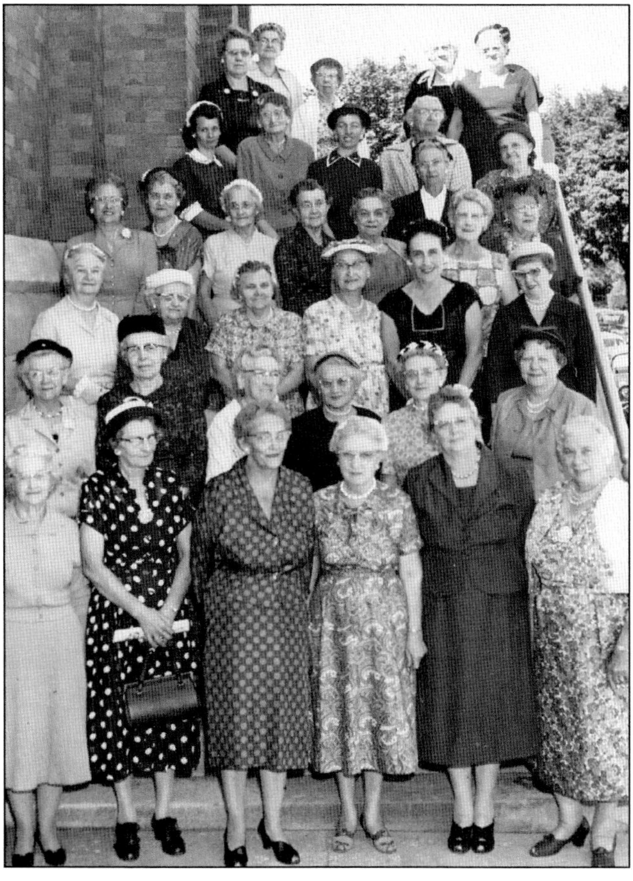

Above, the congregation at West Street Christian Church gathers on a sunny summer's day for a group photograph, about 1950. At left, the ladies' Sunday school class poses for a picture on the steps, around 1960. The ladies are identified as, from left to right, (first row) Ella Wilson, Ethel Huffman, Ruby Fike, Lora Bozell, Adaline Racobs and Hazel Standerford; (second row) Eva Pickett, Hazel Coppock, Hazel Burton, Olive Linderman, Maude Miller, and Maria Jones; (third row) Mayme French, Maude Bolton, Inez Tudor, Lydia Moore, Ruth Russell, and Verna Curtis; (fourth row) Eva Crawford, Chloe Sharum, Lelia Barr, Fay McKinney, Tessie Smitson, Cleo McCulley, and Bessie Kinder; (fifth row) Roxie Emberton, Blanche Ploughe, Dorothy Ploughe, Ethel Self, Pearl Self, and Nellie Hinkle; (sixth row) Bertha Gunkel, Ruby Ray, Flora Teter, Daisy Verguson, and Lelia Jones. (Both, Janet Driver.)

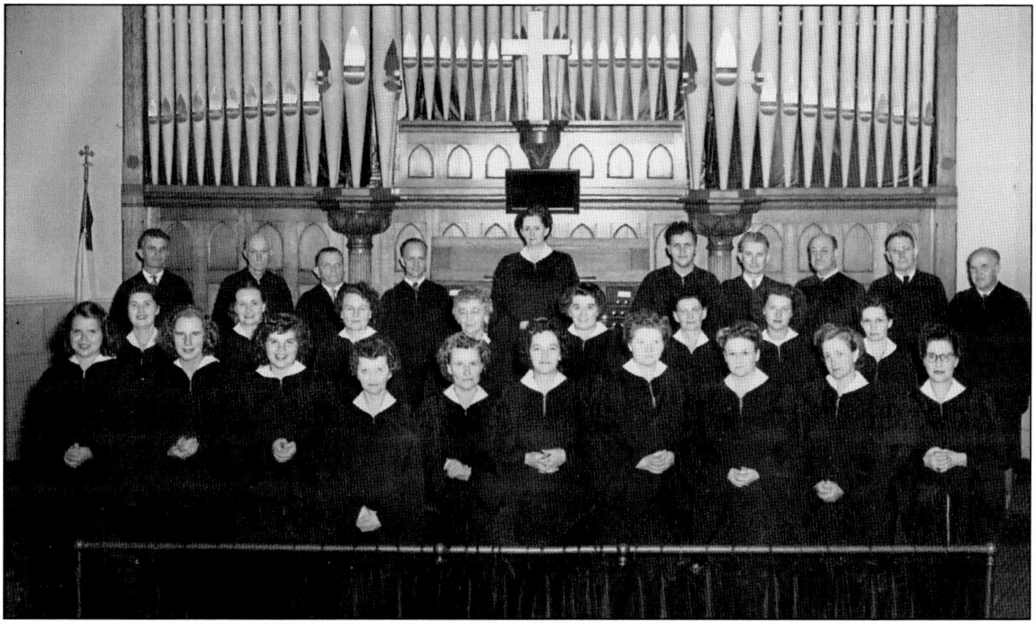

Members of the 1947 Methodist church choir are, from left to right, (first row) Beverly Aaron, Evelyn Rayl, Peggy Aaron, Hazel Swift, Nova Aldridge, Mrs. Steven Spees, Georgia Morehead, Lou Miller, Gladys Stage, and Ruth Regnier; (second row) Mrs. Max Hannum, Doris Morrison, Faye Cline, Mrs. W.E. McKee, Jean Groves, Mary Burdge, Betty Stone, and Ella Durham; (third row) Carl Aldridge, George Richman, Herbert Findling, Bernard Purvis, Helen Mayne, Richard Metcalf, Walter Miller, D.E. Leist, Boyd Thompson, and Louis Foster.

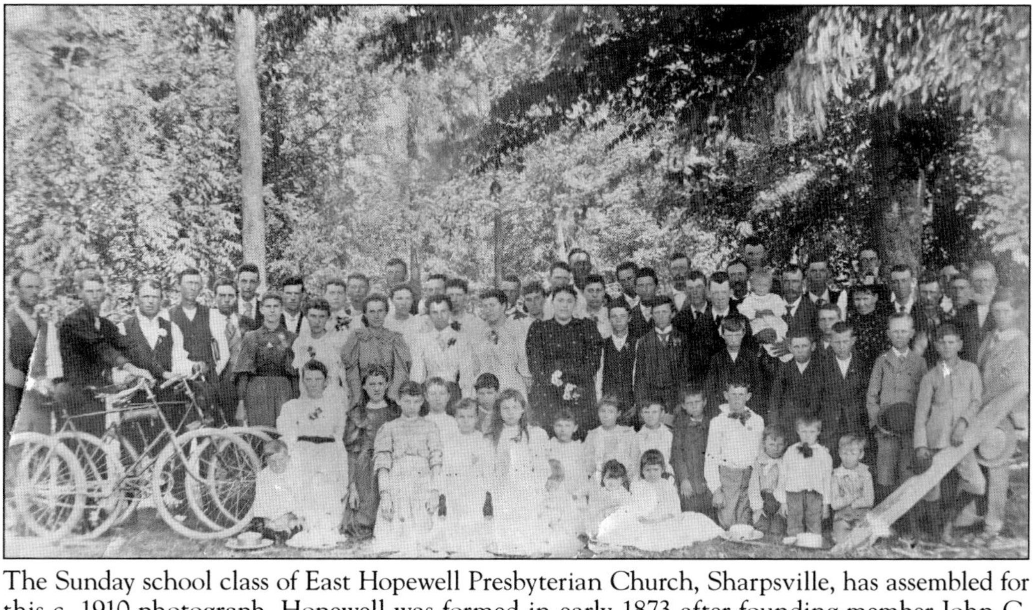

The Sunday school class of East Hopewell Presbyterian Church, Sharpsville, has assembled for this c. 1910 photograph. Hopewell was formed in early 1873 after founding member John C. Henderson made a trip to the Hopewell Presbyterian Church in Franklin, where he received a donation for the new church. The building was completed in the summer of 1874 at a cost of $1,600. (Gae Matchette.)

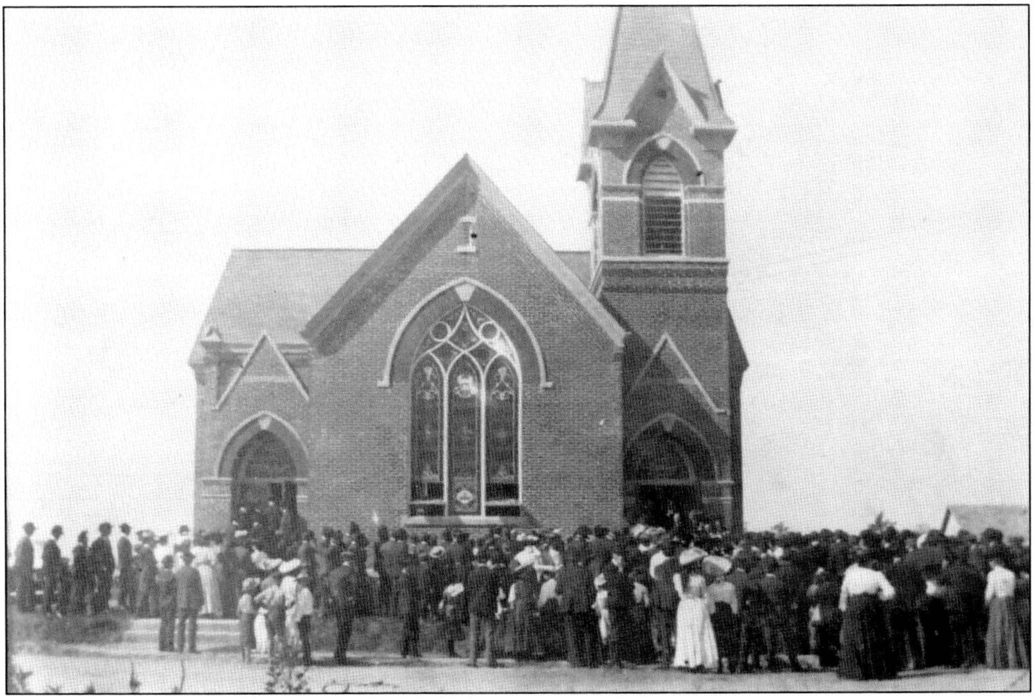

Lutherans had worshipped in Tipton County for nearly 50 years, when, in February 1896, Emanuel Lutheran Church organized in the city of Tipton. Five months later, its congregation dedicated a small frame church at Fairview and Jackson Streets. The members dedicated their new brick church on October 8, 1905, and the frame building became the parish school. The congregation built its present location, south of town, in 1967. (Alice Ricketts.)

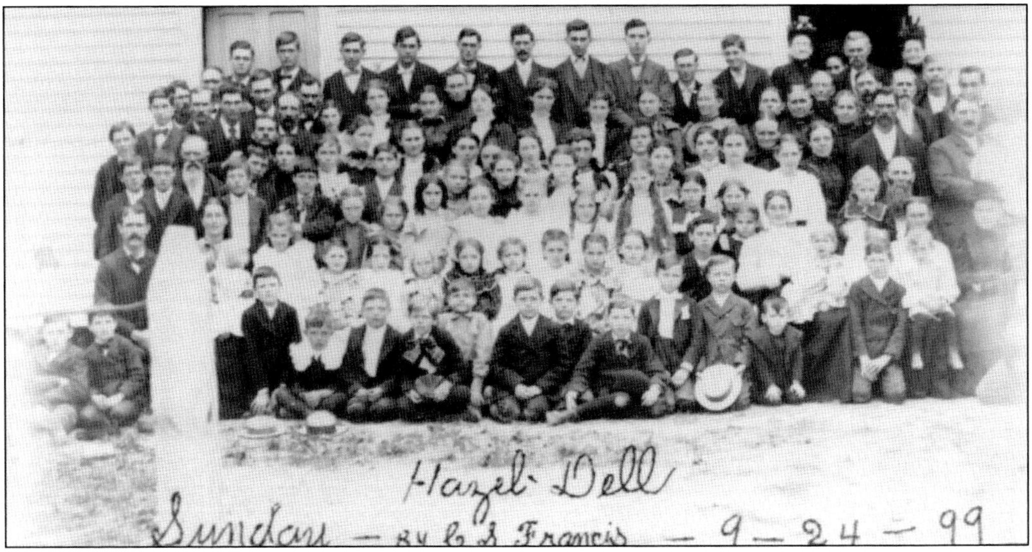

Windfall's Hazel Dell Friends Church congregation poses for this photograph on Sunday, September 24, 1899. The church originally met in the open, surrounded by a dense thicket of hazel. Its first church, built of logs, was replaced in 1880 by the frame structure pictured. The congregation's pastor, George Bragg, whom members affectionately called "The father of Hazel Dell," is the bearded gentleman, second from the left, in the fourth row. (Library archives.)

The steeple of St. John's Catholic Church was destroyed by fire on July 5, 2003, but was quickly rebuilt. Before Tipton County Catholics had a church home, they were served by priests from Peru and Kokomo. Tipton's first Catholic church was a small, wood structure built in 1874. It burned in 1885 and was replaced by the present gray stone church, which has stood on Mill Street since 1891. (*Tribune*.)

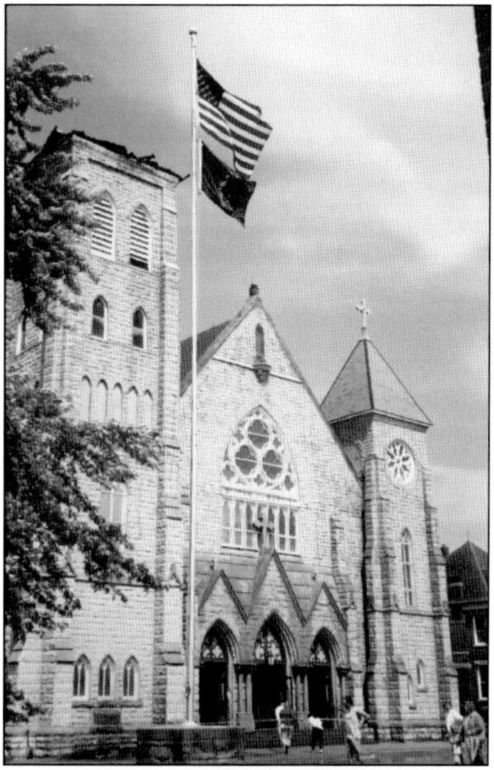

Diane Dane Creasy and cousin Jim Dane of Tipton receive their first communion at St. John's Catholic Church around 1958, when both are eight years old. The two attended St. John's Elementary School from kindergarten through eighth grade. When the church was damaged by fire in 2003, the altar behind the children was spared. (Heather Magee.)

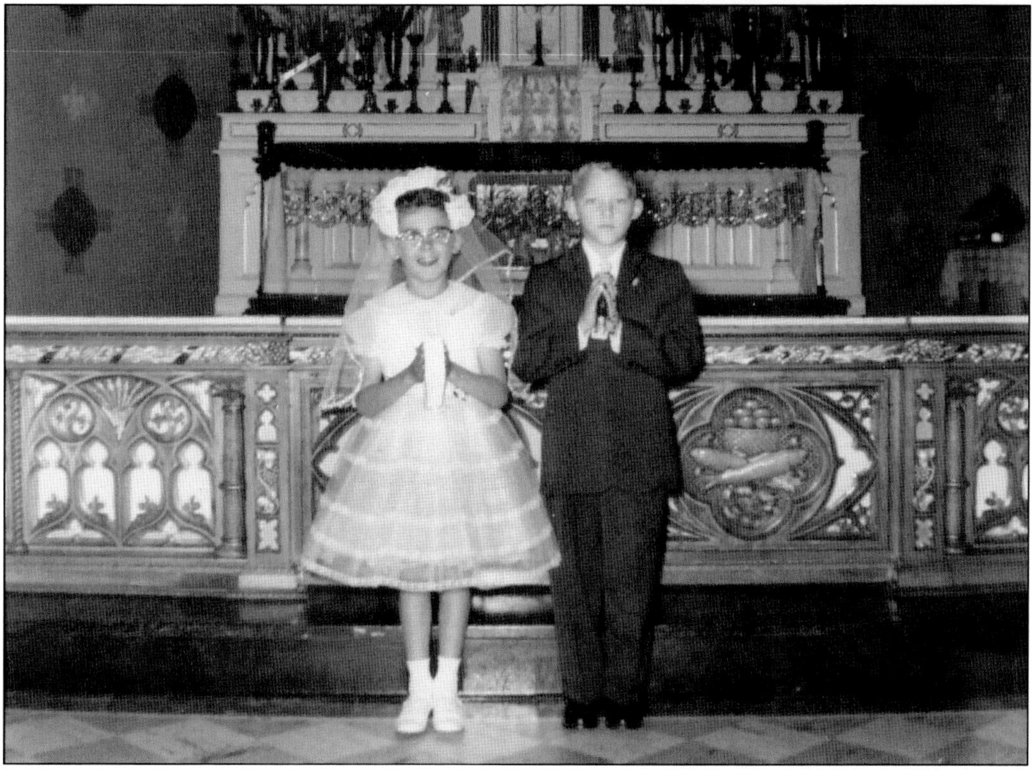

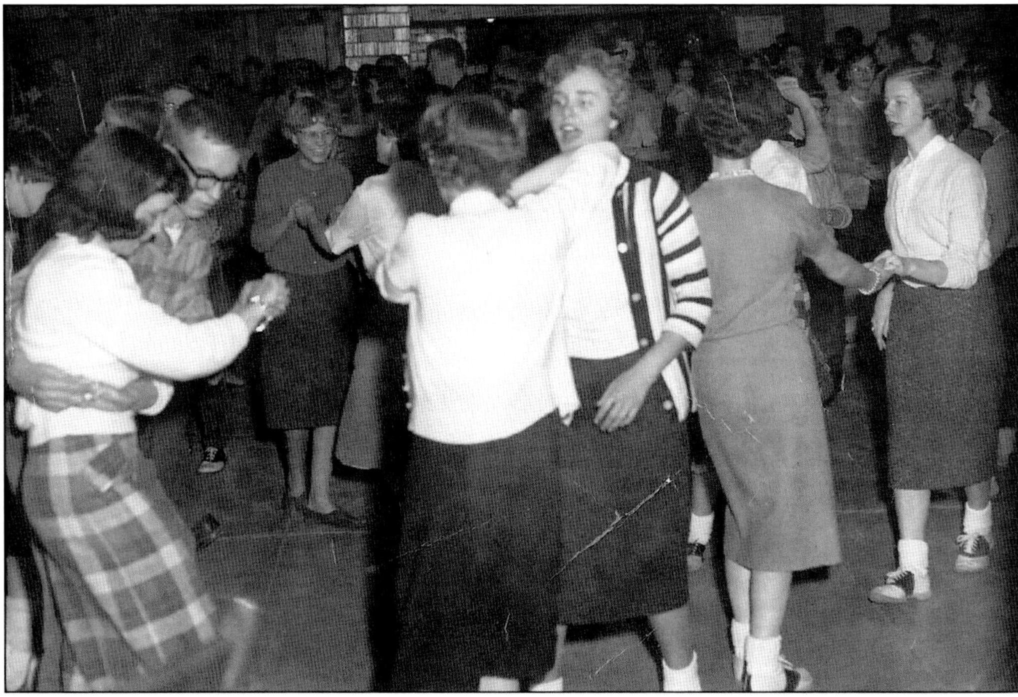

Students dance to rock 'n' roll at the Teen Canteen in Tipton's First Presbyterian Church's basement (above), about 1958. A September 20, 1954, *Tribune* article reports that the church got its start in 1850, after a Presbyterian missionary visited the area from Rush County. A church with seven members was established in the Normanda area and met in members' cabins. Four years later, it and another church near Boxley founded a new church in Tipton on the southeast corner of West and Jefferson Streets. In 1905, a new building (below) was constructed of red brick on the northwest corner of the same intersection. When the building burned some 20 years later, members met in the public library until they raised enough funds to rebuild. The congregation dedicated its new church—the present yellow brick structure—on April 10, 1928. (Both, Elaine Phelps.)

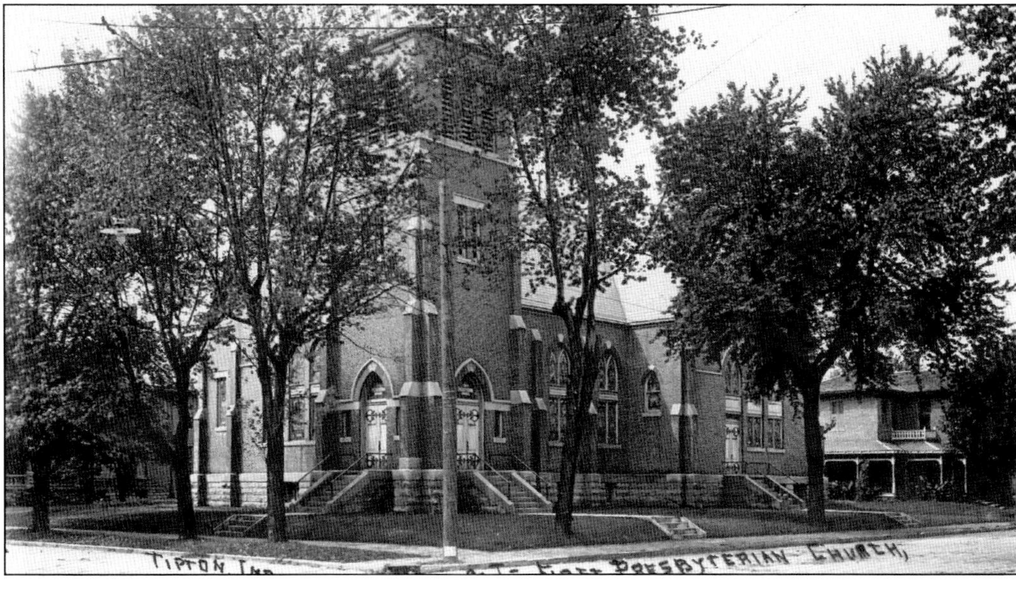

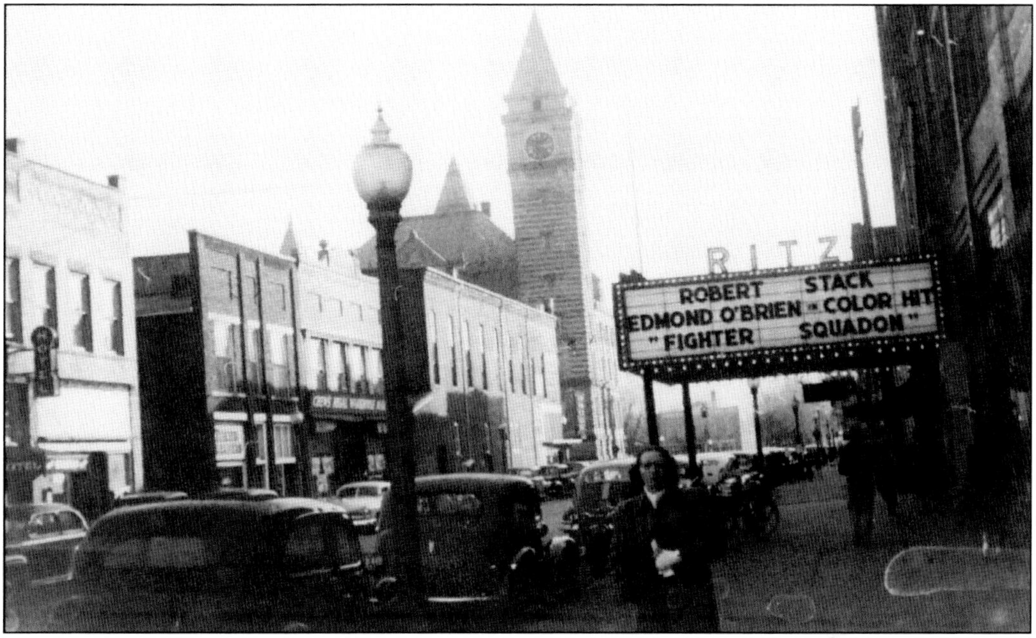

Above, Ruth Illges stops along Main Street near the Ritz Theater, around 1945. For many years, Tipton supported two movie theaters, the Ritz and the Diana. The Ritz took over the former Martz Opera House that opened in 1904 and for decades was a venue for many cultural activities, including musical theater, vaudeville shows, and speakers. Even Francis X. Bushman, the most famous silent-movie actor for his time, once appeared on the Martz's stage. Below, the cast of an early-1900s production at the Martz takes a bow. Established by Nicholas Martz, the theater was gutted by fire April 8, 1929. Rebuilt in 1930, it was renamed the Ritz and remained a popular movie house until it closed in 1956. The building burned again on December 23, 1998. That time, it was a total loss. (Above, Ruth Illges; below, Jeanie and Bob Robinson.)

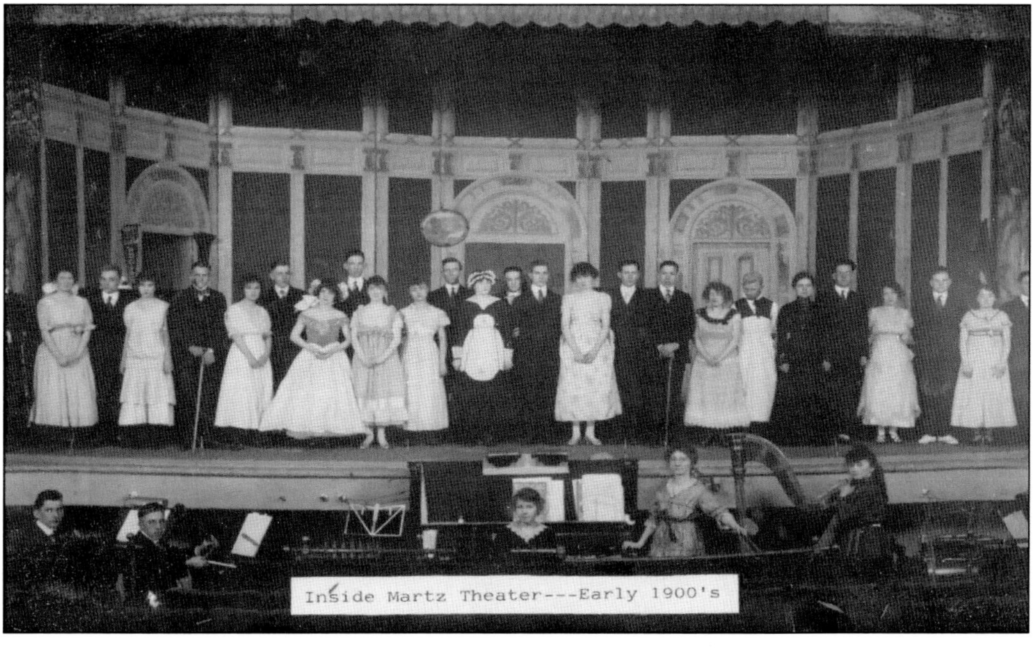

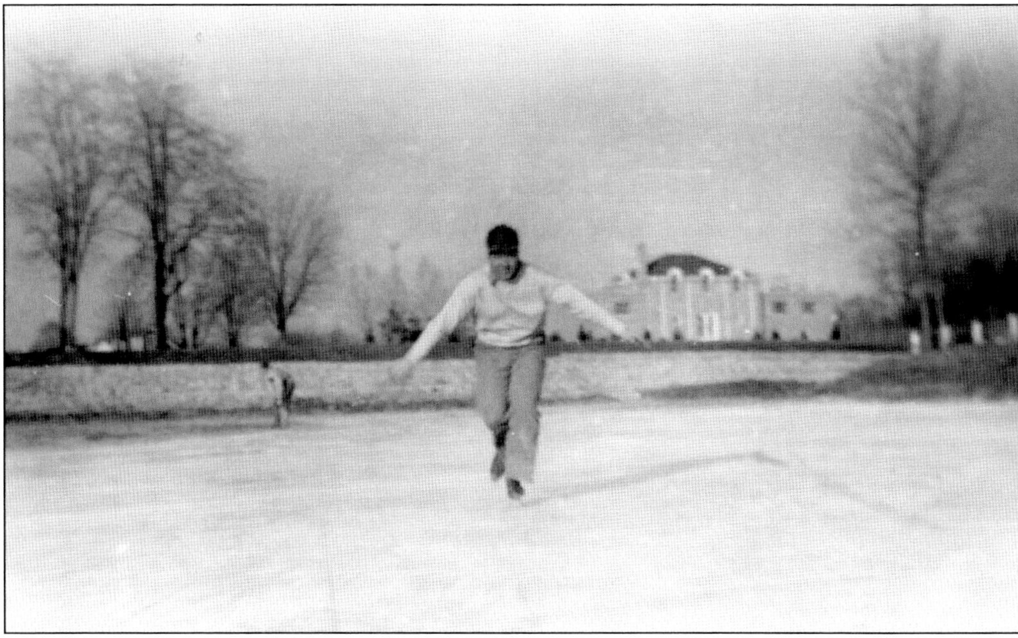

Max Illges skates figure eights at the ice rink in the Tipton Park, about 1940. The rink was located south of Cicero Creek and west of the footbridge. The then new swimming pool building is in the background. Absent from the background is the Boy Scout cabin, which was not built until 1941. (Ruth Illges.)

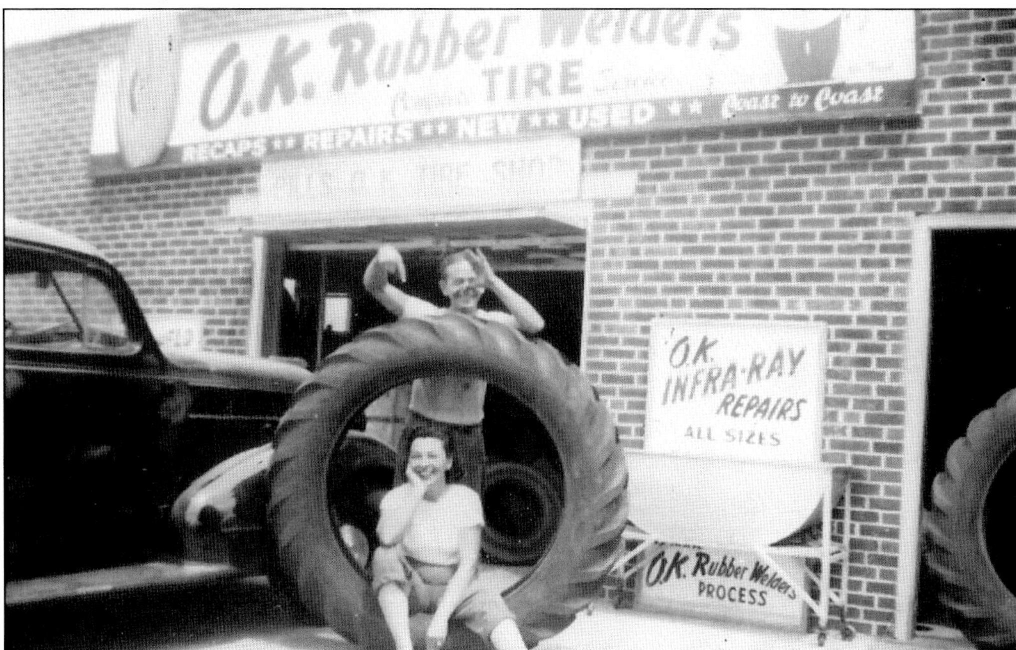

Morris "Bill" and Gwendolyn Stillabower clown for the camera at their business, Bill's OK Tire Shop, a franchise of OK Rubber Welders, located on West Jefferson Street near the electrical power substation. The Stillabowers constructed the building in 1947. They ran the tire shop until they retired in 1973. (Morris Stillabower Jr.)

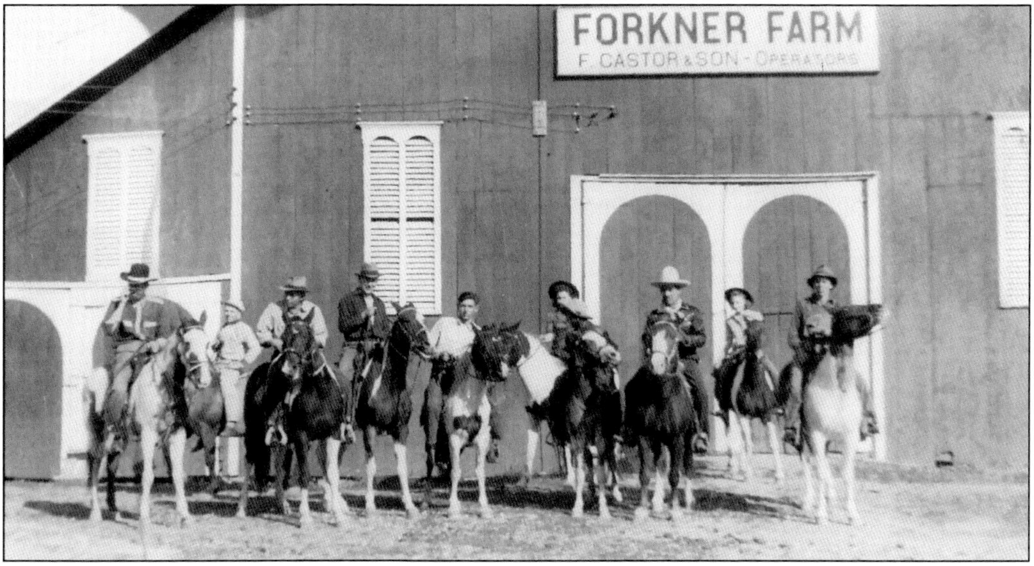

Above, Elmer Ziegler, fourth from the left, enjoys a romp at the Forkner Farm, located at State Road 28 and County Road 400 East, where rodeos occasionally were held in the 1930s and 1940s. Shown below are the members of the "West End Hellcats." Like many youth of the 1920s, they invented their own entertainment. In one of their favorite games, they watched for bumblebees returning to their nest and then, wielding wooden paddles, the boys raided the nest, often getting stung in the process. After eliminating the bees, the boys retrieved the nest and consumed the honey. The photograph was likely taken at the Fourth Street residence of Morris Delbert "Bill" Stillabower, on the right. The other boys are unidentified. (Above, Ken Ziegler; below, Morris Stillabower Jr.)

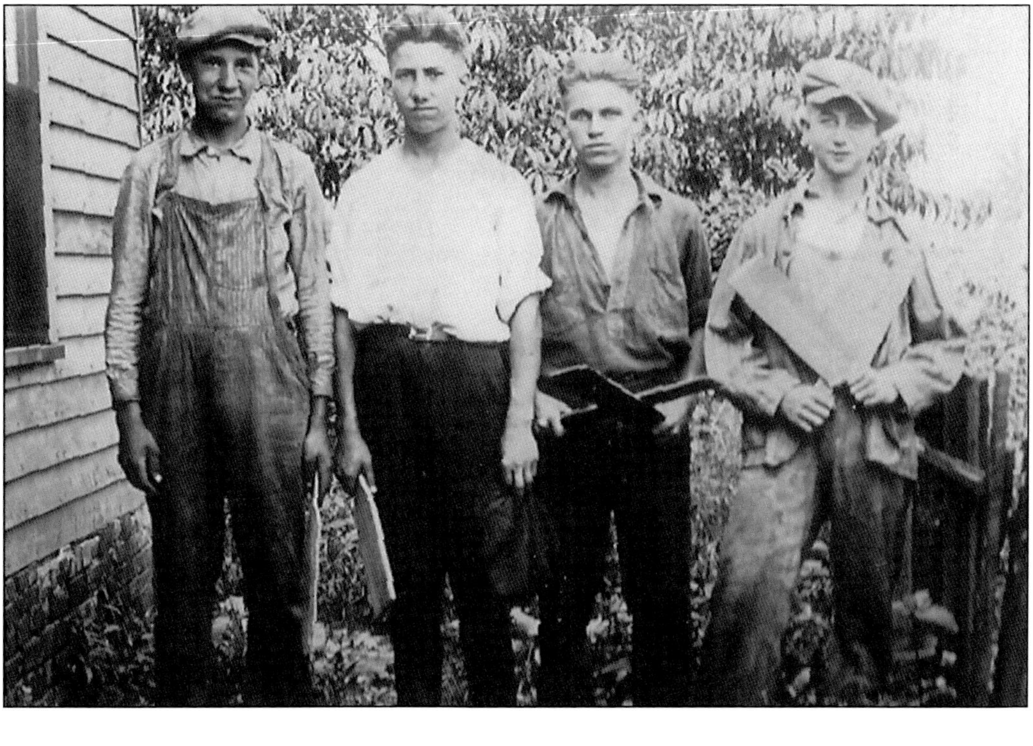

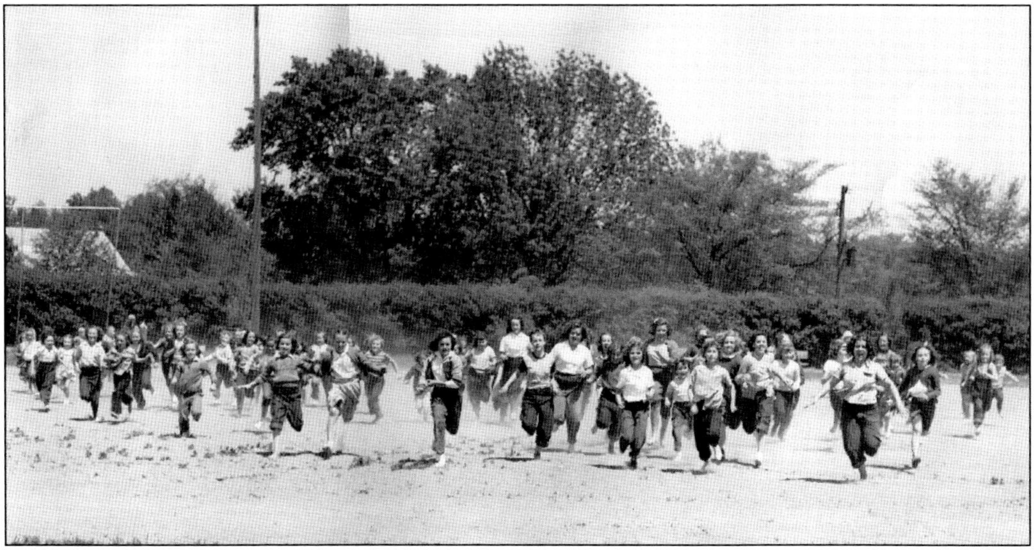

Tipton County children race for their shoes at the 1949 annual Children's Play Day, hosted by Triangle Inn owner Eugene C. Baranowski and other local businesspeople at the Tipton Municipal Park. The events were held each spring from 1949 through 1954 for children throughout the county. This and the cover photograph are included in a May 1949 *Indianapolis Star* magazine feature story. (Gene Baranowsi, with permission of the *Star*.)

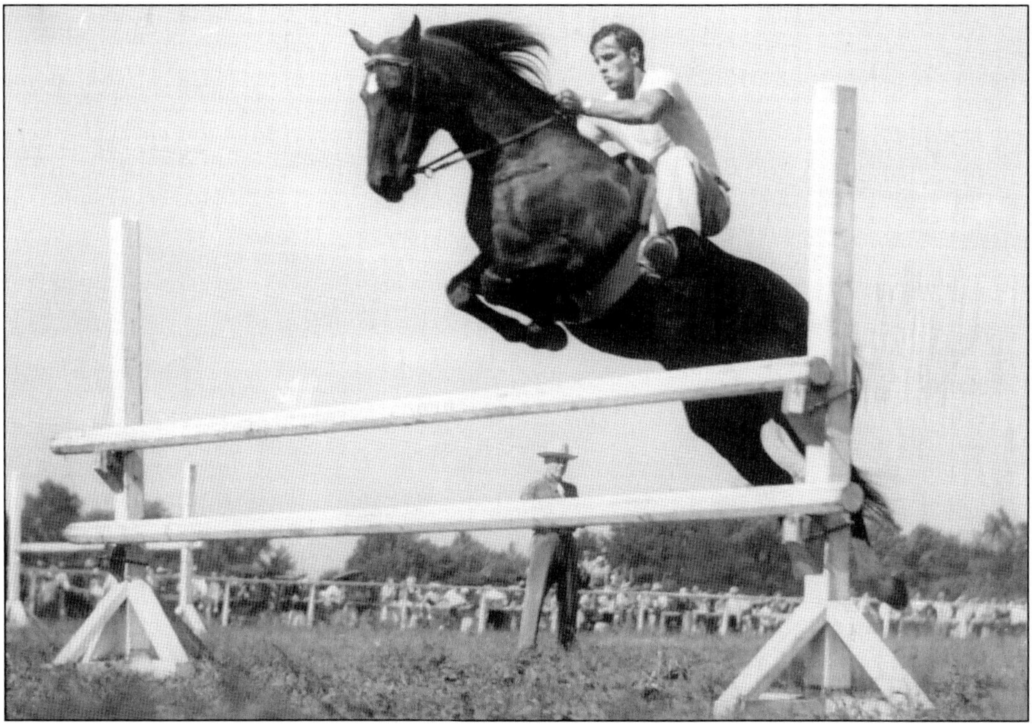

Equestrian E.F. "Bud" Alderson jumps a hurdle during a meet sponsored by the Prairie Township Diamond P. Saddle Club about 1940. Throughout the 1940s and 1950s, the club sponsored riding competitions, including rodeos, at locations throughout the county. Alderson was one of the more accomplished riders, often claiming a top prize. (Madonna Alderson.)

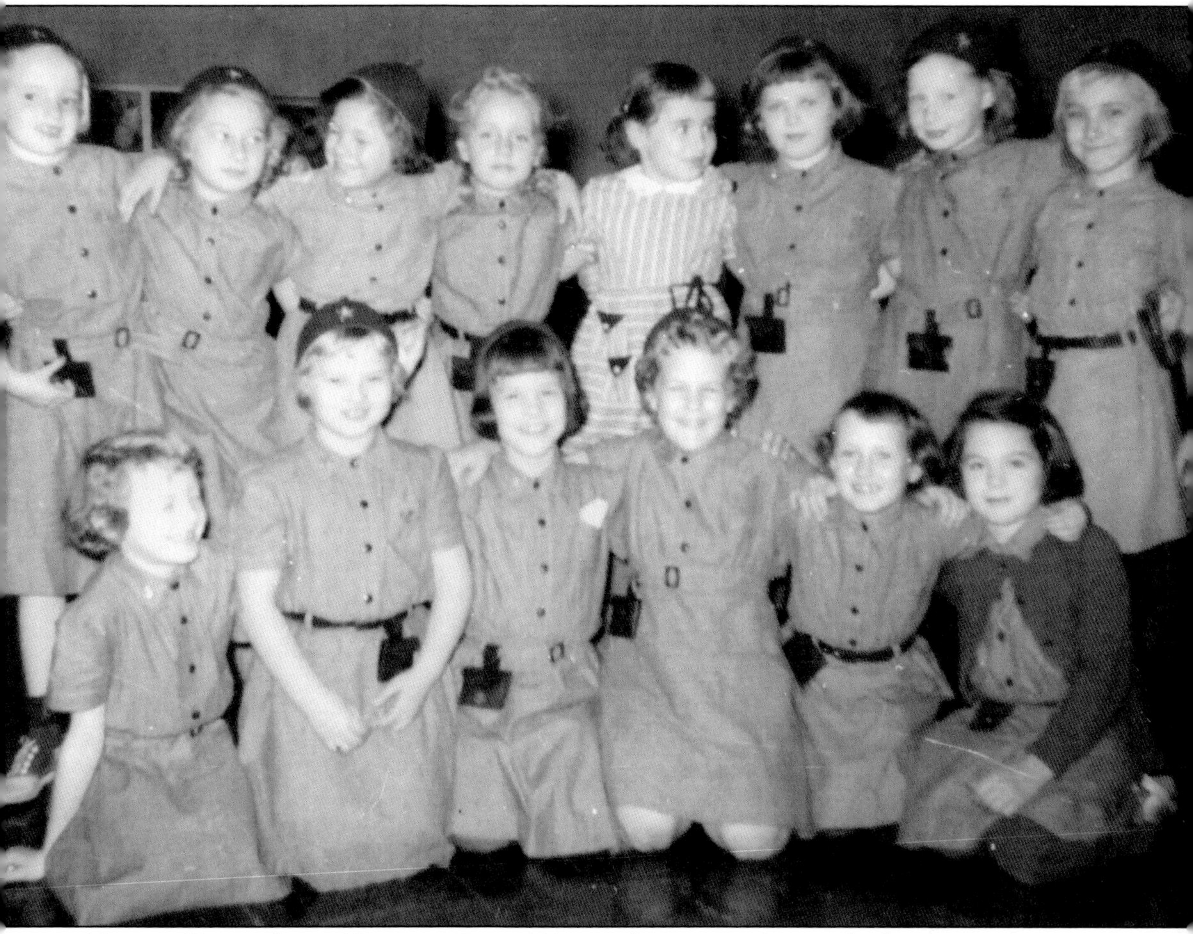

About 1955, members of Brownie Troop 350 pose for a group shot in the basement of Tipton's First Presbyterian Church, where they met each month for several years. The girls started meeting as Jefferson Elementary School second graders and stayed together as Girl Scouts and ultimately Senior Scouts. Through the years, their leaders included Bobbi Ramsay, Louise Bowers, Helen Leininger, and June Thornton. The Brownies are, from left to right, (first row) Debbie Campbell, Jane Ann Cooper, Debby McIntosh, Karyn Harkness, Marcia Green, and Janet Ramsay; (second row) Nadine Haley, Janis Thornton, Sandy Farmer, Jennifer Wiggins, Nancy Stout, Wendy ?, Mary Martha Purvis, and Linda Bowers. Ten members of the original troop received their curved bars in a ceremony on May 23, 1962. The curved bar is the highest rank in the intermediate program, equivalent to the Eagle rank in Boy Scouts. At that time, only 11 other Girl Scouts in Tipton County had earned the distinction.

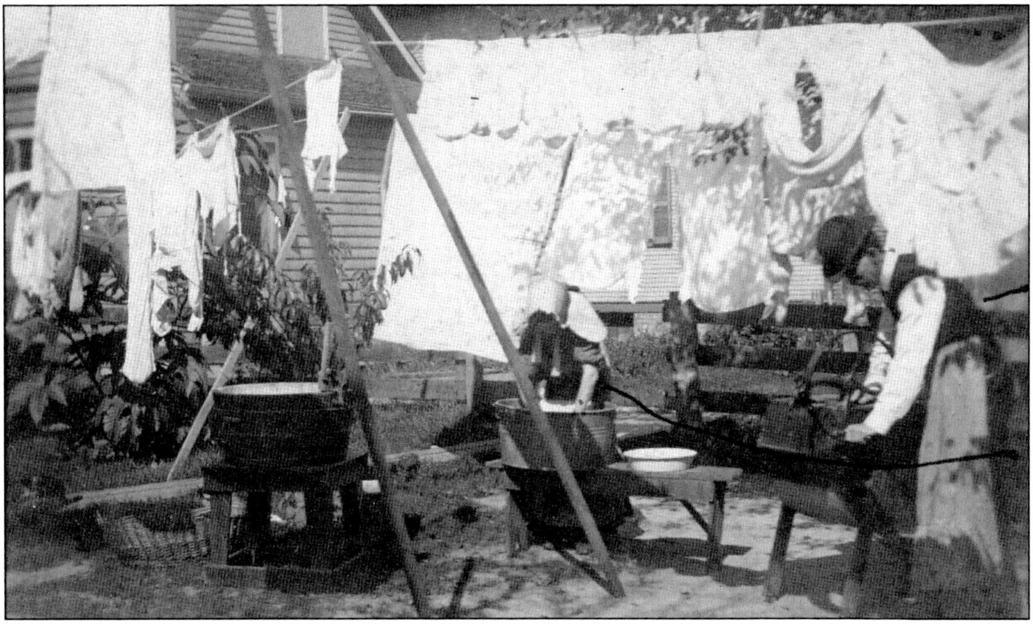

It is washday for Blanche Koker, left, and her brother Walter Duncan, hard at work in the backyard of their mother, Opal, in Goldsmith. The c. 1910 photograph depicts the all-day event, with Duncan rotating the agitator wheel on the washtub while Koker tends to the rinse. A hand ringer is attached to the tub on the right. On the clothesline overhead, the laundry billows in the breeze. (Viola Jones.)

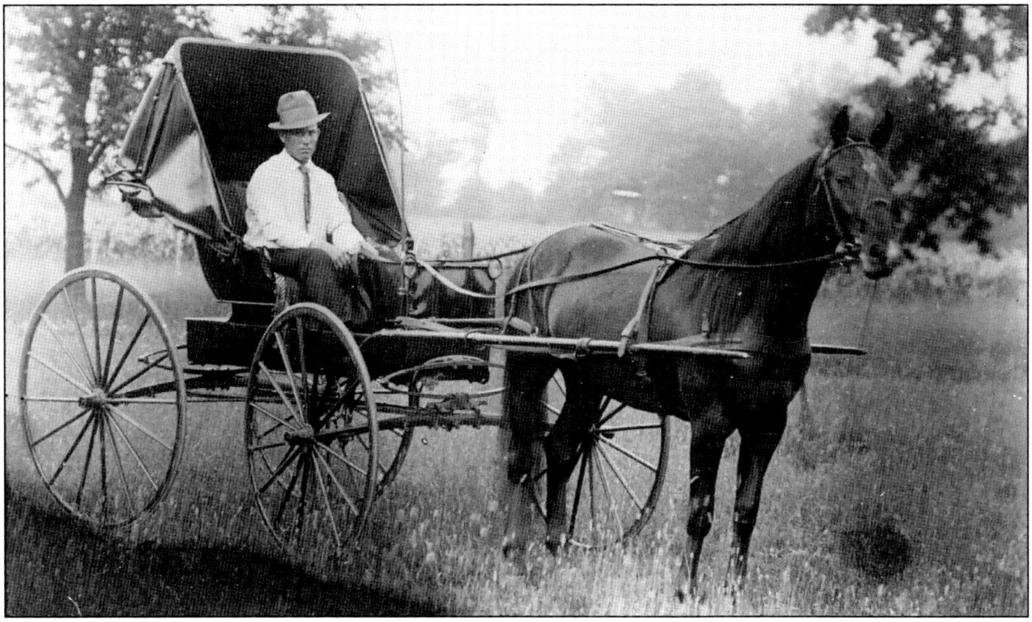

Tiffin Miller, at age 20, is seated in his rig, which he called his "courting buggy." This picture was taken in the Goldsmith area in 1907. Miller was born in 1887 in Tipton County, and like his father, Frank, became a farmer. Miller and his wife, Edith, had six children, including Fred, who still resides in the Goldsmith area. Miller died unexpectedly in 1932 of pneumonia. (Fred and Julie Miller.)

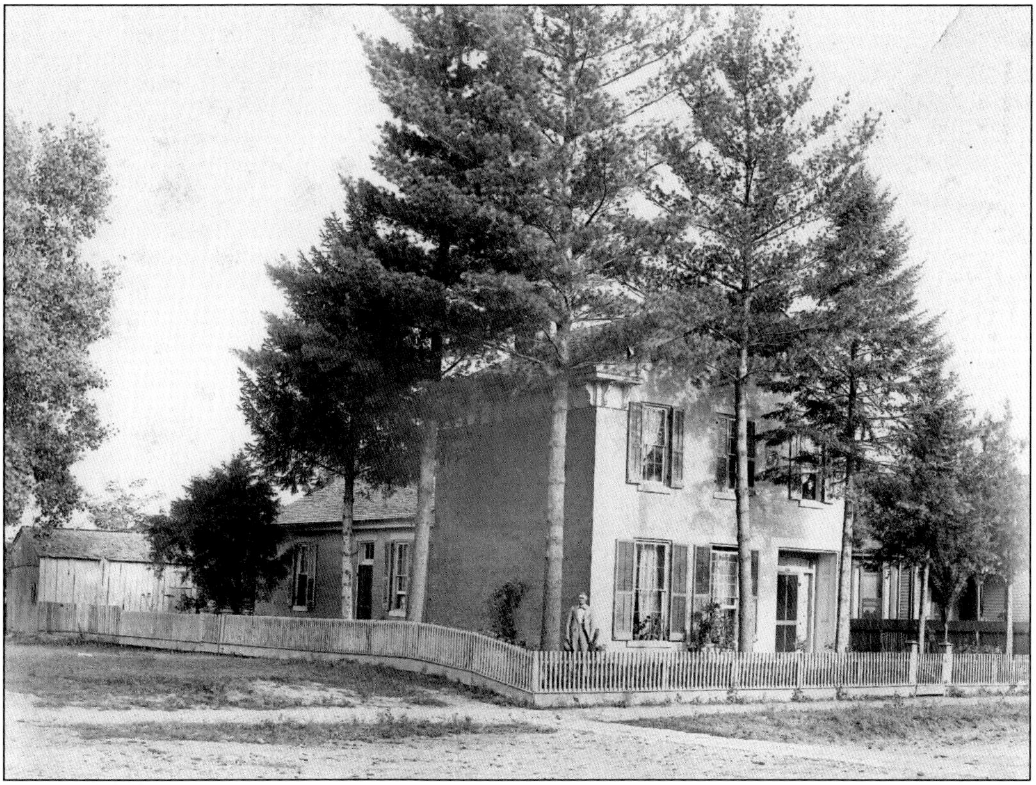

Tipton businessman Joseph A. Lewis was born in 1860 in this house, located on the northwest corner of West and Washington Streets. He lived his entire life in this house and died there August 27, 1939. His wife, Alice, can be seen looking out the upstairs window. Lewis is standing in the yard.

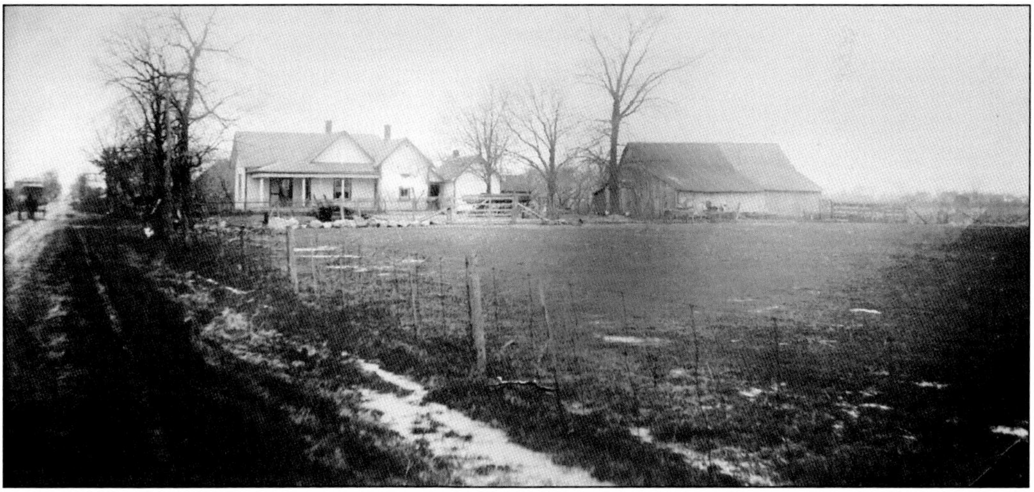

This photograph looks west at Fred and Julie Miller's house alongside State Road 28 near Tetersburg, around 1910. At the far left, a horse and buggy travel eastward on the dirt road, which was not paved until 1929. The Millers' neighbor Ralph "Hank" Teter worked for the construction company that cemented the state road when he was a boy. He recalls earning 30¢ per hour. (Fred and Julie Miller.)

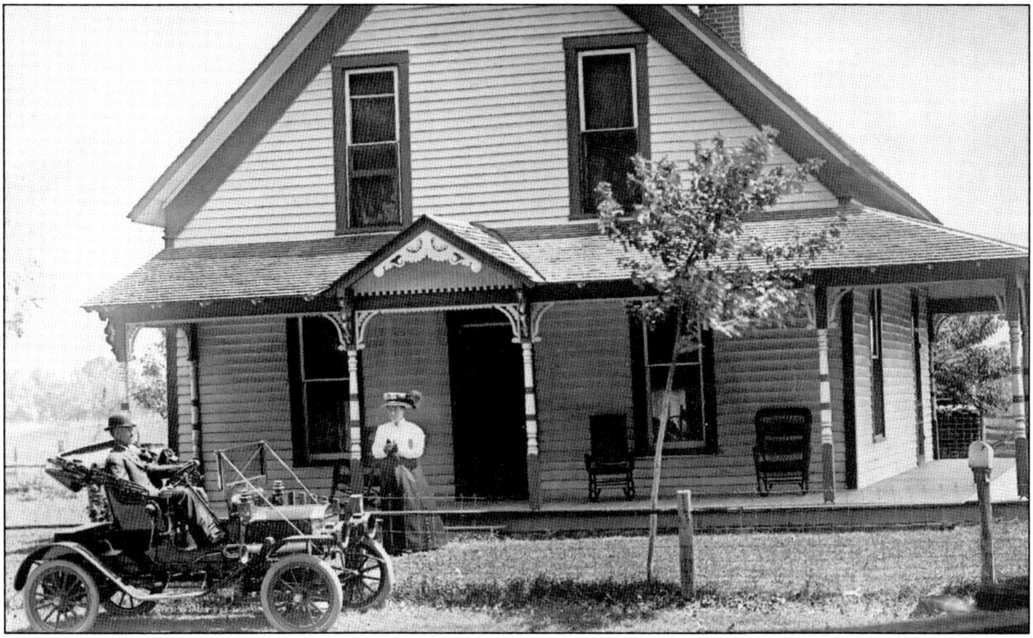

This house, located across from Old Settler's Woods in Goldsmith, is still there. Driving the car is John T. Ellis, nicknamed "Buck." Standing is his wife, Susan, nicknamed "Tude." The house was built on one acre, a gift from Susan's parents, Enos and Susan Hinkle. The Hinkles gave each of their 12 children an acre on which to build a home. The Ellises had no children. (David Cox.)

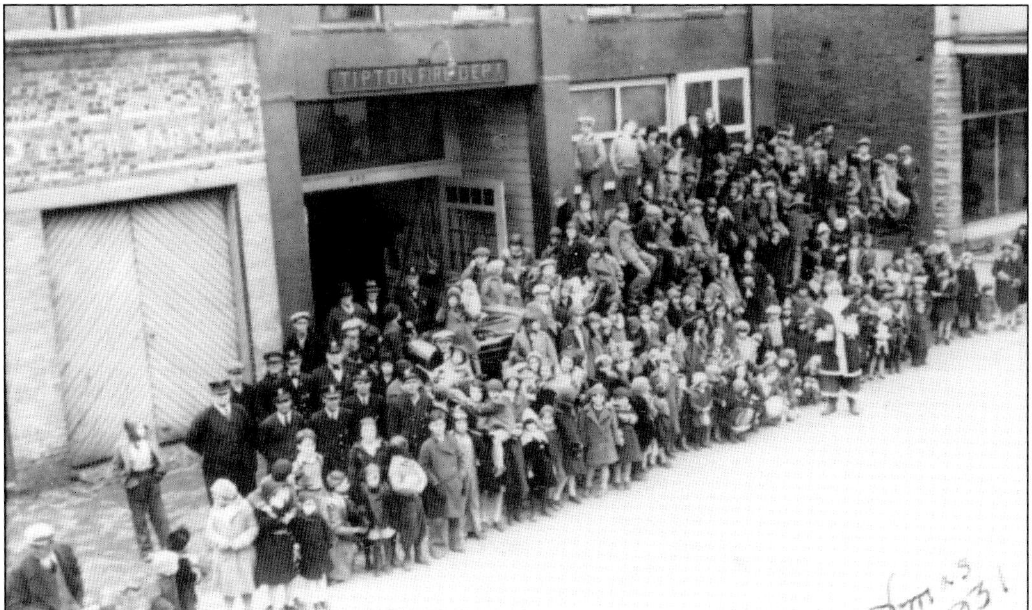

The Tipton Fire Department spent weeks refurbishing used toys and collecting clothing, food, and money for needy families and children for Christmas 1931. As an additional treat, every child who came to the fire station between 10:00 and 11:00 a.m. Christmas morning received a special gift—candy, an orange, an apple, popcorn, and a bag of nuts—from Santa himself. They all pose for this Christmas morning photograph. (Library archives.)

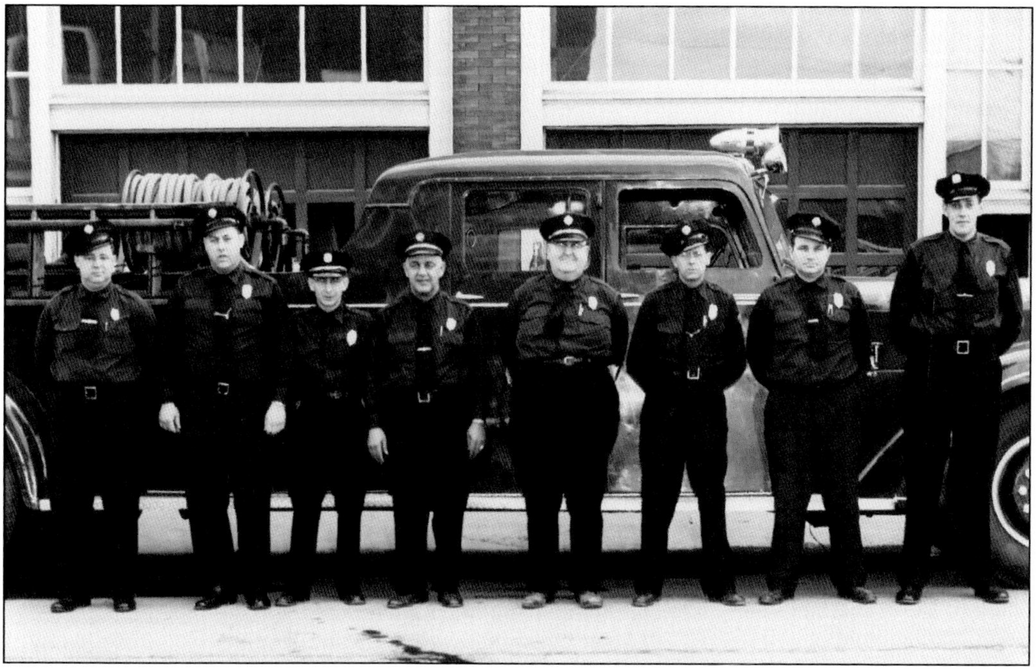

On a sunny day, around 1948, members of the Tipton Fire Department have lined up for this picture with their 1948 Buffalo Pumper. The men are, from left to right, Bob Durham, Chuck Logan, Jack Boes, Landis Fields, Lowell Kinder, Zeck Cardwell, Jack McCullough, and Bob Wesner. (Library archives.)

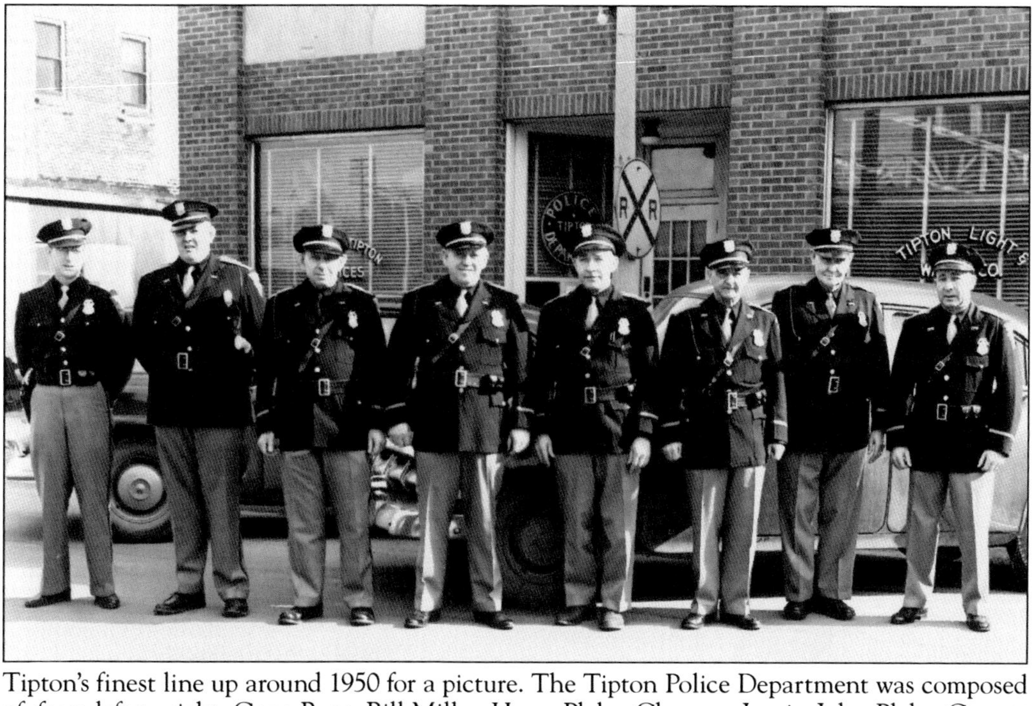

Tipton's finest line up around 1950 for a picture. The Tipton Police Department was composed of, from left to right, Gene Boes, Bill Miller, Harry Plake, Clarence Jarvis, John Plake, Garrett Jackson, Paul Egler, and Bill Basey. (Library archives.)

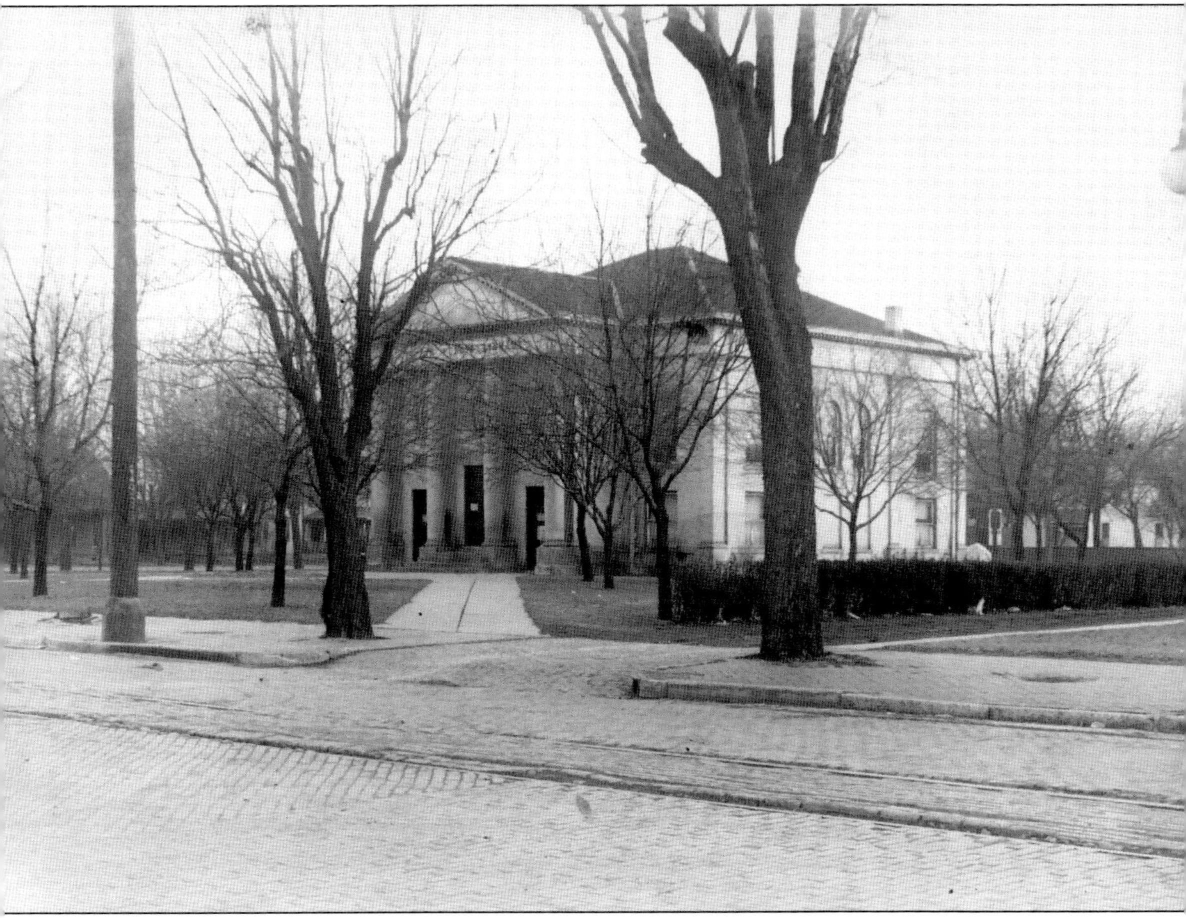

Numerous efforts had been made to establish a library in Tipton. Then, the evening of March 11, 1901, Ida Matthews boldly suggested to her fellow Literary and Suffrage Club members that a public library might be a worthwhile community project. A few months later, after starting a small library on the third floor of the courthouse, Matthews wrote to the patron saint of libraries, Andrew Carnegie. Many letters later, Carnegie gifted $10,000 to the City of Tipton on the condition that the city provide a site for the library building and guarantee $1,000 a year for its maintenance. The city immediately accepted the terms and launched the project. The library cornerstone was laid October 15, 1902. The Tipton Public Library became the Tipton County Library in July 1942, when the county commissioners appropriated $5,000 for library services. Tipton's beautiful Carnegie library remained a treasured community centerpiece until 1980, when, amid a clamor of protests, it was razed and replaced with a modern facility. (Library archives.)

Six

SCHOOLS AND SPORTS

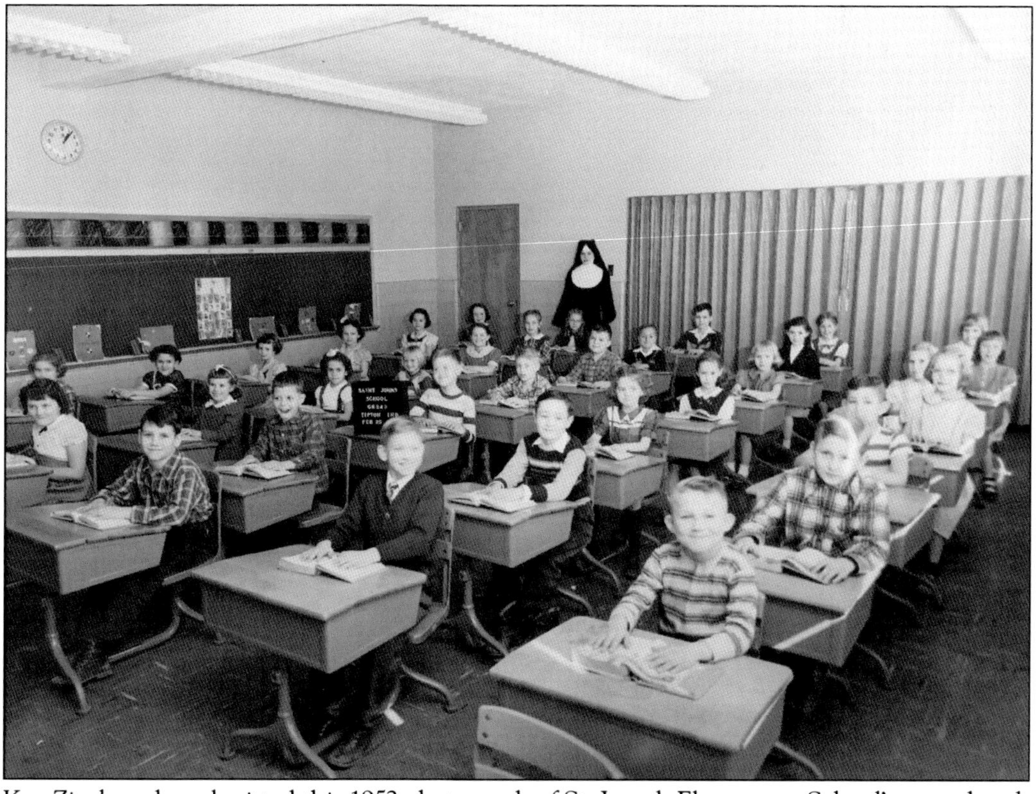

Ken Ziegler, who submitted this 1952 photograph of St. Joseph Elementary School's second-and-third-grade class, is the boy with the ornery smile seated second from the front in the center row. The teacher, Sr. Maria Goretti, stands at the back of the room. The school was only two years old when this picture was taken. The county's first school was taught in 1840 in a small cabin in Madison Township.

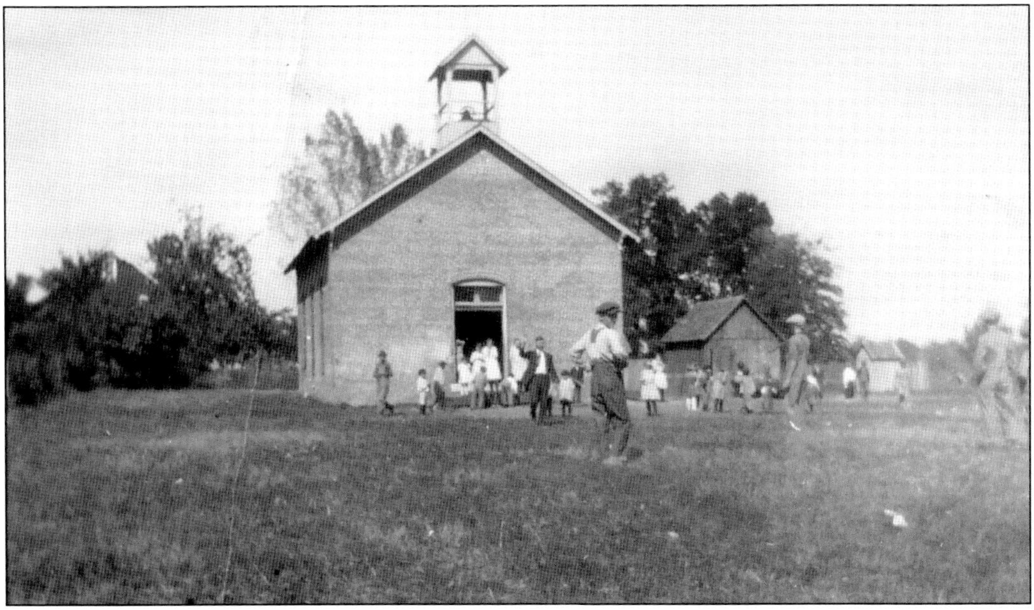

This picture at Independence School, located four miles west of Tipton, is dated October 1, 1923. The school, built in 1901, was part of an unplatted community known as Independence, or Parker's Mill, composed of six homes. The teacher, waving from the center of the photograph, is identified as Earl Foster. The school operated until 1953, when Lincoln School opened. Today, the building is an antique store. (Library archives.)

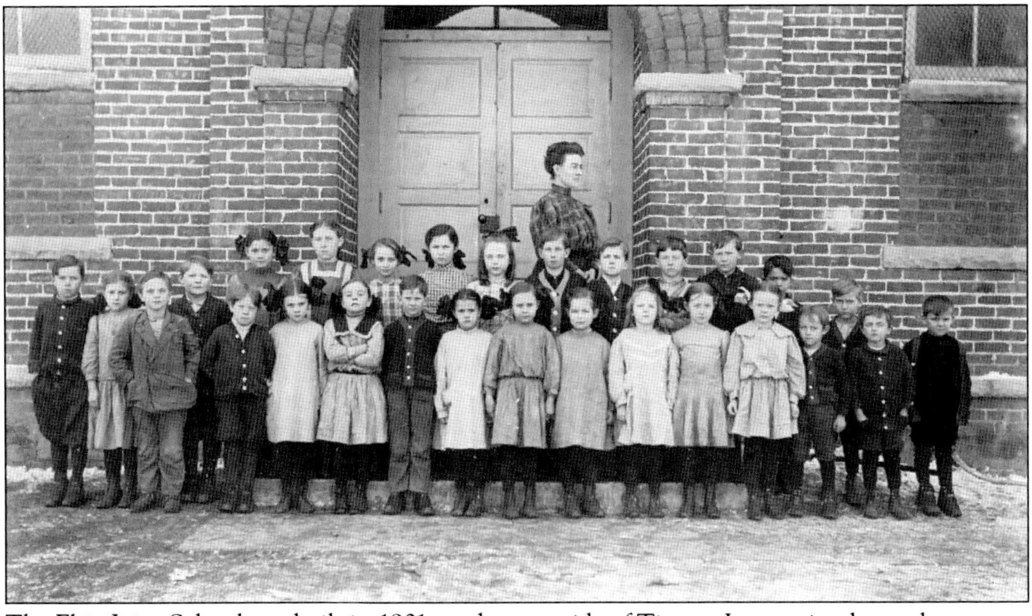

The Ekin Joint School was built in 1901 on the west side of Tipton. It contained two classrooms, each accommodating four grades. Teacher Sally Miller Fox is shown in this 1910–1911 photograph with her second-grade class. Of the students, only Pearl Thompson Pickett (third from the left in front row), the donor's grandmother, is identified. (Penny Manier.)

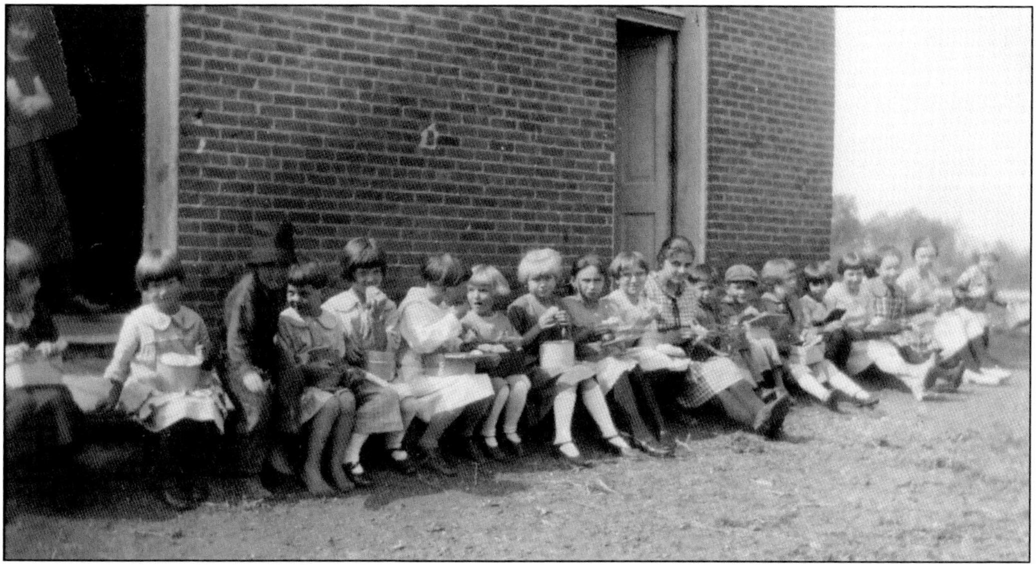

Elementary-aged children line the outside wall of Clay School to eat their lunches out of their lunch buckets. The photograph is dated October 1, 1923. The school, built in 1896 in Cicero Township, was located at what is now County Roads 300 West and 500 South. (Library archives.)

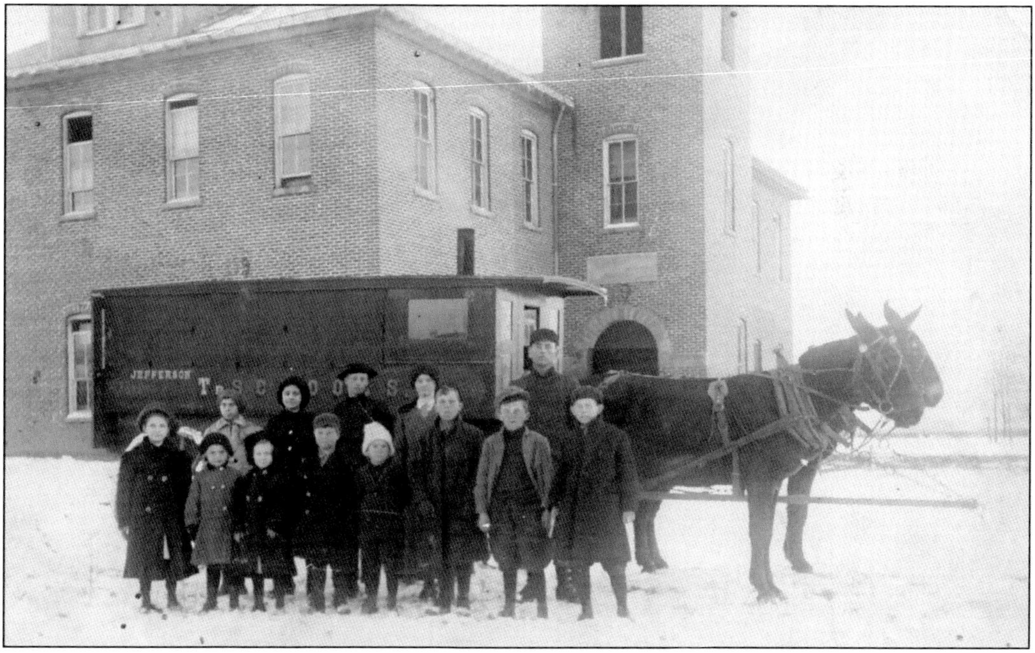

Students stand outside Jefferson School in Kempton, about 1910, alongside the horse-drawn school hack. The school was Kempton's first brick school and served both elementary and high school students. It was built in 1888 at the intersection of Main and College Streets. W.R. Dunham was principal for many years. (Alice Ricketts.)

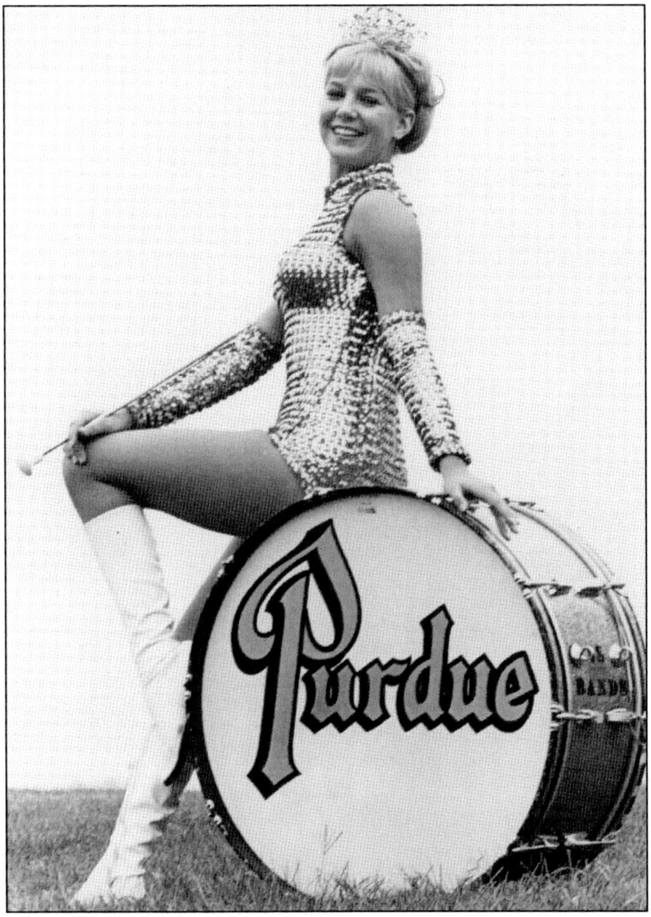

Selita Sue Smith had been a champion twirler most of her life when she was picked Purdue University's Golden Girl. The 1969 Sharpsville High School graduate held the honored title until she graduated Purdue in 1973. Today, she is an executive at Red Gold Inc., in Elwood. The Golden Girl tradition started in 1954. Since then, there have been 28 Golden Girls. Selita Sue Smith was No. 8. (Selita Reichart.)

The 1946 Sharpsville High School Band, directed by Catherine Hiatt (standing fifth from right), raised fans' spirits at the school's home games and took part in community celebrations. It also earned many first-place awards at the state contest. Two of the members—twirler Jane Hawkins (standing third from the left) and tuba player Max Henderson (standing ninth from the left)—later married. Principal J. Paul Kendall is also shown. (Gae Matchette.)

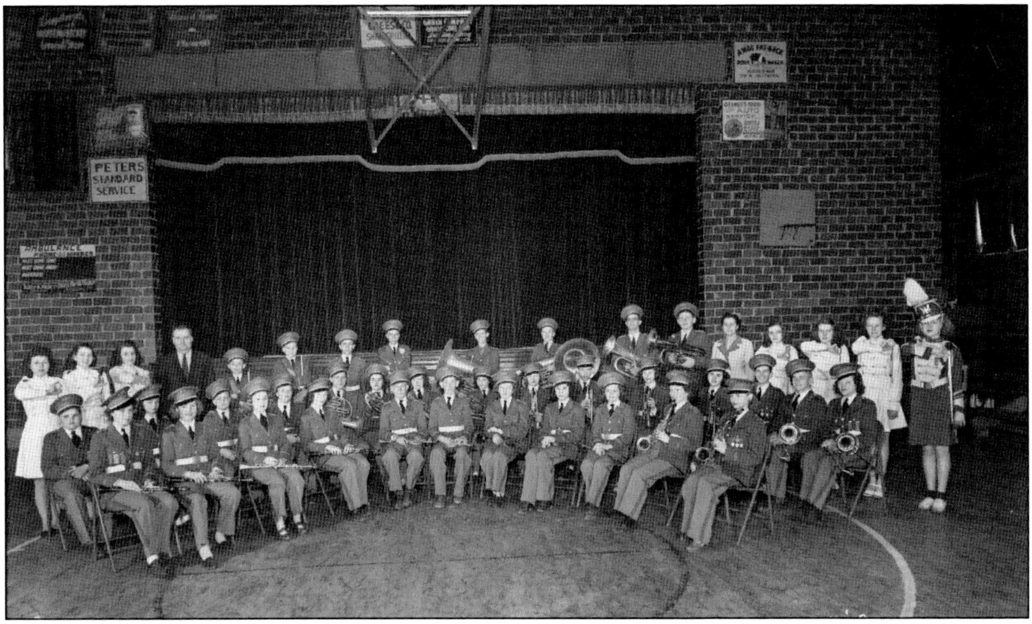

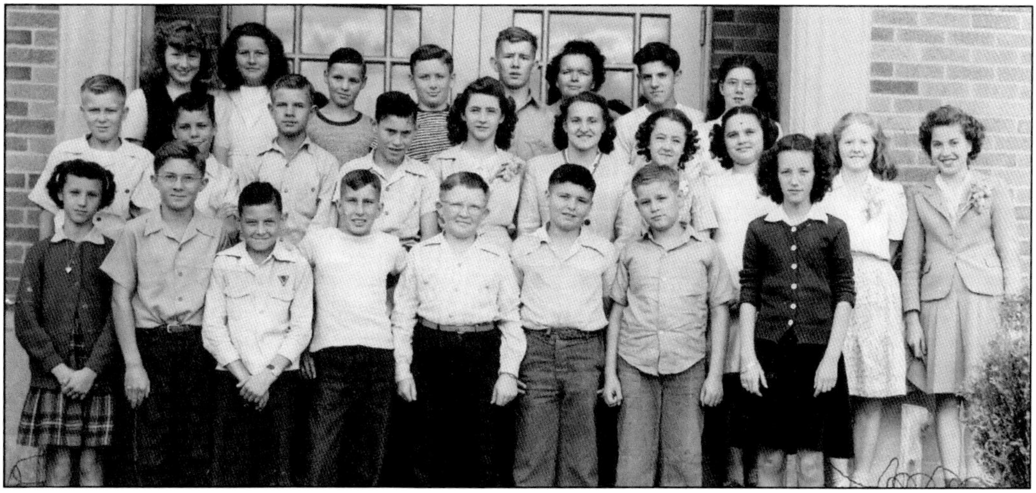

The 1947–1948 Hobbs Junior High class poses for a picture. Shown are, from left to right, (first row) Bonnie Heflin, Ralph Kauffman, Paul Julius, Nathan Fouch, Larry Clouser, Doyle Hobbs, Oliver Flowers, and Sue Bogue; (second row) Billy Davis, Jake Barnes, Charles Jack, Larue Fecher, Wilma Stuckard, Delores Miller, Jean Stuckard, Sherry Hinds, Jean Bogue, and Olive Fecher; (third row) Nelda Legg, Opal Lacey, Phillip Henderson, Garland Dellinger, George Booher, teacher Jeanette Apple, Robert Kintner, and unidentified. (Paul Julius.)

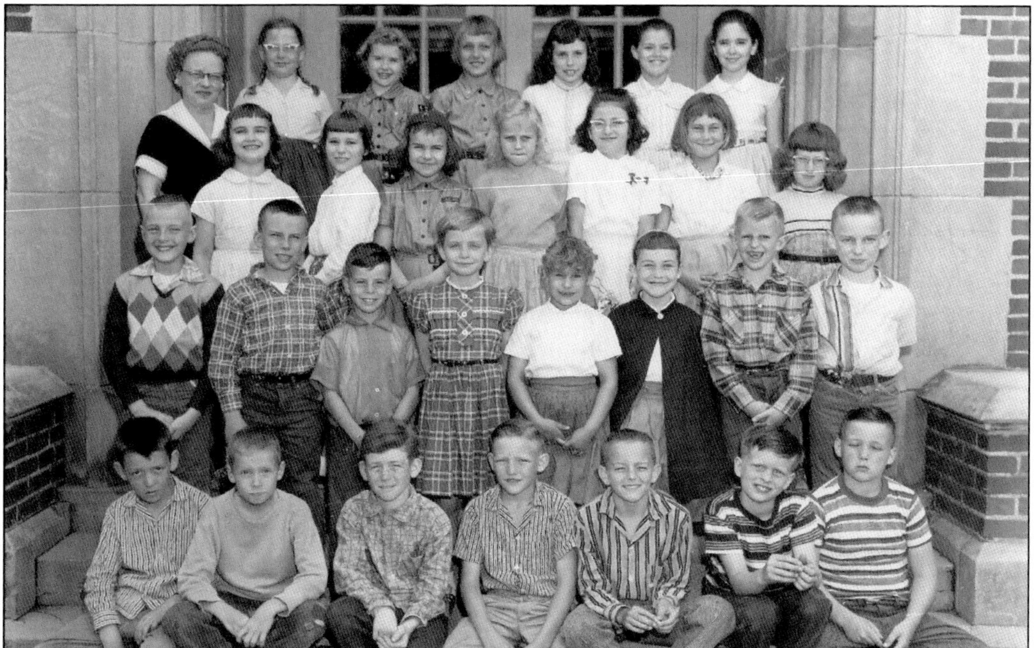

Teacher Betty Jones poses with her third-grade class in the spring of 1958 in front of Tipton's Jefferson School. The kids are, from left to right, (first row) Charlie King, Tom Fletcher, Terry Netherton, Ronnie Driver, unidentified, unidentified, and Forest Hook; (second row) Jeff Campbell, Steve Deering, Jerry Shirley, Cathy Addington, Linda Worsham, Linda Angell, Steve Haley, and Barry Bou; (third row) Patty Piper, Deana Stockwell, Paula Luttrell, unidentified, Ann Durr, Kay Cain, and Linda Reecer; (fourth row) Jones, Cindy Kincaid, Doris Skidmore, Franchon Giffin, Linda Dulworth, Kathy Watson, and Diane Haley. (Heather Magee.)

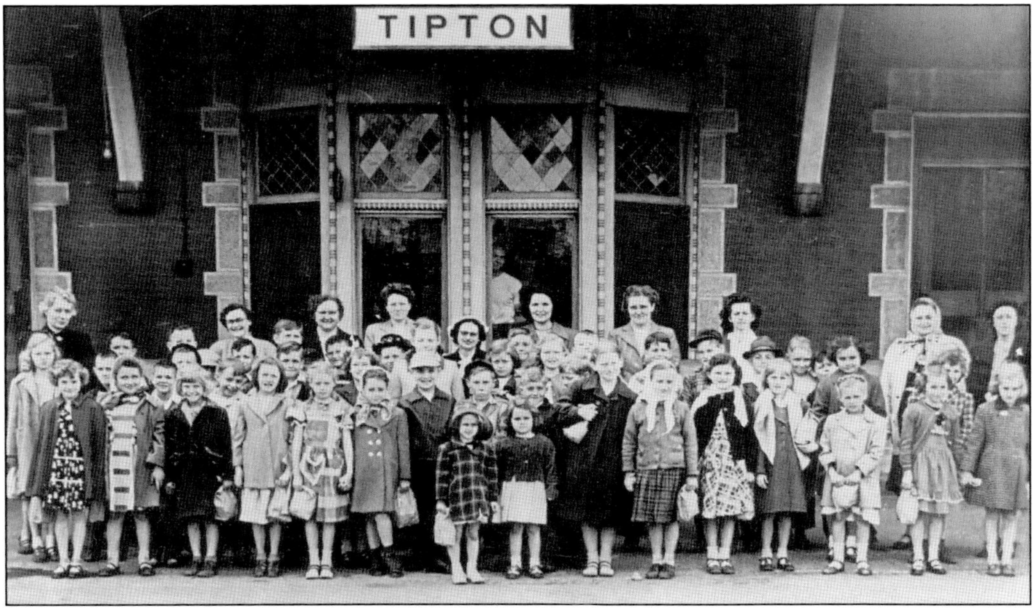

For many years, Tipton's Third Ward School third graders packed a brown bag lunch and ventured out for an annual field trip, a 26-mile train ride from the Tipton depot to Frankfort's roundhouse. This picture was taken in 1950. Janet Driver, who submitted it, is fifth from the right in the first row. The man looking out the window is unidentified, but he obviously is enjoying the children's excitement over their impending adventure. (Janet Driver.)

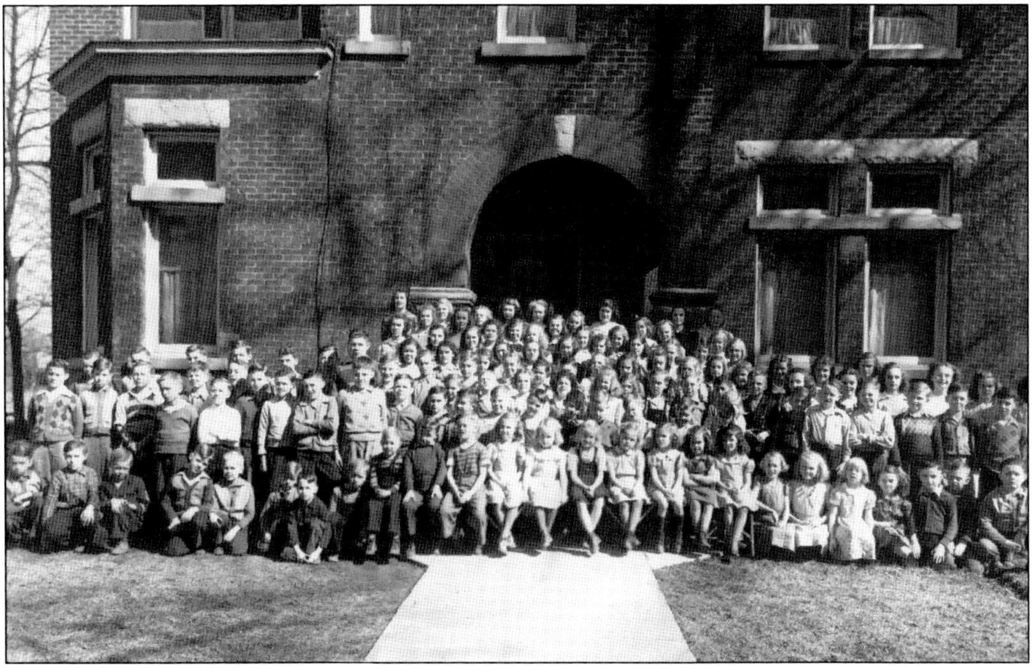

St. John's Elementary School students gather outside the original Catholic school building in the late 1940s. The school was constructed in 1891 at the corner of Mill and North Streets. St. John's students were taught by secular educators until the Sisters of St. Joseph arrived from Watertown, New York, in 1888. A new school was built in 1950. (Rosemary Comer.)

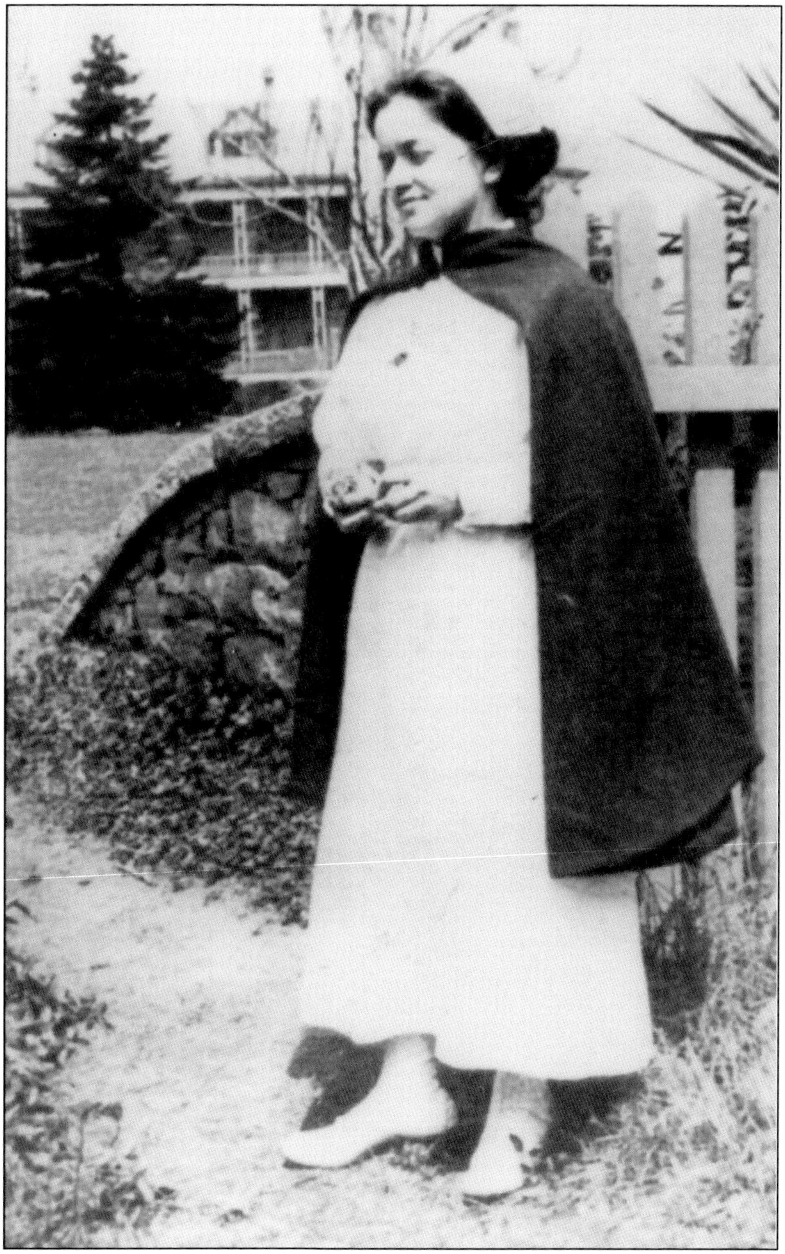

Maude Welsh served Tipton County as its health nurse for 34 years. Tiny in physical stature, Welsh was known for her boundless energy and selfless devotion to the county's sick and disabled, especially children. Elementary school students throughout the county loved her, yet they dreaded her annual visits that subjected them to the prick of a tiny, four-prong needle used to administer tuberculosis tests. Long before Welsh joined Tipton County's public health staff, she earned her nursing degree from Indiana University and volunteered with the Army Nurse Corps during World War I. After the war, she studied, practiced, and taught pediatric nursing in Cleveland, St. Louis, Indianapolis, and Ann Arbor. Welsh spent the rest of her career in Tipton, retiring in 1971 at the age of 81, leaving an enduring legacy of compassion and respect. She died in 1990 at the age of 100. (Library archives.)

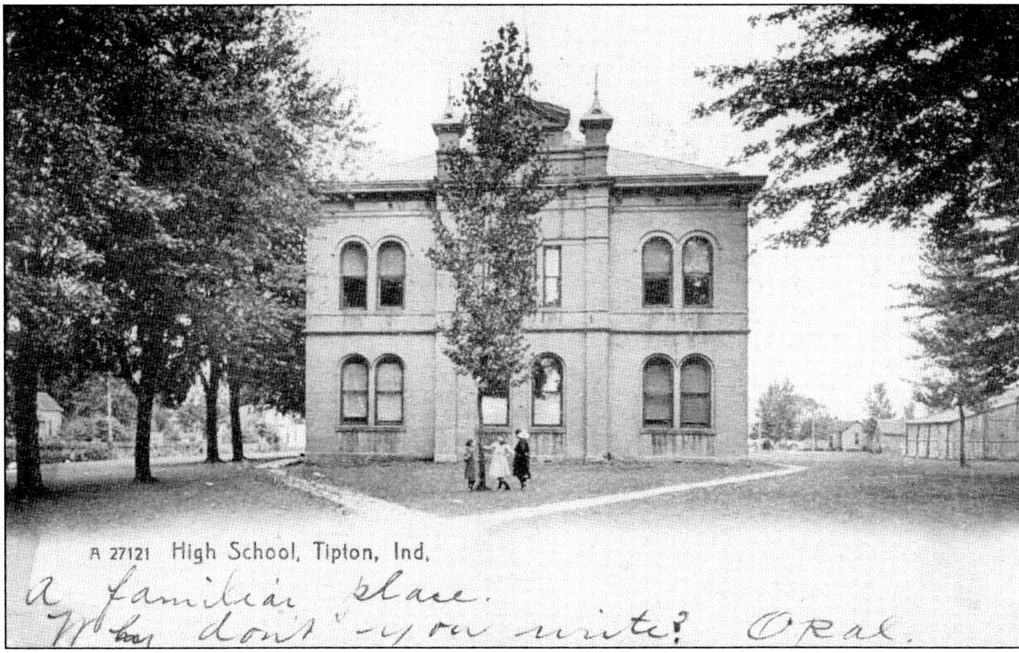

Tipton's first high school (above), built for $1,500 on West Jefferson Street on land that would become the site of Jefferson Elementary School in 1920 and the C.W. Mount Community Center in the 1980s, graduated its first class in 1876. It was composed of seven students. Initially, the building was a township school, with the first floor dedicated to elementary grades and its second floor used by grades 9 though 12. A new high school opened in 1908 at Main and North Streets. The photograph below, dated winter 1961, shows the building in its final year as Tipton High School. From the fall of 1961 through 1971, it housed only junior high students. High schoolers started their 1961–1962 academic year at a new school, located near the city's southern city limits. (Above, Alice Ricketts; below, Rick Curnutt.)

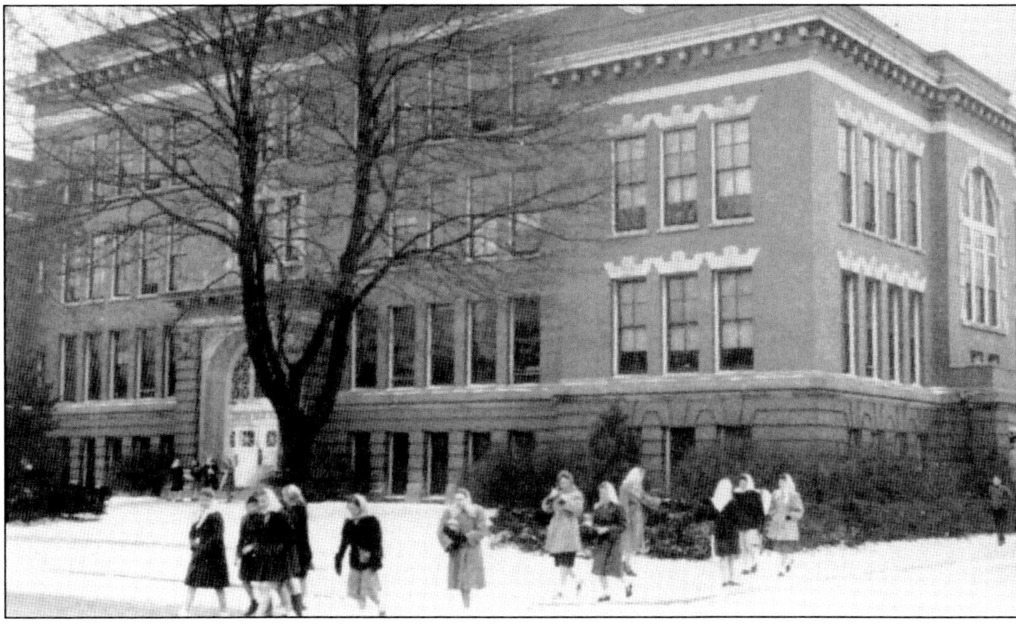

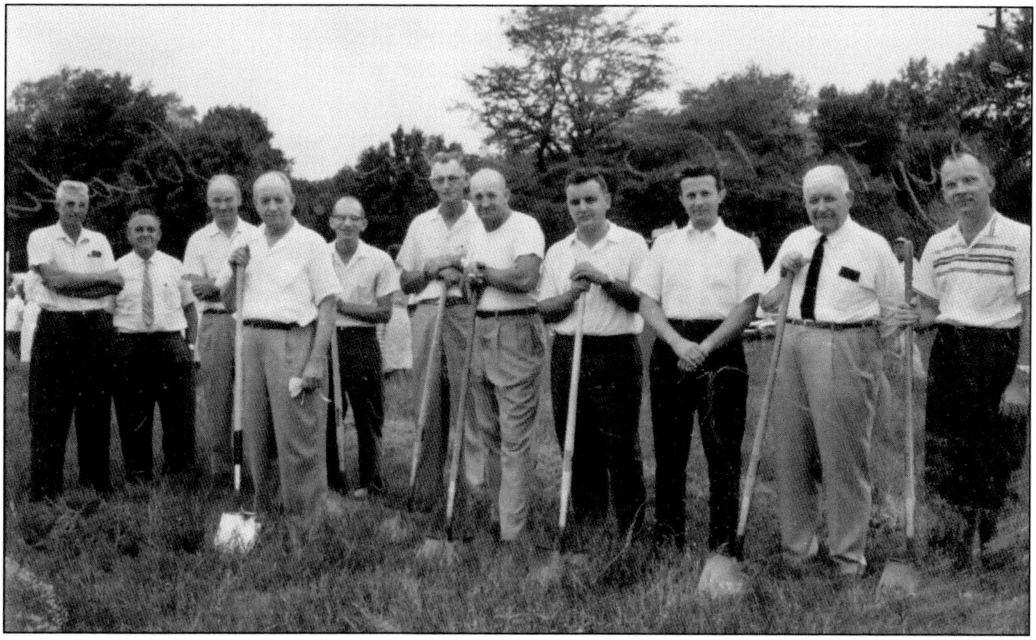

On the morning of August 28, 1959, two years before the new high school would be ready for occupancy, a crowd has gathered at the future site for the ceremonial ground-breaking. Those turning a shovelful of dirt are, from left to right, Troy Hutto, unidentified, unidentified, C.B. Stemen, Cornelius "Bus" Fox, Harold Planck, unidentified, Jim Francis, Harry Reasner, unidentified, and Ward Riffe. (Library archives.)

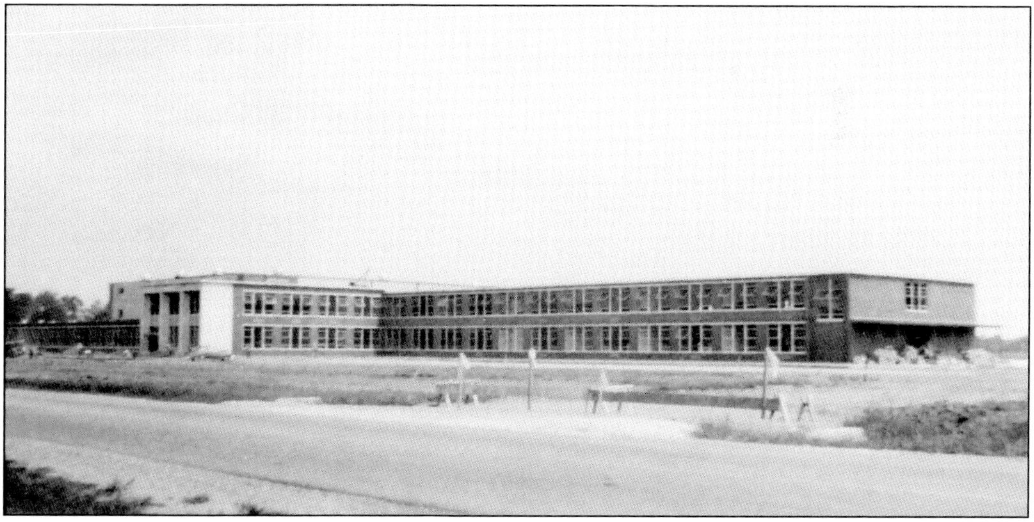

The newly constructed, fully modern Tipton High School, situated on South Main Street, was ready for the 1961–1962 school year. Built at a cost of about $2.1 million, the sprawling facility offered students many amenities never previously available to them. Features included several new and expanded courses, a farm shop, a printing press, a cafeteria, proximity to the football field, many more classrooms, a full-service library, and a cavernous gymnasium with seating to accommodate 3,400. (Rick Curnutt.)

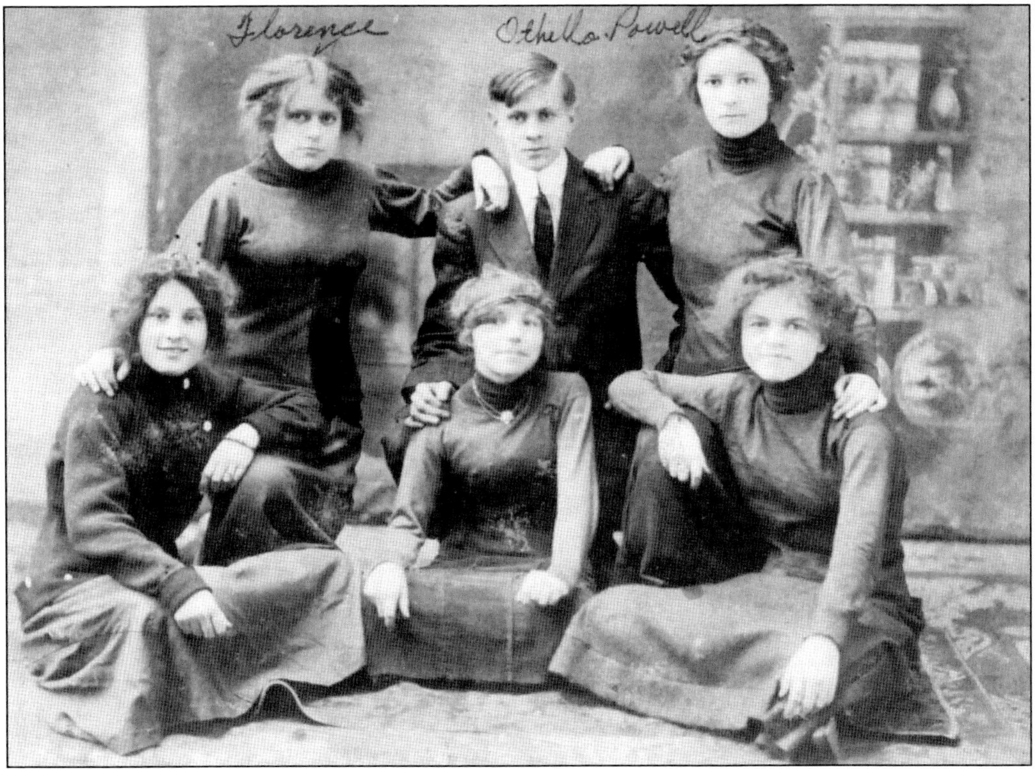

Tipton High School's first girls' basketball team was formed during the 1912–1913 school year. In this photograph are, from left to right, (first row) Margaret Nicholson, forward; June Hooten, forward; and Patricia Langan, guard; (second row) Florence Brown, guard; Othello Powell, coach; and Charlotte Qualters, center. (Library archives.)

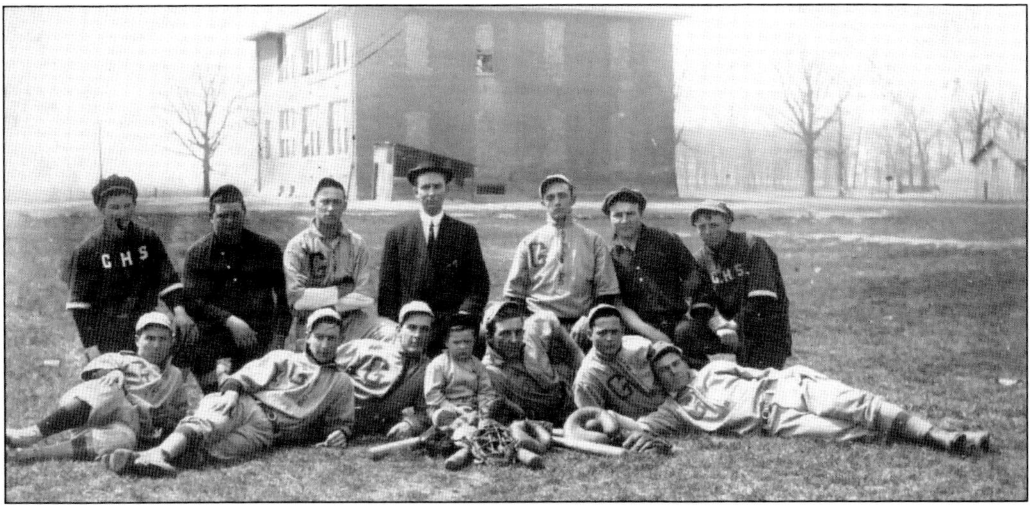

Community baseball teams provided popular Sunday afternoon recreation for athletes and spectators alike during the first part of the last century. The Goldsmith Athletics was one of the county's finest, challenging teams from surrounding counties and towns—even Indianapolis—for many seasons. This undated photograph likely was taken during spring training, around 1913. None of the players or the manager is identified. (Alice Ricketts.)

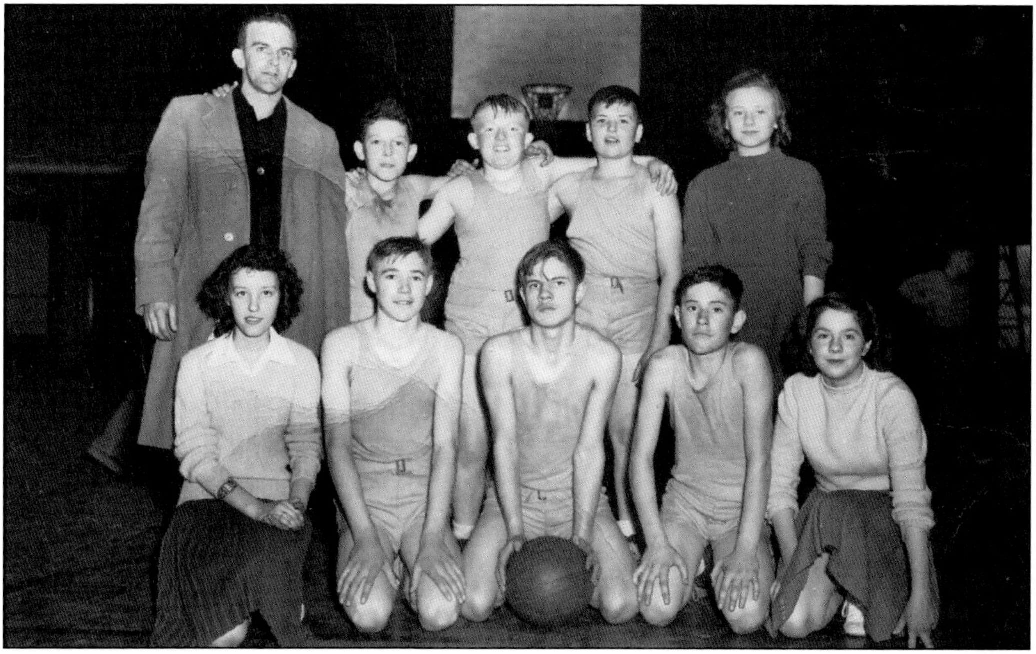

Hobbs Elementary School basketball team and cheerleaders gather after they won the 1948 "kids tournament." Pictured are, from left to right, (first row) Eva Sue Bogue, Everett Stiner, Charles Jack, Larue Fecher, and Betty Deverback; (second row) coach Verl Grimme, Paul Julius, Larry Clouser, Doyle Hobbs, and Darlene Overdorf. (Paul Julius.)

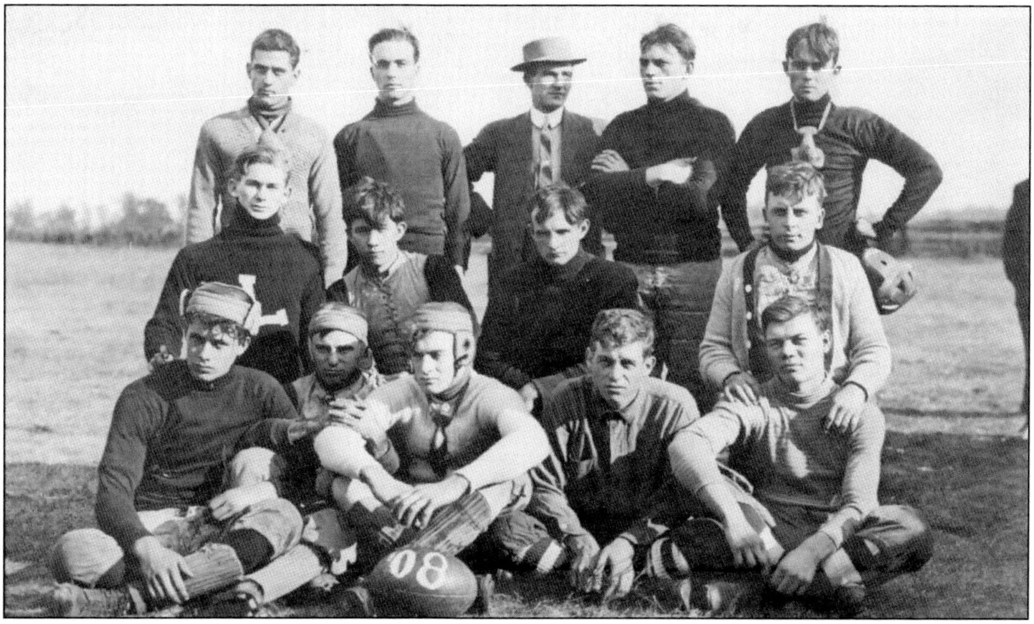

Describing a noble but disappointing football season, the 1909 Tipton High School yearbook nonetheless has only praise for its 1908 team, consisting of Monroe Hughes, Paul Van Buskirk, Herschel Francis, Verne Wagstaff, Herman O'Hara, Roderick Renner, Ray Glenn, Merle Brown, Dennis Thompson, Dudley Wagstaff, L.H. Brookbank, Eugene Teter, Ray Kirtley, and Frank Richey. (Library archives.)

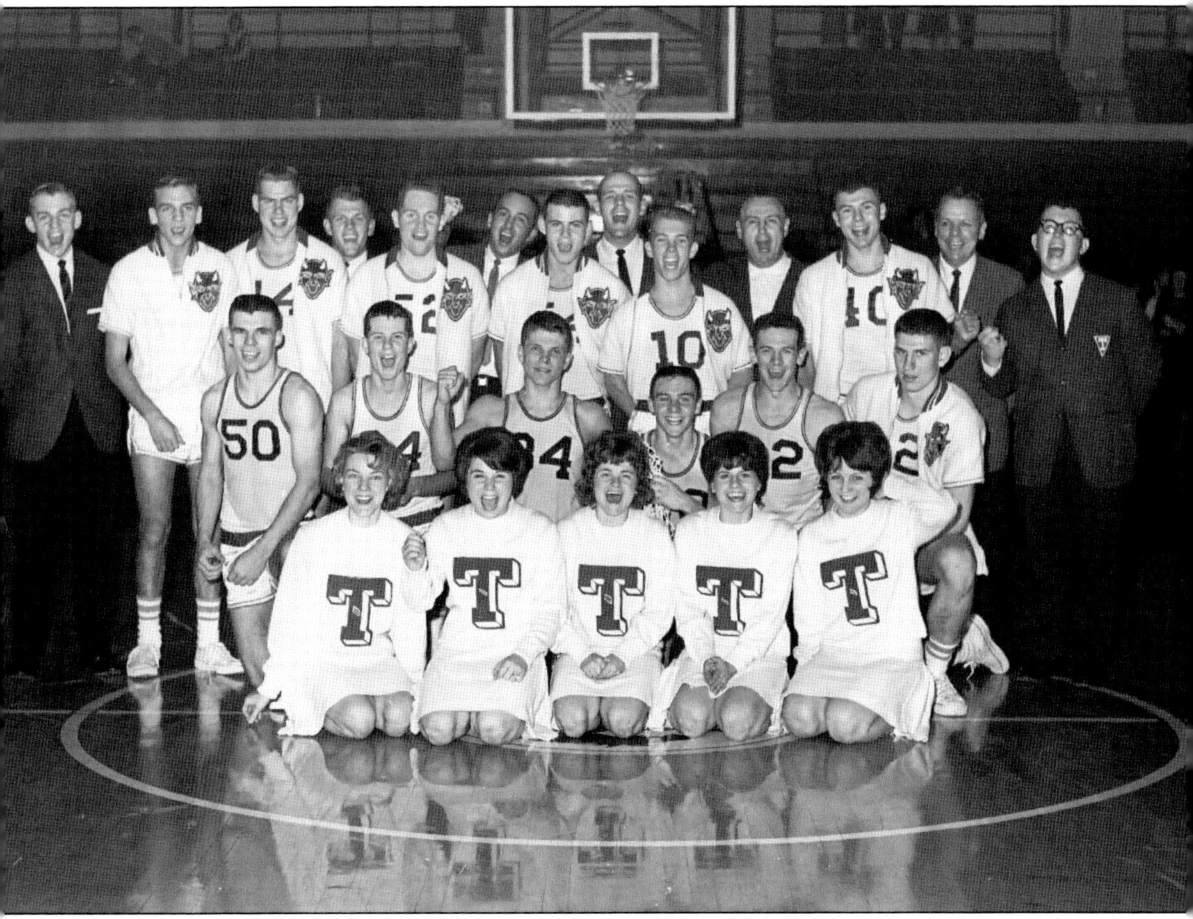

Not since 1936 had a Tipton basketball team been rated No. 1, and not since 1947 had one progressed past a sectional in its quest to nab a state championship title. Then, for a while in early 1964, THS's 1963–1964 basketball team was rated No. 1, sparking speculation about a state tournament win. However, after delivering the state tournament's semifinalists—Huntington and Lafayette Jefferson High Schools—their only losses during regular-season play, the Blue Devils lost their sectional in a crushing nail-biter. The team poses for a victory photograph on December 27, 1963, after beating No. 1–rated Lafayette Jeff, 72-67, at Lafayette during its holiday tournament. Pictured are, from left to right, (first row) Annie Bowers, Sandy Green, Jeannie Welchel, Artha Schulenberg, and Julie Foster; (second row) Bill Moore, Don Curnutt, Dan Crouch, Dick McIntosh, Harvey Harmon, and Clarence "Butch" Myers; (third row) Forest Addington, Steve Hackett, Lex Boyd, Phil Sullivan, Steve Van Horn, John Woods, Bill Elliott, assistant coach John Moses, Mike Captain, head coach Dick Barr, Keith Smith, THS principal Charles Edwards, and Roland Beatty. (Bill Moore.)

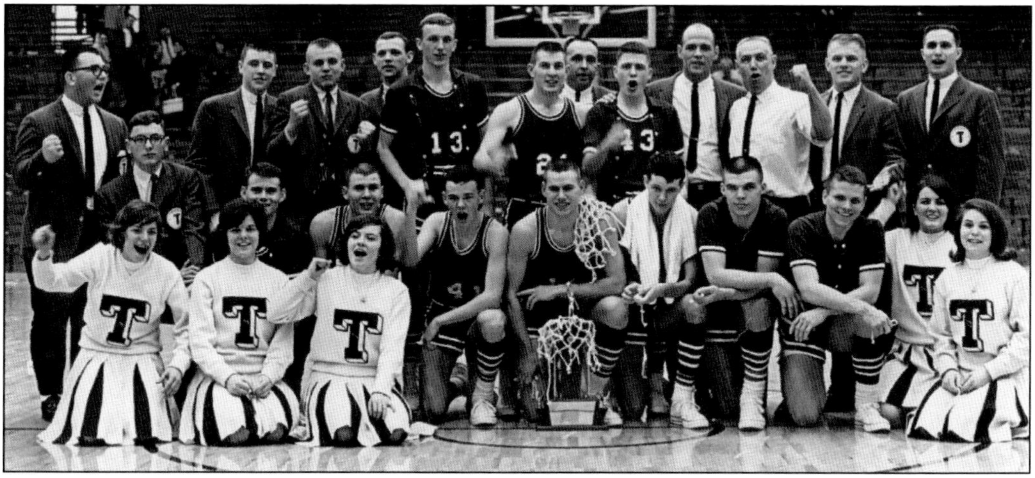

Tipton's hope was realized the following year, when the 1964–1965 team fulfilled the promise by claiming the sectional victory—the school's first since 1947—beating archrival Noblesville in the final game. The Devils advanced to their regional contest but were eliminated after the first game. Tipton did not win another sectional until 1986. In the photograph above, taken after the sectional win, are THS's 1964–1965 basketball team and cheerleaders. The cheerleaders are, from left to right, Lois Lambert, Debby McIntosh, Becky Morris, Julie Foster, and Sandy Green. Also pictured are, from left to right, (sitting) David Quigley, Bill Elliott, Keith Smith, Jim Harmon, Lex Boyd, Don Curnutt, Bill Moore, and Dan Crouch; (standing) Roland Beatty, Terry McIntosh, Forest Addington, Ron Long, Garry Meyer, Jim Hannah, John Woods, Jerry Carter, assistant coach John Moses, head coach Dick Barr, Phil Sullivan, and George Walter. (Rick Curnutt.)

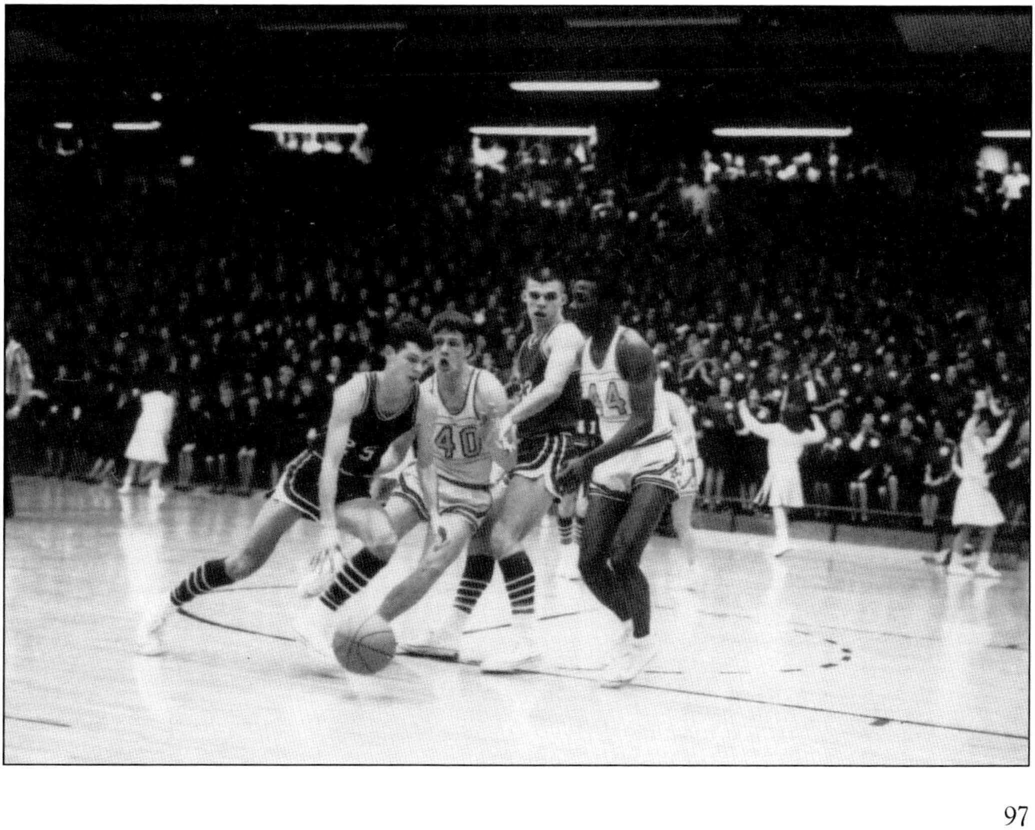

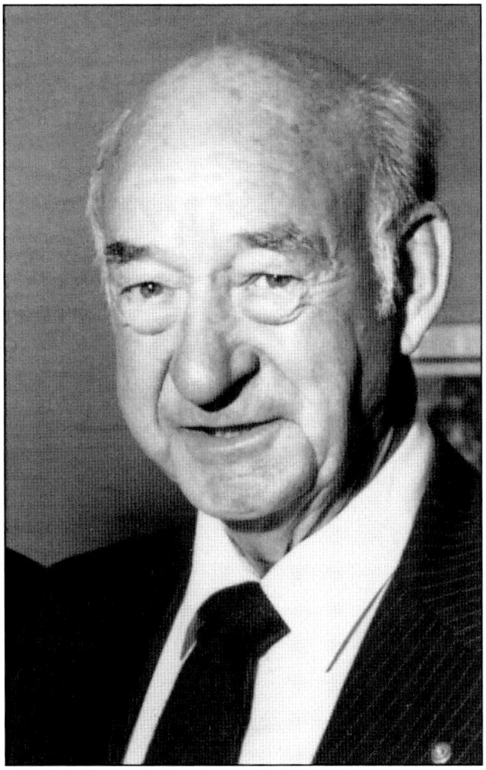

Mark Ertel was a standout on Tipton's 1935–1936 basketball team. His ability earned him a spot on Notre Dame's varsity squad for three years and in the college all-star game. Graduating in 1940, he played three seasons with the Indianapolis Kautskys and the US Navy officers' team at Miami, winning 36 of 38 games. He was inducted into the Indiana Basketball Hall of Fame in 1985. (Gary Ertel.)

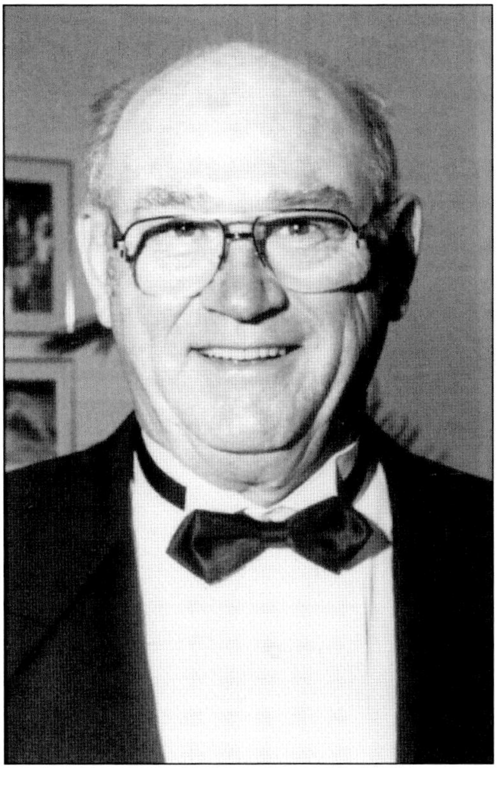

James Ertel was a three-year, all-conference Tipton basketball player, graduating in 1942. Considered one of his era's top pivotmen, he was picked for the 1942 Indiana All-Star team. With the war raging, he put college on hold and entered the military. He graduated Purdue University in 1949 after earning two basketball letters. Ertel became a career teacher and coach and was a 1990 Hall of Fame inductee. (Gary Ertel.)

Dick McIntosh was a three-year Tipton varsity basketball starter, named Central Indiana Conference Player of the Year, and a member of the Indiana All-Star team. Graduating THS in 1964, he continued his basketball career at the University of Georgia, where he was named to the Academic All-Conference in 1966 and 1967 and the 1967 Little Man All-American team. He was inducted into the Indiana Basketball Hall of fame in 2003. (Terry McIntosh.)

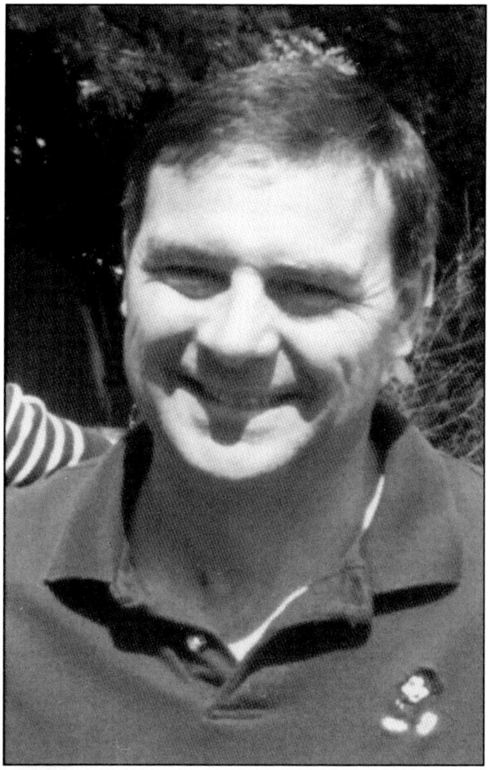

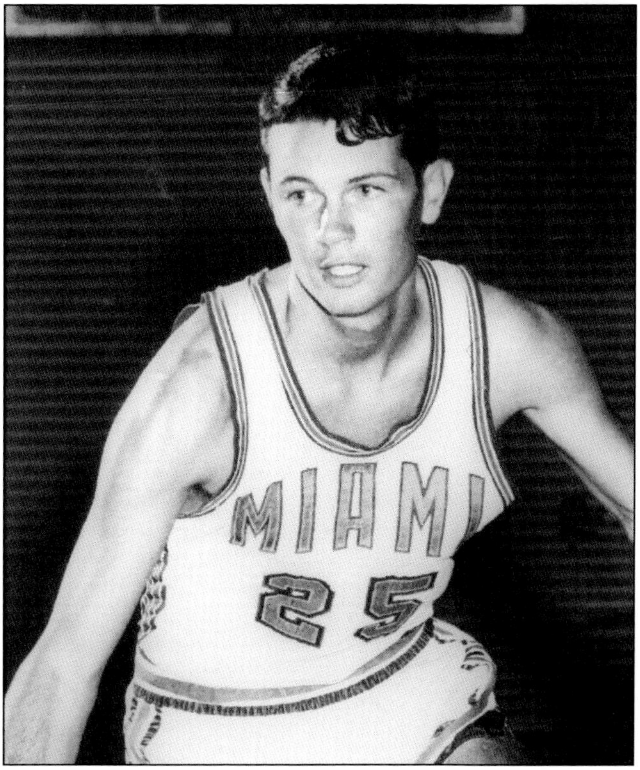

A 1965 THS graduate, Don Curnutt played varsity for three seasons at the University of Miami, averaging 26.1 points for a 77-game career. Graduating in 1970, he earned all-American honors and signed a one-year contract with the Pacers. Called "the greatest shooting guard in the history of the University of Miami," he was inducted into the Indiana Basketball Hall of Fame in 2001. (Rick Curnutt.)

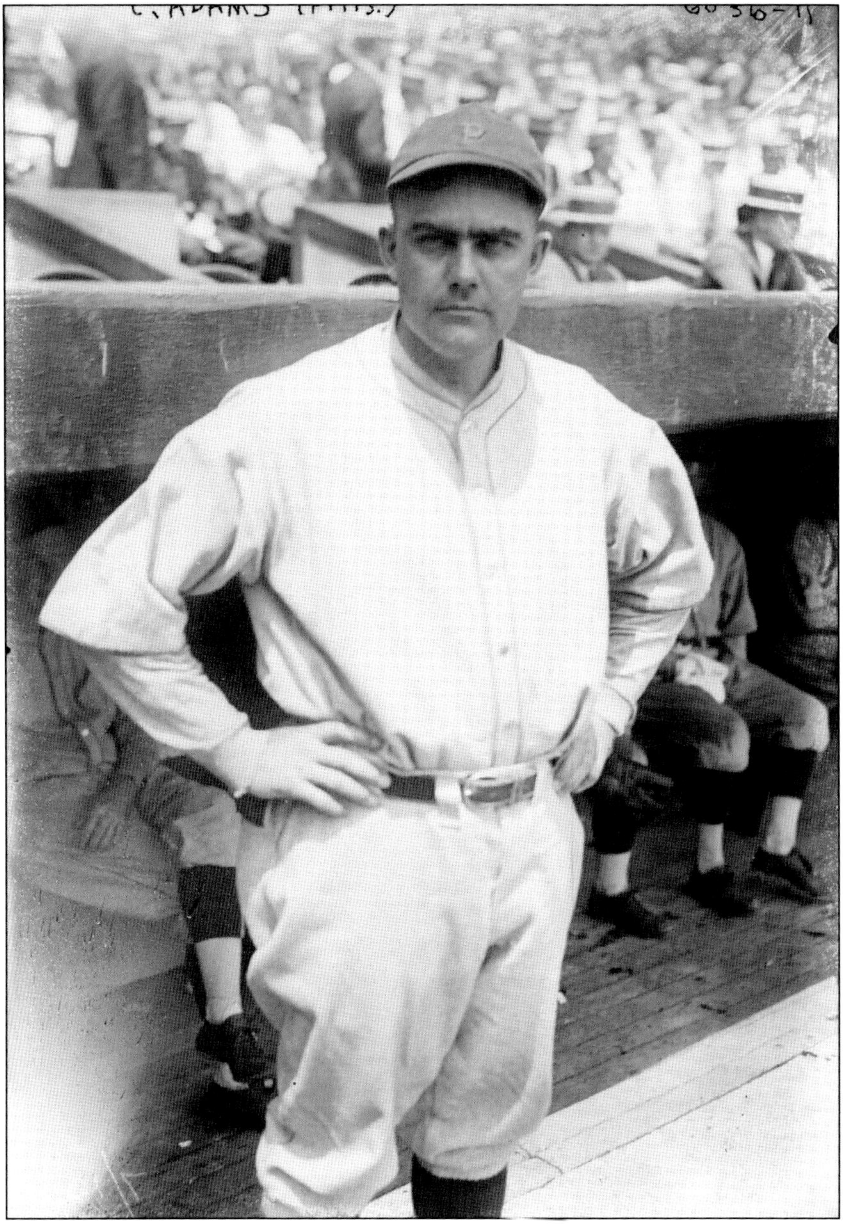

Charles "Babe" Adams was born on a farm in Prairie Township, near Kempton, May 18, 1882. Adams started his professional baseball career in 1904. After one game with the St. Louis Cardinals, he was sent back to the minors. In 1907, he led the Class A Western League in victories. The Pittsburgh Pirates took notice and purchased his contract. After four games with the Pirates, Adams was sent back to the minors. That time, he perfected his pitch and started winning games. He returned to the Pirates in 1909, joining their pitching staff. The 27-year-old's 7-2 finish helped clench the American League pennant for the Pirates that year and then led the team to a World Series victory over the Detroit Tigers. It was a remarkable feat for a rookie season. During the celebration back in Pittsburgh, fans gave the loudest ovation to Adams; they considered him a hero. He went on to play 16 more seasons in the big leagues and retired in 1926. He died in 1968 on his farm in Silver Spring, Maryland. (Library of Congress.)

Seven

Events and Celebrations

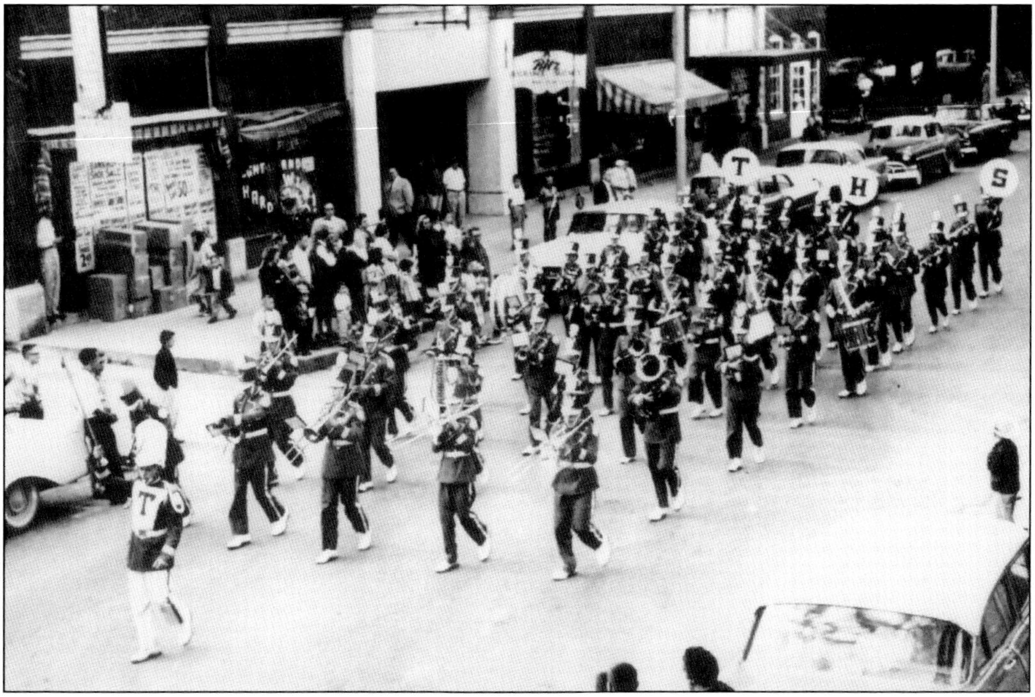

Debuting new blue uniforms, the Tipton High School marching band energizes the homecoming parade on Friday, September 27, 1957, as it progresses southward along Main Street toward Jefferson Street. That evening, the Tipton Blue Devils dominated the football field, racking up their first win of the season, beating Jackson Central 48-6. (Rick Curnutt.)

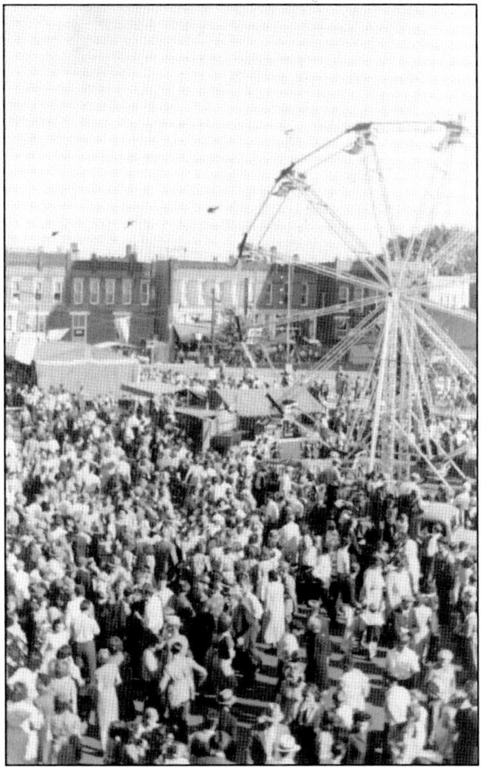

For one Friday and Saturday near the end of the harvest season in late October 1939 through 1941, thousands packed Tipton's downtown area to enjoy the Corn Festival, an event calling attention to the county's outstanding corn production. The fun-filled celebration featured a parade, food, vendors, games, a husking bee, a corn king and queen coronation, a greased pig race, band concerts, aerial acts, husband-calling and hog-calling competitions, a milking contest, and a Ferris wheel. The popular events were discontinued in 1942 due to the war and never resumed. Below, the 1939 Corn Festival queen and her court wend through town on their designated float. The queen's float was one of the festival parade's centerpieces. (Left, library archives; below, Ruth Illges.)

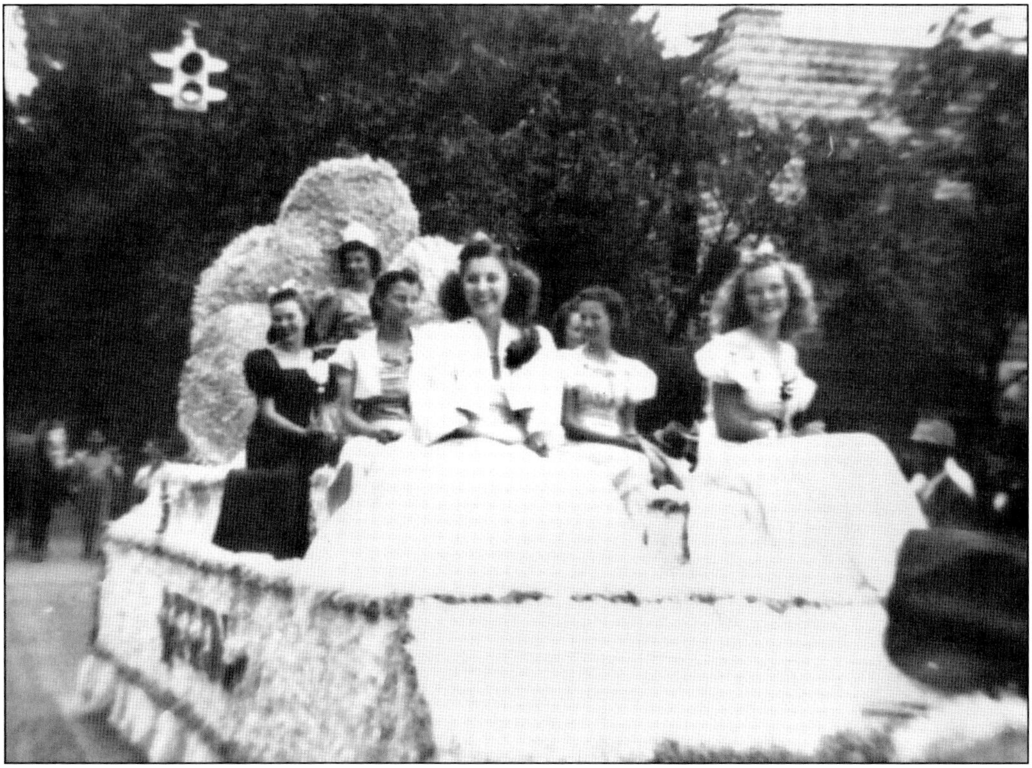

Drum major Kenny Hamilton leads the Tipton High School marching band west along Jefferson Street during the parade that kicked off the county's first annual Corn Festival in October 1939. The *Tribune* called the parade "the most colorful and impressive event of its kind staged in Tipton County for years." (Ruth Illges.)

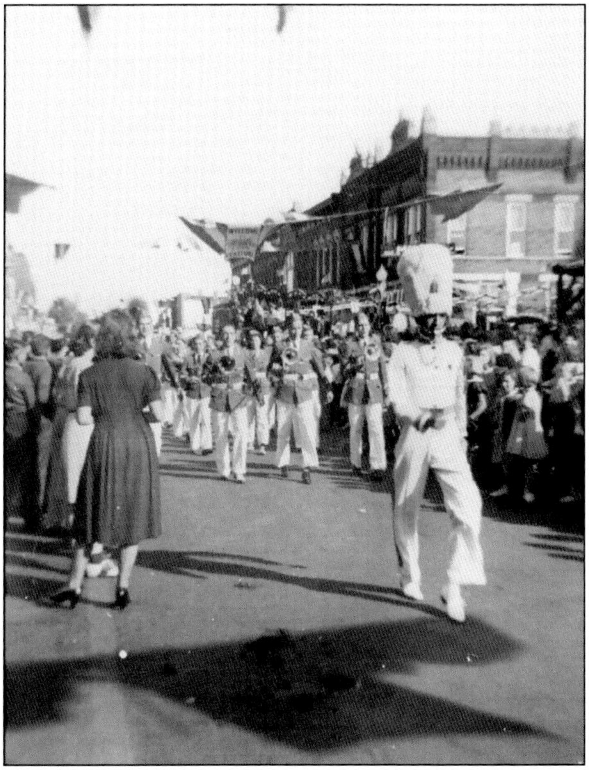

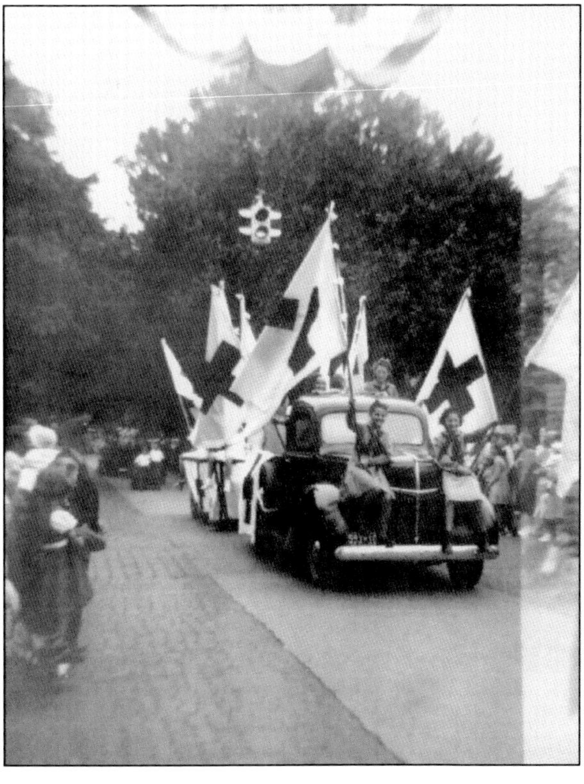

Members of the American Junior Red Cross wave flags as they promenade south on Main Street during the 1939 Corn Festival parade. At the time of this photograph, more than 1,200 area students belonged to Tipton County's Junior Red Cross, a popular service program that taught the value of service, safety, good health, and world understanding. Its motto was "We serve." (Ruth Illges.)

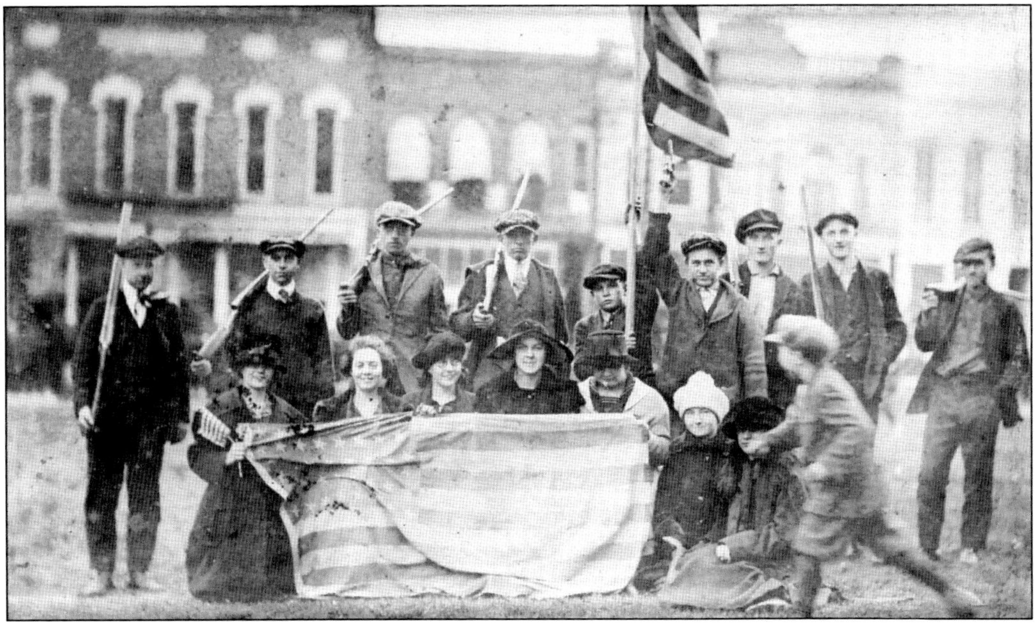

News of the Germans' surrender ending World War I reached Tipton at 2:00 a.m. November 11, 1918. According to that day's *Tipton Daily Tribune*, every whistle and noisemaker in the city broke loose, and the clamor continued through the night and into the day. Several Tipton residents decided the town needed a celebration, and so Tipton celebrated. Fame Canning Factory donated several hundred five-gallon tin cans, and hundreds of townspeople marched the streets banging on their improvised drums. They were joined by workers from local factories and businesses. By 1:00 p.m., according to the *Tribune*, the demonstration had turned the town "topsy-turvy." These photographs are believed to be from that celebration. Both were taken on the front lawn of the Tipton County Courthouse. (Both, Alice Ricketts.)

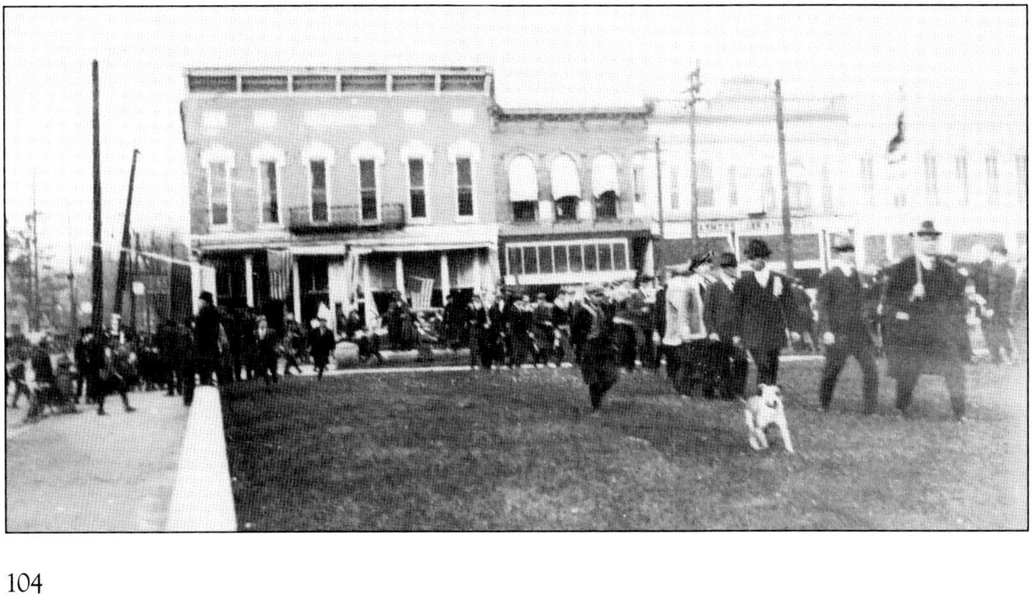

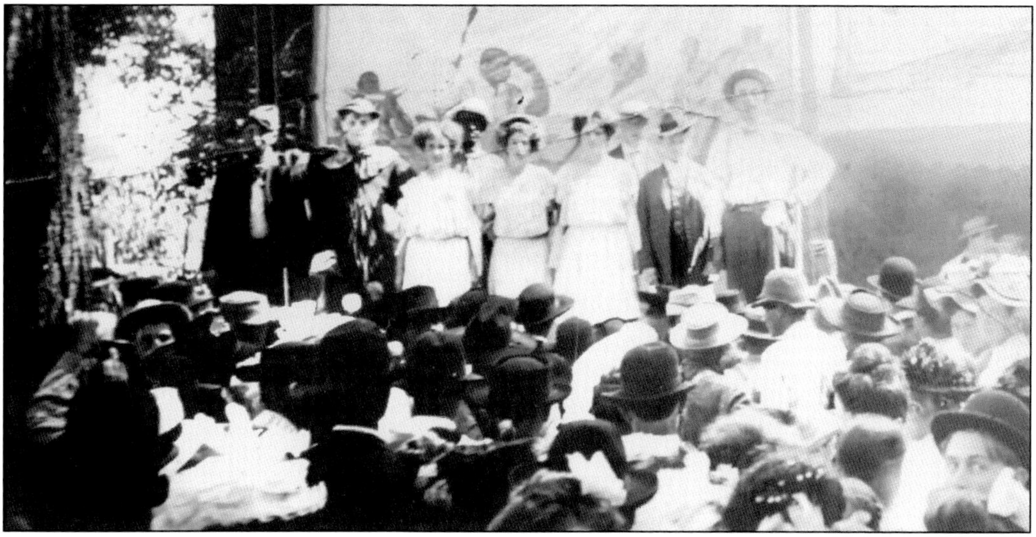

In the early part of the 20th century, traveling theater groups often made stops along railroad routes and performed in makeshift venues, sometimes hastily constructed in a woods. This group is shown performing in Ekin. They arrived by train at Goldsmith and journeyed on to their destination by horse and buggy. (Penny Manier.)

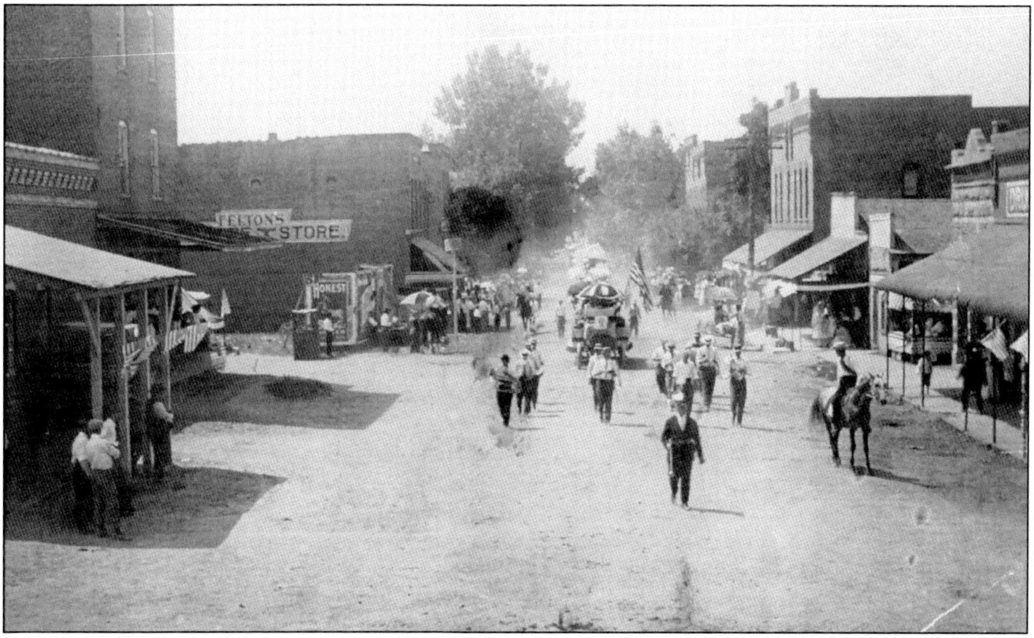

Spectators line the main street of Sharpsville for a good old-fashioned Fourth of July parade, about 1911. Following the Sharpsville Band is a line of festive floats. The stores are decked out in stars and stripes, and at the end of the route, a picnic and games are likely waiting. (Virginia Chambers.)

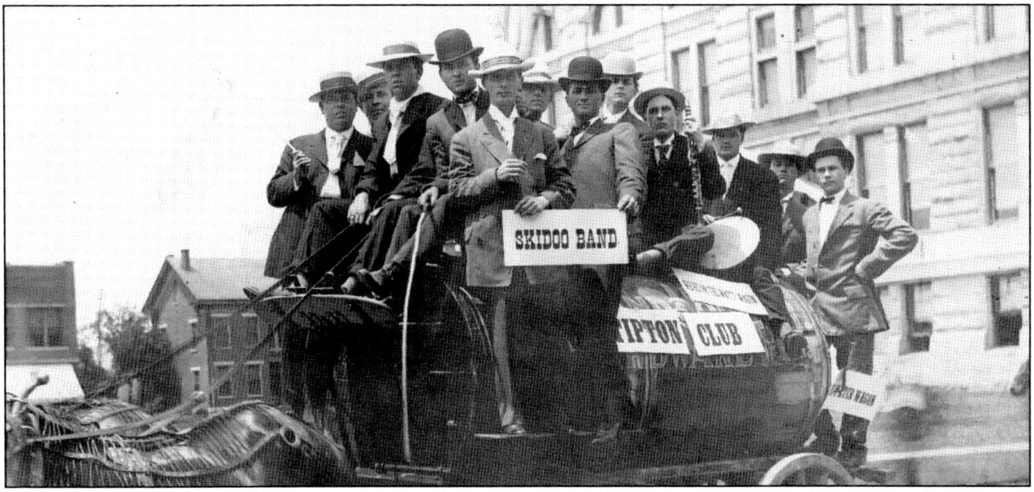

The Skidoo Band performed at dances, parties, and social events in the early 1900s. Also shown in this photograph, taken on the southeast side of the courthouse, are members of the Tipton Club, a young men's organization. A 1936 *Tribune* article identifies some of the men pictured as, in no particular order, Frank Vawter, William Nelson, Lawrence and J. Carl Shiel, Fred Schick, G.J. Oglebay, Garnet Dodds, and L.O. Behymer. (Alice Ricketts.)

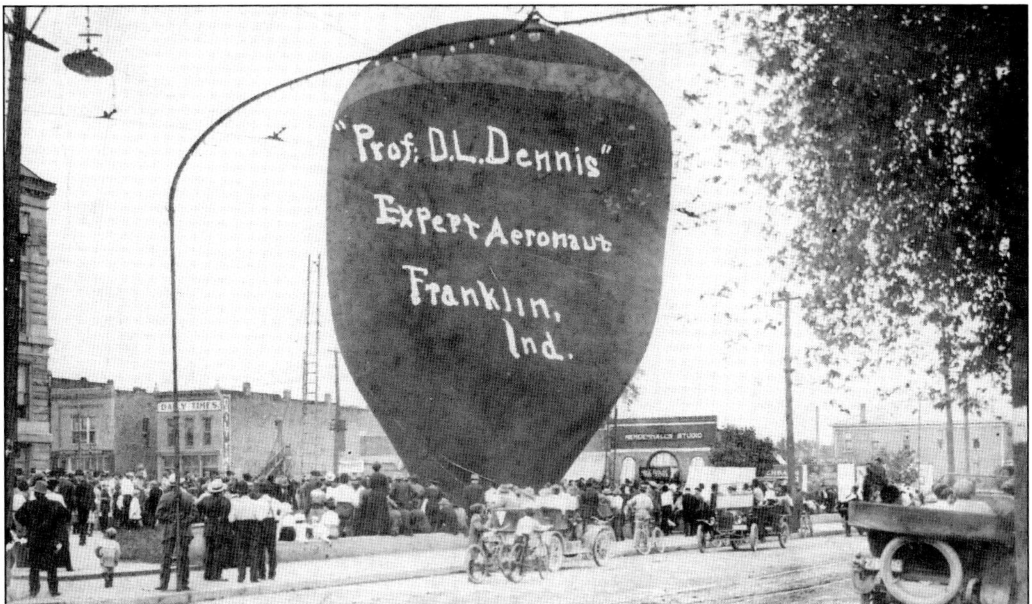

In the early part of the 20th century, balloonist Prof. D.L. Dennis from Franklin, Indiana, was touted as the most daring aeronaut in the country and was often featured at county fairs and town carnivals. In this undated photograph, a crowd has assembled on the south side of the Tipton County Courthouse to witness the famous daredevil make another of his acclaimed balloon ascents. (Alice Ricketts.)

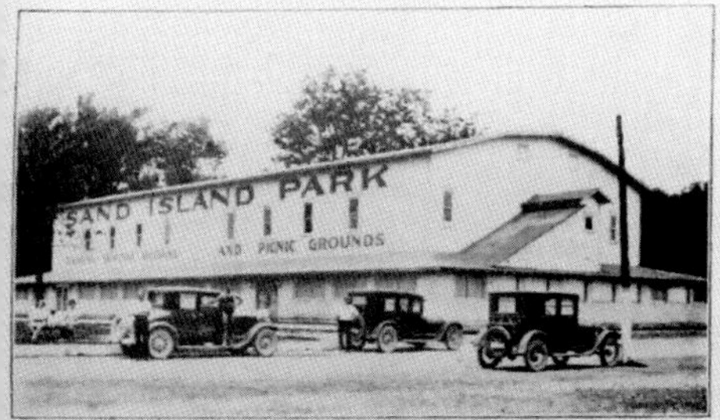

DANCE HALL AND SKATING RINK

Persons in picture, left to right: Martha Russell, Nenoa Highbaugh, Mrs. J. N. Russell, George Werner, Glen Werner, J. N. Russell.

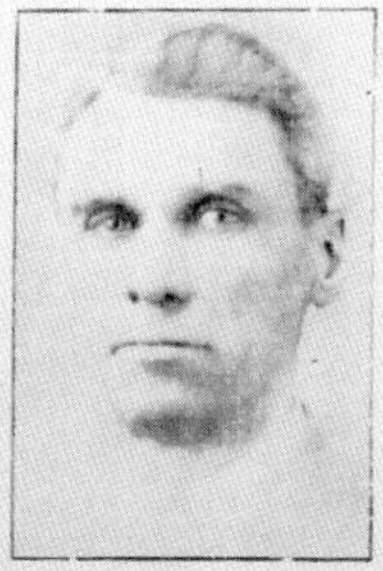

J. N. RUSSELL, Proprietor

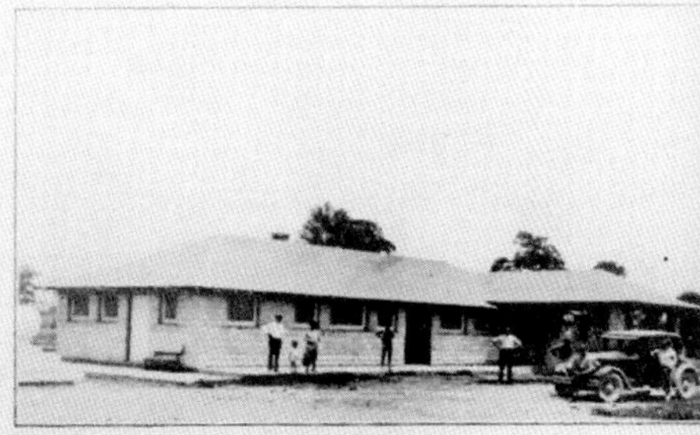

TEA ROOM

Persons in picture, left to right: J. N. Russell, Nenoa Highbaugh, Mrs. J. N. Russell, Glen Werner, George Werner, Amos Comer, John E. Lower, Martha Russell.

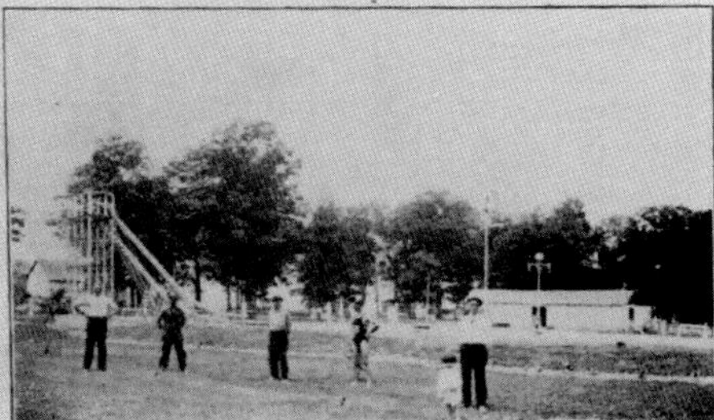

SWIMMING POOL

Persons in picture, left to right: George Werner, Amos Comer, John E. Lower, Glen Wetner, Nonoa Highbaugh, J. N. Russell.

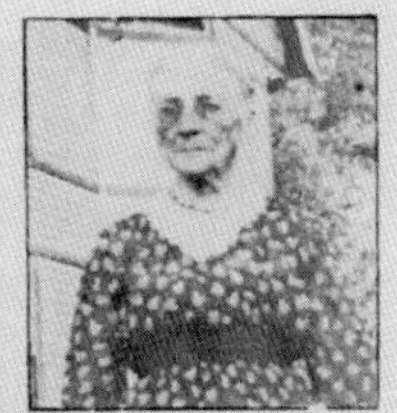

MRS. AMANDA J. (SELLARS) RUSSELL
Age 96
Mother of the Proprietor

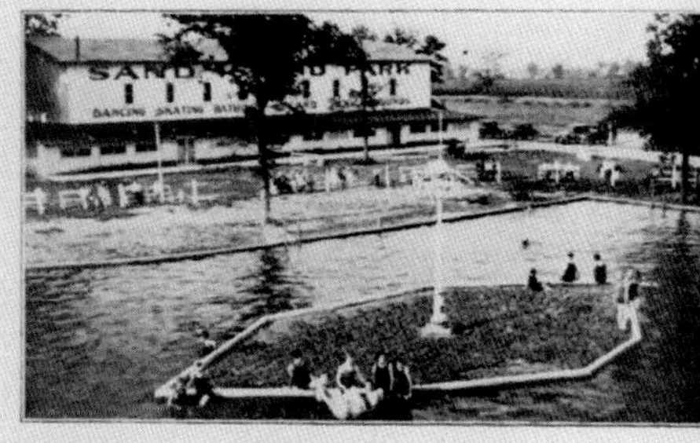

SWIMMING POOL
With Bathers in Action

SAND ISLAND AMUSEMENT PARK

Located one-fourth mile west of Tipton on lands known as the Harry Woodruff farm, on State Road 28. Construction and building work begun Sept. 9, 1924, and it was completed and opened to the public Dec. 21, 1924. The park is nicely situated in a beautiful grove of native trees, abundant shade and splendid well water. This tract of land contains fifty acres, and is provided with a free tourist camp, open to the public. The dance hall is 100x130, provided with one of the best dance floors in the state, with roller skating rink on second floor. The swimming pool is 135x200 feet, constructed with cement throughout. In the central part of this pool is an artificial island, constructed of sand, which gives the place its name—Sand Island. It is due to Mr. Russell that this amusement park was built, affording the public a nice place for amusement and recreation. The Tipton County Fair Association has its buildings and race track on a portion of this tract of land and conducts a free fair annually.

Sand Island occupied 50 acres just west of Tipton. It featured a dance hall, skating rink, a tearoom, campgrounds, and a swimming pool with an artificial island of sand at its center—hence the park's name. Sand Island opened Sunday, December 21, 1924, amid protests from area churches that the park's operation on the Sabbath would surely lead youth astray. According to a *Tribune* article, churches warned, "Permit this encroachment to grow and we will soon have no day of rest." But grow it did. By summer, Sand Island's dances, baseball games, racing, swimming, and 10-minute airplane rides attracted thousands of patrons—even on Sundays. However, after the park changed hands some five years later, the new owner used the racetrack for auto racing and slowly phased out the rest of the park. He opened a slaughterhouse there in 1933 and later tore down the dance hall and converted the swimming pool to a catfish pond. Model Canning Factory took over the tearoom. Today, not a trace of the park remains. (Library archives.)

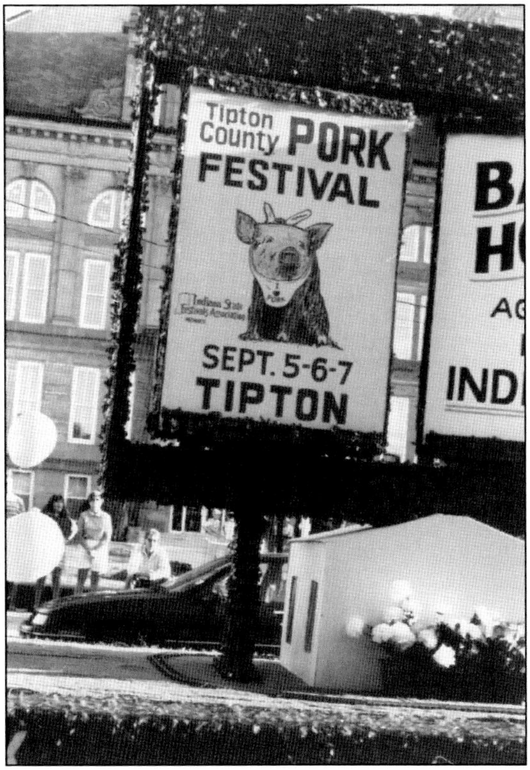

Tipton has been synonymous with its Pork Festival since 1969. Originally intended as a one-time affair to help promote the local association of pork producers, the first festival had not even ended before organizers recognized its overwhelming success, prompting a buzz that an annual event had just been born. The September 15, 1969, *Tribune* reports that thousands of visitors poured into Tipton that weekend. Occupying the courthouse lawn, the festival offered an assortment of pork dishes for breakfast, lunch, and dinner while hosting a variety of games and contests—greased pig riding, egg tossing, and husband and hog calling—with trophies. A 100-unit parade threaded through town led by Maj. Gen. Jesse McIntosh and featured bands from area schools, civil defense units, fire trucks, horse patrols, and dozens of floats. The Tipton Merchants Association's float won first place that first year. Below, Uncle Sam coaxes a handshake from a toddler who is enjoying the parade. (Left, Ron Byal; below, *Tribune*.)

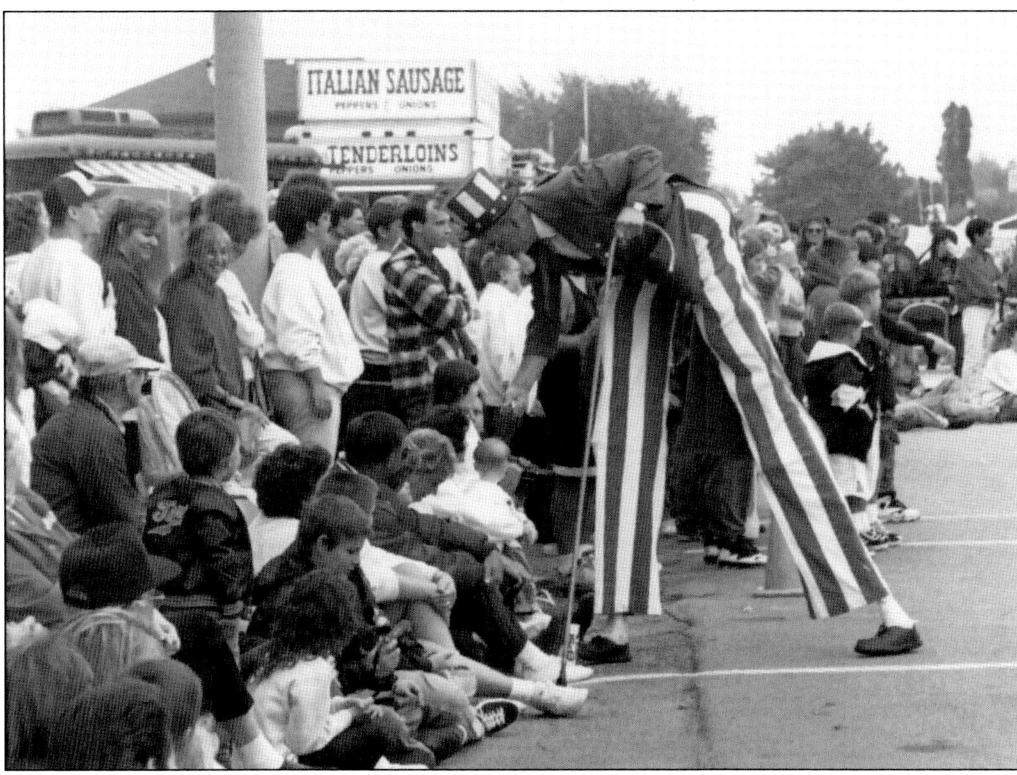

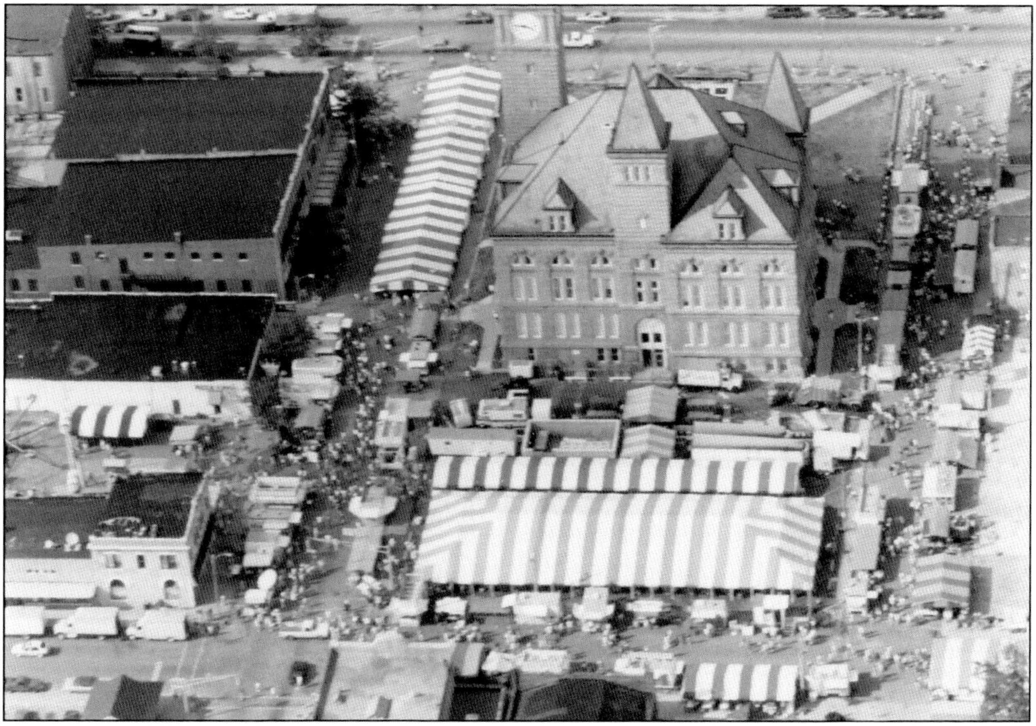

An aerial view reveals the crowd pouring into downtown Tipton at 3:45 p.m. on the opening day of the 1991 Pork Festival. That year, an estimated 20,000 people converged around the courthouse square to hear recording artist Jimmy Ryser, who headlined the entertainment roster. (Ron Byal.)

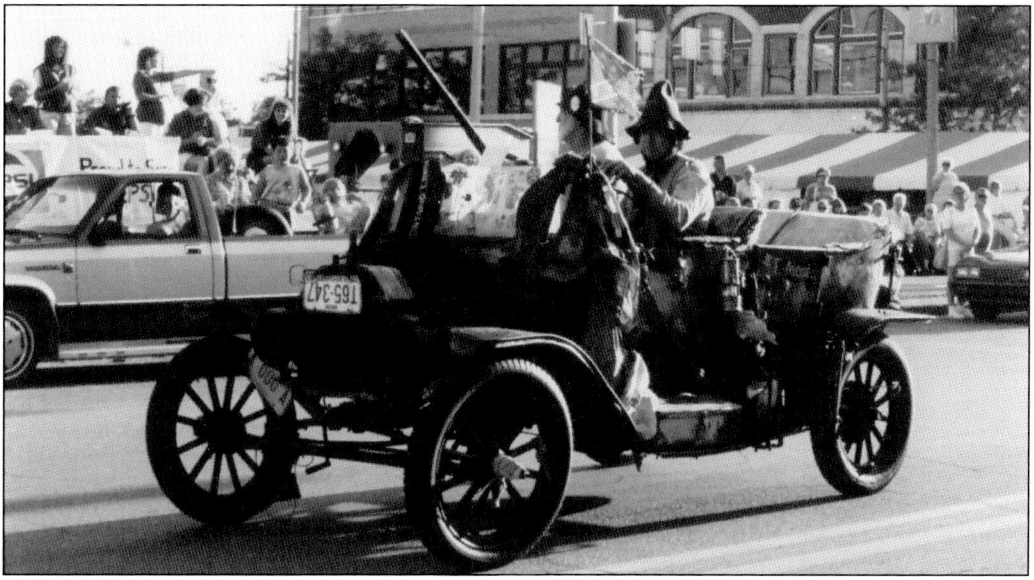

The hillbillies were among the favorite celebrities at many Pork Festivals throughout the 1980s and 1990s. Driving their Model T and waving their tattered Rebel flag, the duo were unofficial ambassadors for fun and good times. Here, the ragtag team draws cheers from the spectators lining the street for the Saturday afternoon parade in 1991. (Ron Byal.)

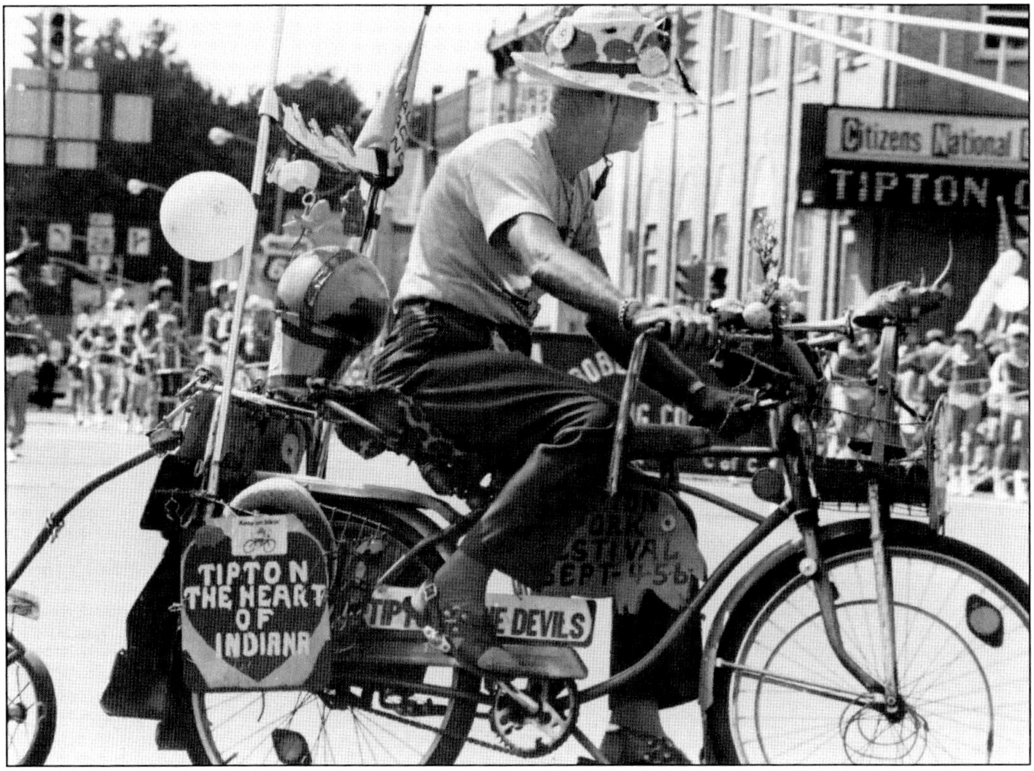

For years, Tipton resident Mitch Kelley was seen riding his bicycle around the streets of Tipton and became a familiar part of the Pork Festival parades. He is shown here stopping traffic at Main and Jefferson Streets in the 1989 parade. (Library archives.)

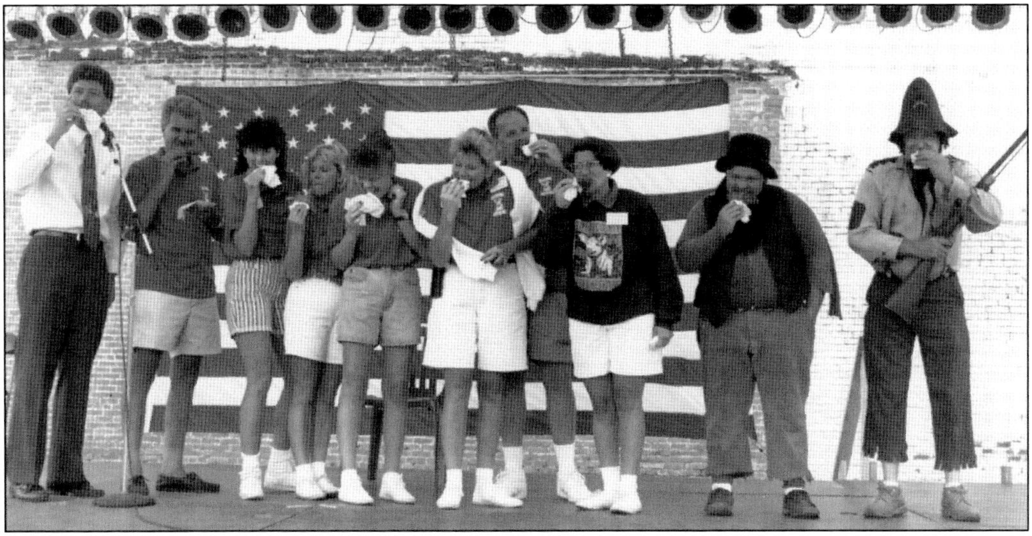

Tipton County Pork Festival VIPs (Very Important Pork-lovers) wrap their chops around the festival's signature commodity—a hot, juicy barbecued pork chop—at the official opening of the 1995 event. Pictured are, from left to right, Brett Curnutt, Tom De Shon, Kim Good, Carrie Burton, Becky Watkins, Jenny Cavanaugh, Rick Smith, Jacque Clements, John Alley, and E.J. Hayes. (*Tribune*.)

Eight

Patriots and Presidents

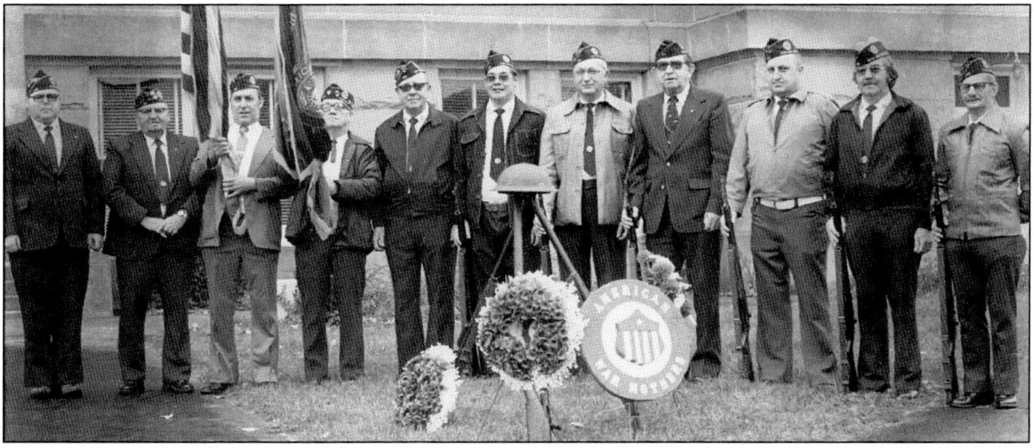

Tipton American Legion Post No. 46 Firing Squad Color Guard members led the 1978 Veterans Day memorial services on the Tipton County Courthouse north lawn. Wreaths, stacked rifles, and a World War I helmet were placed by American Legion units personnel. Pictured are, from left to right, then post commander Larry Cain, Bill Frost, Bob Barga, Bill Sutton, Bob Biltz, Bob Purvis, Bill Carter, Eldon Cage, Jim Biddle, Max Illges, and Alfred "Shorty" Hawkins. (Ruth Illges.)

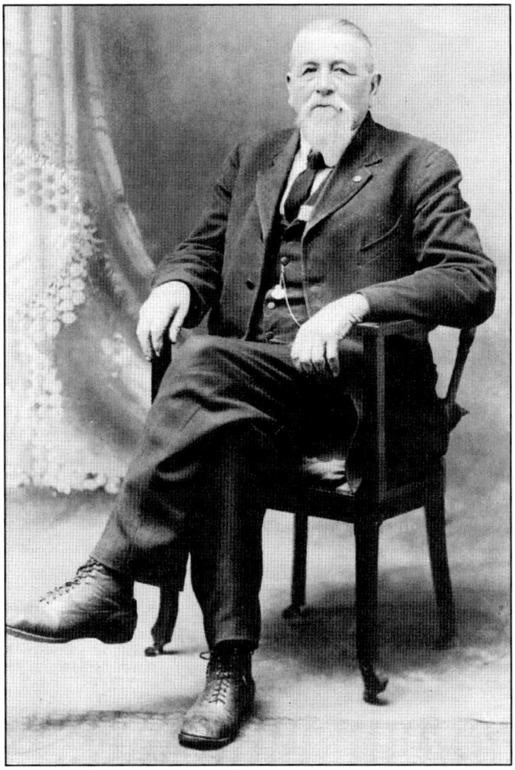

Shown left, Capt. Thomas Paul was born in 1824 in Henry County. He claimed both his grandfathers fought in the Revolutionary War under Gen. George Washington. Paul moved to Tipton County in 1855 and worked at the sawmill. When the Civil War broke out, he enlisted with the 11th Indiana Volunteer Regiment and fought some of the war's bloodiest battles, while steadily moving up through the ranks. At the time of his death on July 22, 1918, he was one of Tipton County's oldest and most revered residents. His obituary, headlined "Captain Thomas Paul Goes Into Eternal Bivouac," paid tribute to his military accomplishments, stating, "Bravely he marched to that field where he made the last stand, and there he was finally mustered out, but all who know him deeply regret this day when he was handed his final discharge." He was 94. Shown below, Jonathan Darke volunteered with the 26th Indiana Regiment, Company C, in 1861. Darke was a resident of Sharpsville, where he was the town's blacksmith. He died June 8, 1911, at the age of 83. (Both, library archives.)

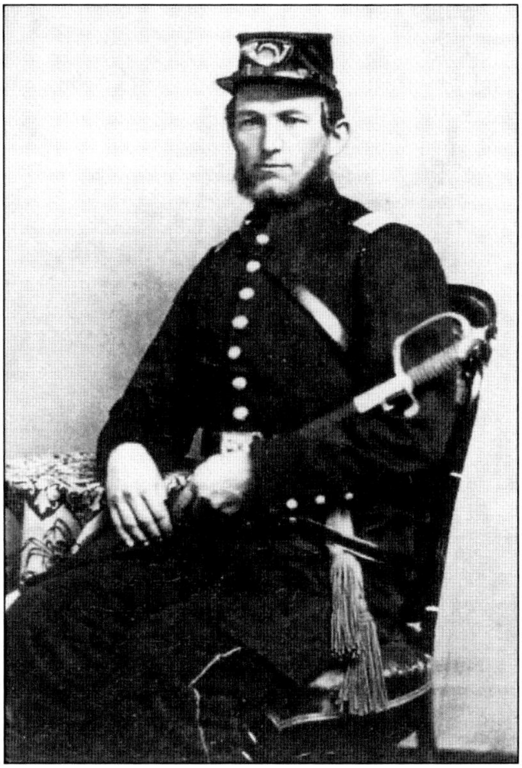

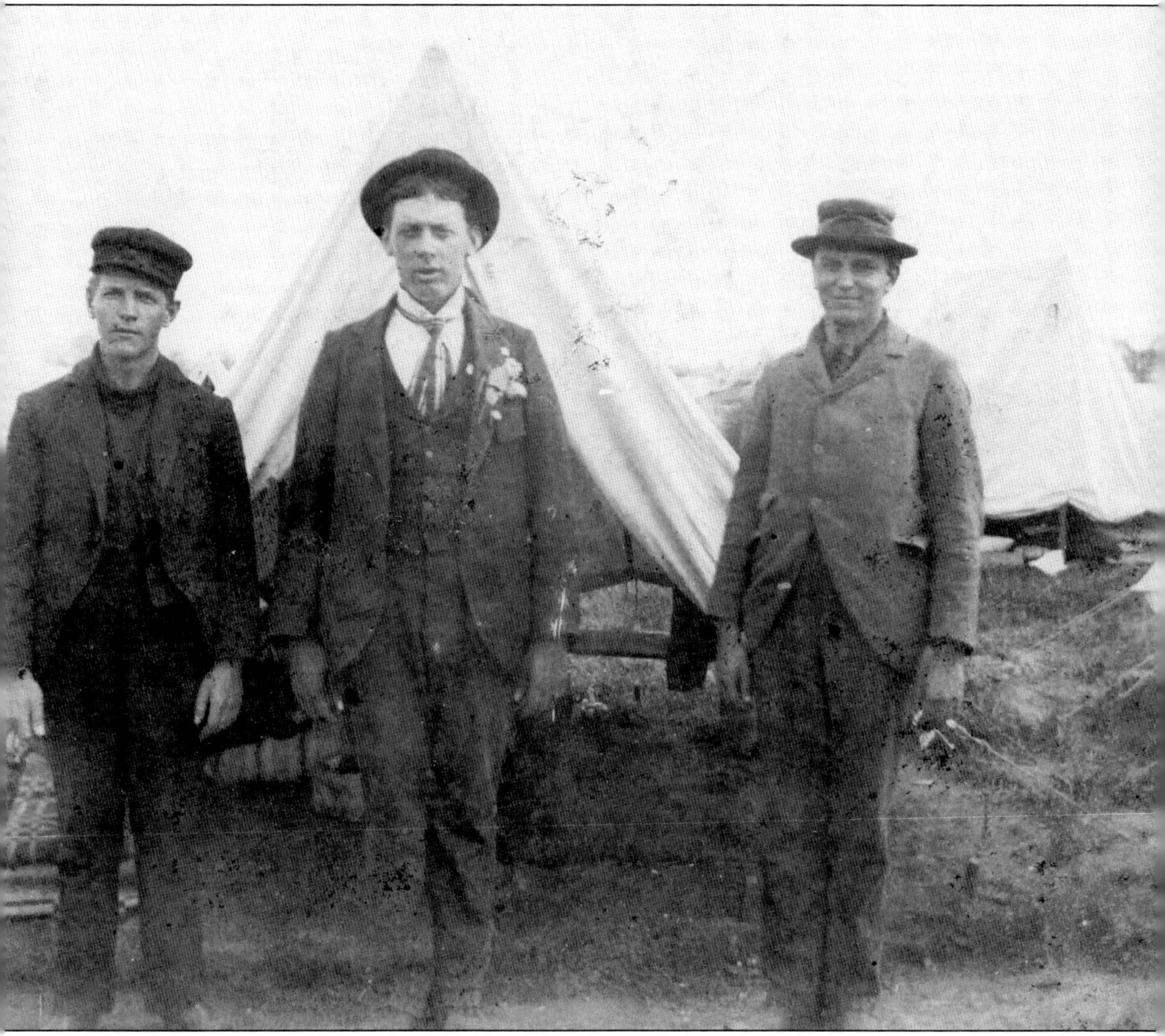

When the battleship *Maine* exploded in Havana Harbor in February 1898, killing more than 250 American seamen, Americans knew war with Spain was imminent. Friday, April 22, 1898, Pres. William McKinley called for volunteers. By Saturday night, a company had organized in Tipton. The following Monday night, the company received a telegram ordering them to report immediately to Camp Mount Indianapolis. At noon Tuesday, approximately 125 men fell in line behind the Tipton Cornet Band and marched to the depot, where hundreds had assembled to see them off. Amid tears and cheers, the young men boarded the train and off they went, each remembering the *Maine*. The Tipton men became part of the 160th Indiana Volunteer Infantry, and although none experienced actual warfare, they were ready, they were willing, and they were patriotic Americans. Pictured are, from left to right, C.W. Mount, Harry Mitchell, and Allen Gifford during training at Camp Mount. (Library archives.)

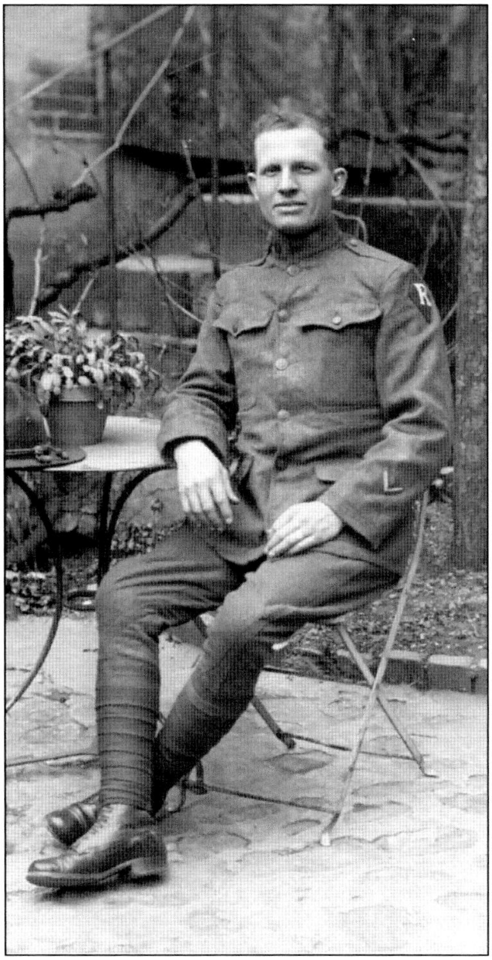

Tipton County native Everett Newkirk served with the US Army during World War I in France, where he poses for this photograph. After the war, Newkirk went to work for the Santa Fe Railway, necessitating his relocation to Santa Ana, California. He died there on April 20, 1955.

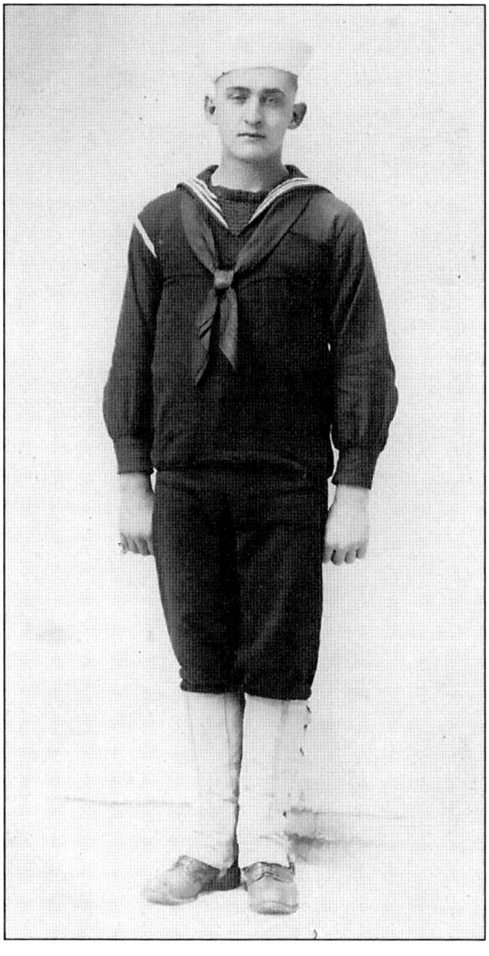

Elmer C. Doversberger, a native of Tipton County, served in the US Navy during World War I. He was sent to the North Atlantic in 1917. He was a lifelong farmer and became one of the county's first contract seed growers for Pioneer Seed Company. He died February 15, 1957, at the age of 57. (Larry Rump.)

Raymond Vair, left, was on leave from the Army around 1943, when he visited his little nephew, Billy Funke, age 7, in Jackson Station, where the family lived. Little Bill was obviously impressed with his uncle and did his best to emulate him—from his formal military stance to his garrison cap. (Catherine and William Funke.)

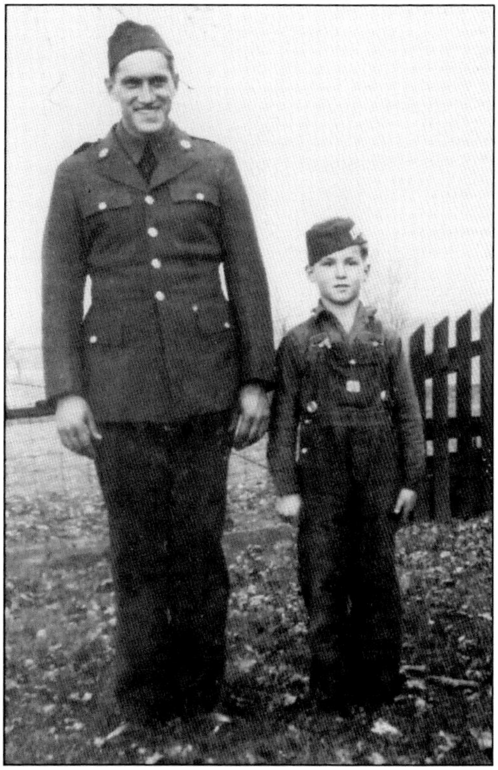

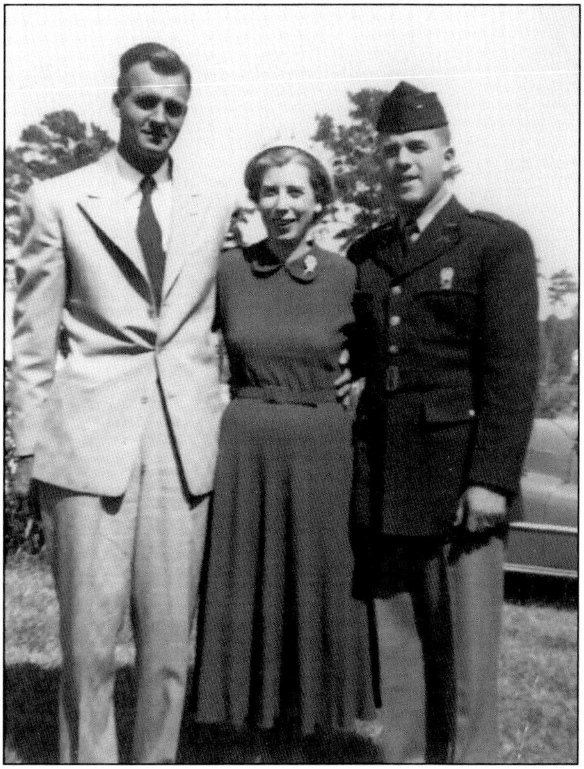

John L. and Martha Walker pose with son John C. following his graduation at Fort Benning, Georgia, Infantry School. When John's orders to serve in Korea were cancelled, he was reassigned to Alabama's National Guard. Discharged in 1953, he joined the family business, Tipton Produce Company, located in the 100 block of North West Street. It moved to East Jefferson Street in 1956. Hy-Line Chicks bought it in 1963. (John Walker.)

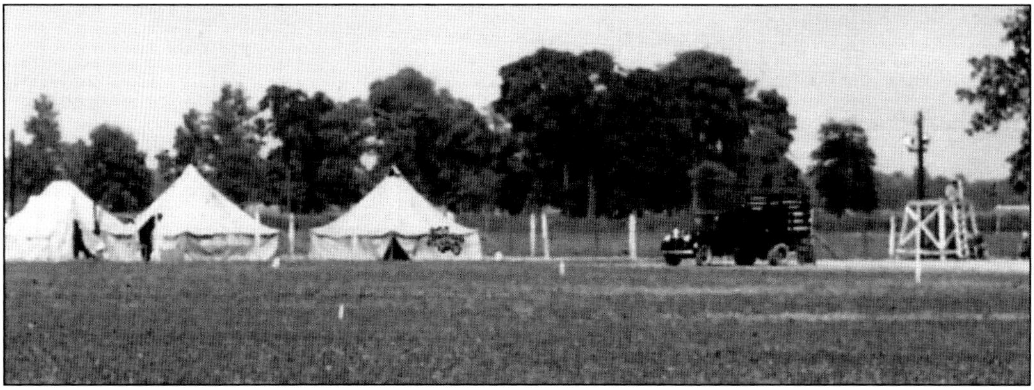

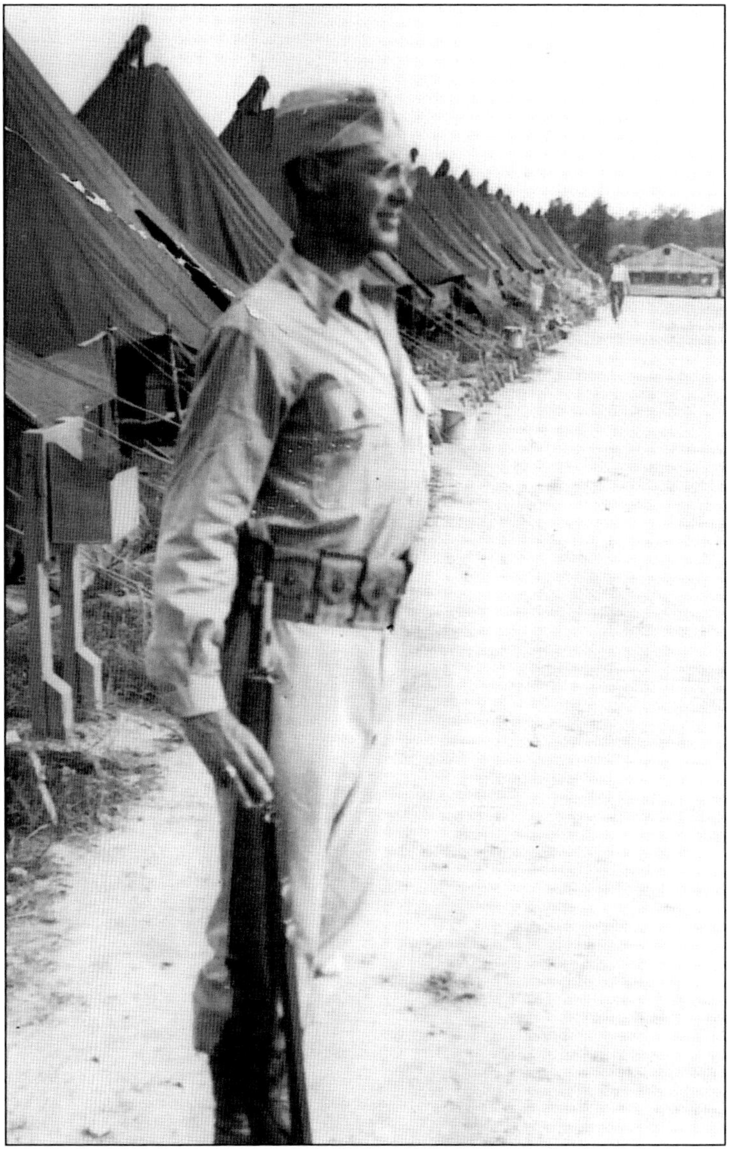

During the summers of 1944 and 1945, Windfall became home to hundreds of German prisoners of war. Living in a tent city near the high school, the POWs worked at county farms and factories, filling the labor shortage brought by the war. Reportedly, the prisoners were intelligent, courteous, and excellent workers, earning 40¢ an hour for their labor. Approximately 400 American servicemen watched over the 30-acre, L-shaped, wire-enclosed area. At left, Army sergeant Russell Stevens stands guard inside the camp. During his assignment in Windfall, Stevens and his wife, Margaret, lived with Henry and Ellen Zehner. After the harvest season, the prisoners were removed to a Kansas detention camp. The Windfall camp was one of several in Indiana administered by Camp Atterbury. (Both, Tipton County Historical Society.)

Arthur Manlove, left, was born in Tipton in 1901. He enlisted in the Navy in 1923 and made it his career. Warrant Officer Electrician Manlove was killed in action on December 7, 1941, at Pearl Harbor. Two years later, an escort ship, the USS *Manlove* (DE-36), was named for him. Two other Manlove family members, cousins, also perished in the war. Donald Manlove, a Marine, died on the island of Peleliu. Floyd Griggs died in Germany during the Battle of the Bulge, while serving in the Army. The officer pictured alongside Manlove is unidentified. Below, William E. Tidler Jr., a Marine parachute rigger serving during the Vietnam War, smiles for a photographer at the Fifth Special Forces Camp near Da Nang in 1968. Tidler returned to civilian life in Tipton early the next year. (Right, Manlove family; below, Bill Tidler.)

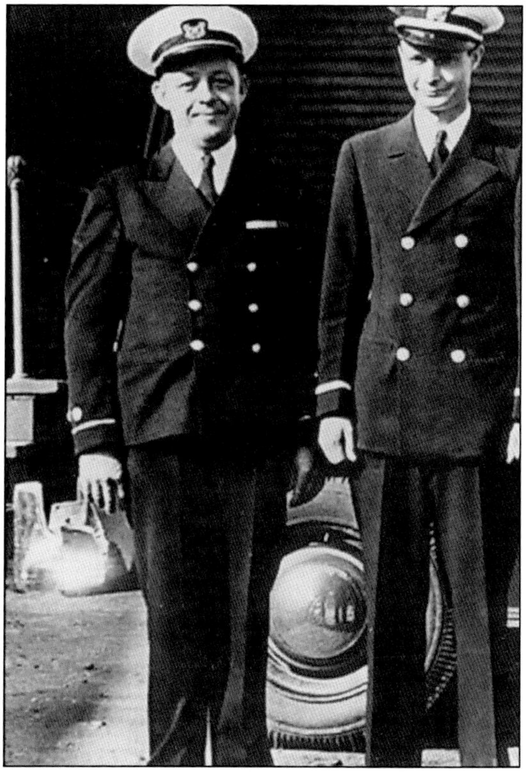

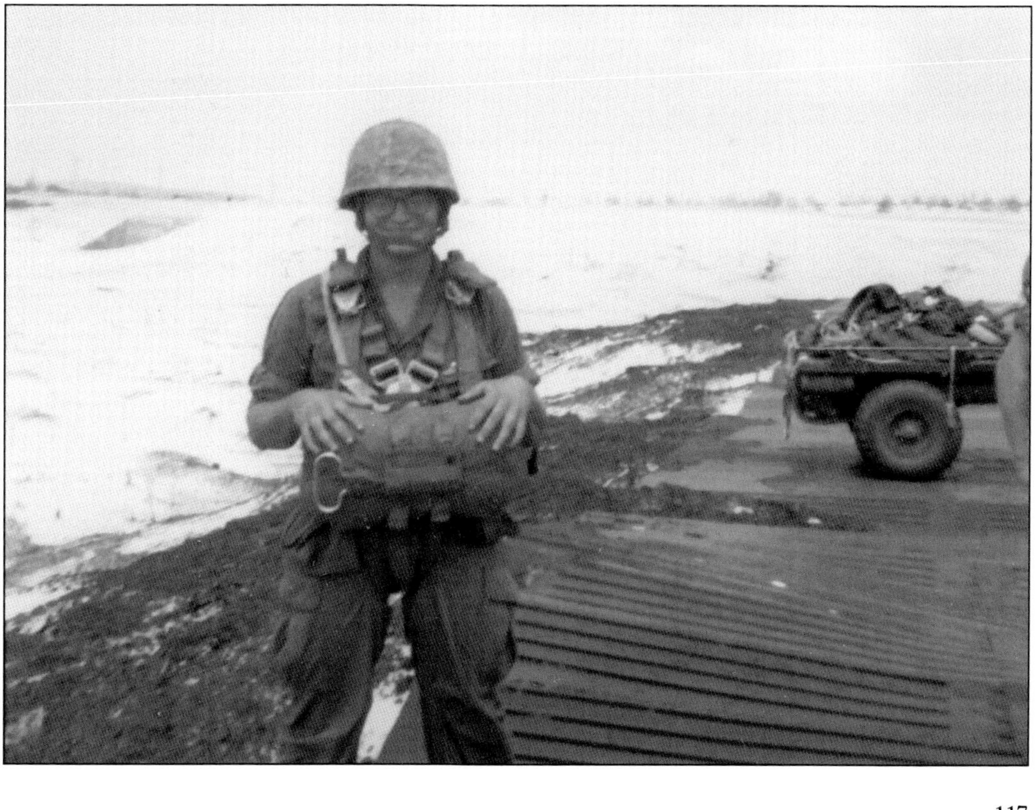

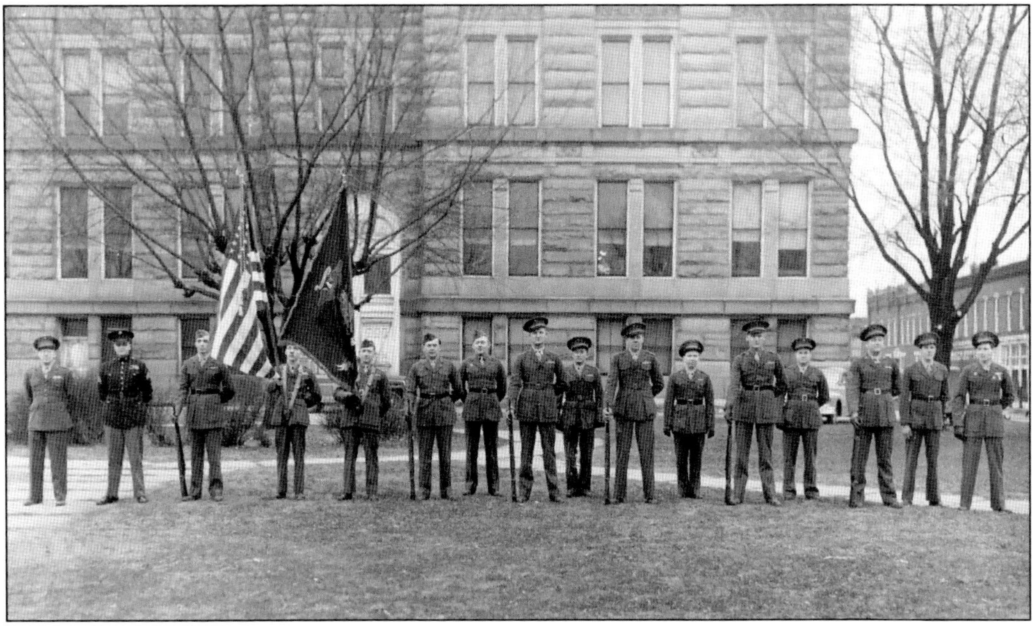

Above, a Marine honor guard takes part in a late-1940s military ceremony on the south side of the Tipton County Courthouse. Only Robert Lett, sixth from the left, is identified. Below are members of Company E, 2nd Battalion of the Indiana National Guard based in Tipton, about 1948. Identified are (first row, from left to right) unidentified, Oliver Posey, Cebe Woods, Wayne Luttrell, Gene Boes, Gene Coy, Charlie McIntosh, Dan Mattingly, and Maurice Thompson; Max Illges is seated in the second row, second from the right. (Above, Tom Lett; below, Ruth Illges.)

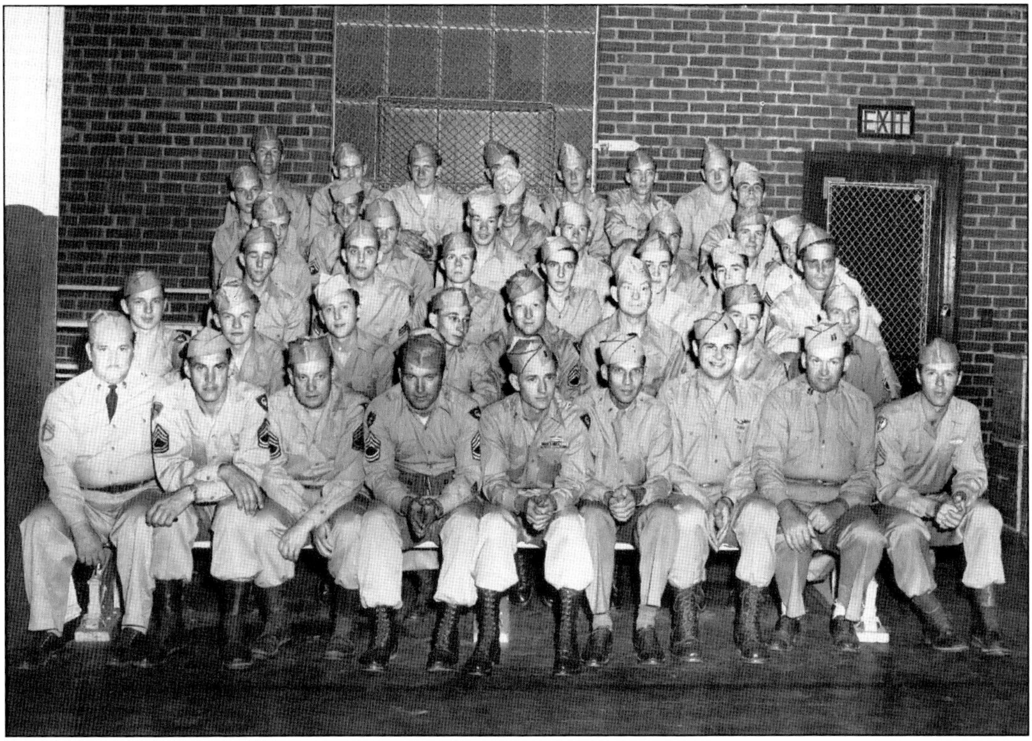

Friends, family, and military officials came to Tipton Sunday afternoon, April 24, 1977, when Maj. Gen. Jesse E. McIntosh, former commander of the 38th Infantry Division of the Indiana National Guard, was buried in Fairview Cemetery with full military honors. A caisson bearing his body slowly proceeded through the city he lived in most of his life, while an Army helicopter hovered overhead and a riderless horse bearing reversed boots in its stirrups trailed the flag-draped coffin. General McIntosh, a much-decorated veteran of World Wars I and II, died April 21, 1977, in a Tipton nursing home after a military career spanning 62 years. His son Robert died in action during World War II. (Right, Terry McIntosh; below, Ruth Illges.)

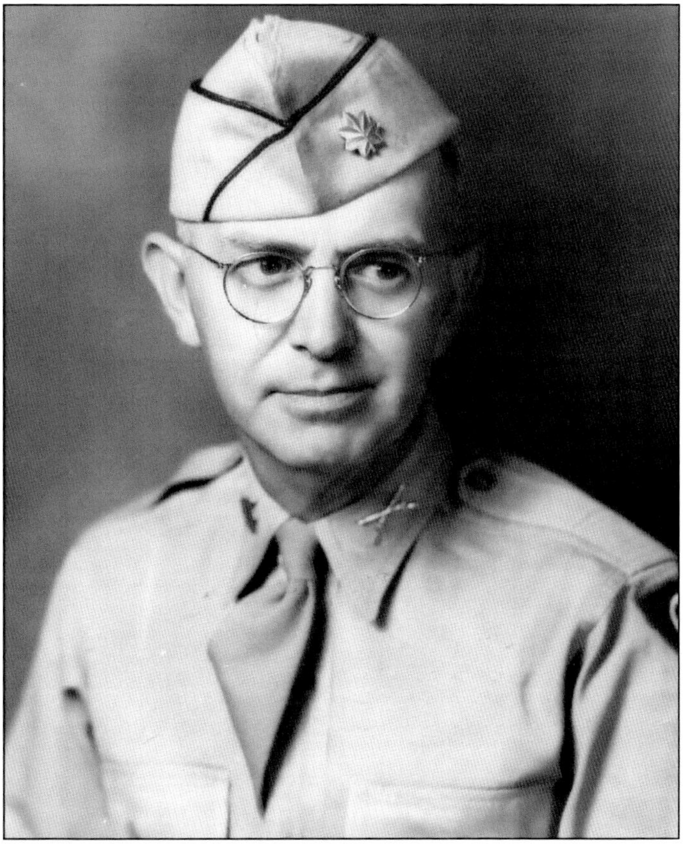

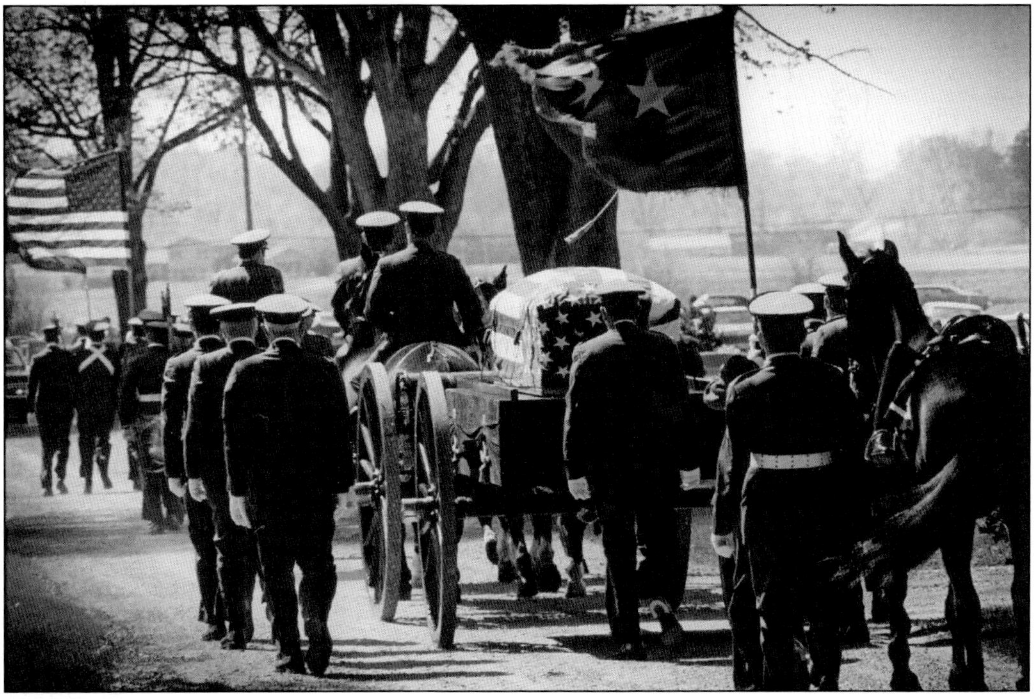

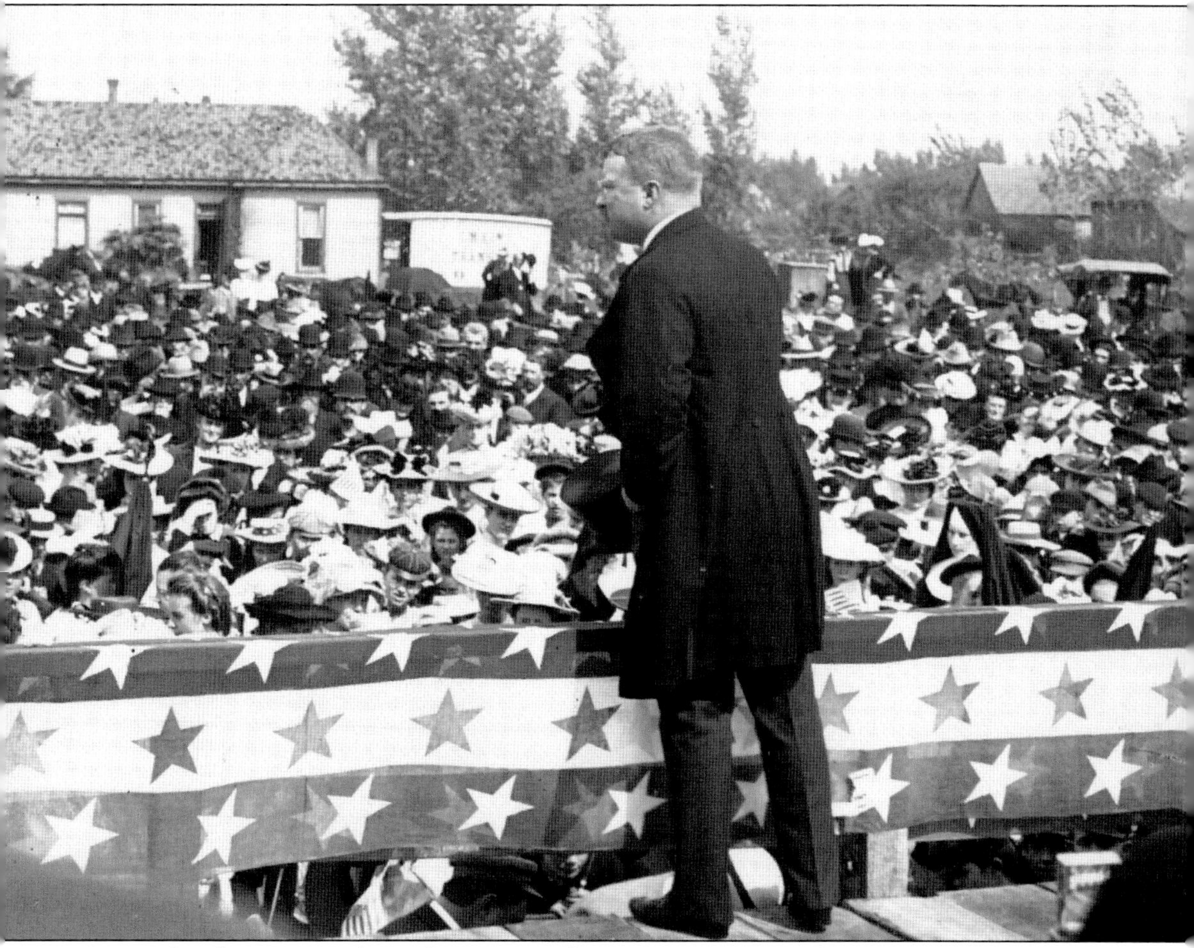

Pres. Theodore Roosevelt speaks to a crowd in Tipton on September 23, 1902, as part of his "Northwestern Tour." Traveling by train, Roosevelt's third Indiana stop that day was Tipton, having delivered speeches in Logansport and nearby Kokomo. A few days prior, President Roosevelt had suffered a leg injury in a carriage accident in Baltimore, Maryland. Since then, his leg had become badly infected, and as he spoke in Tipton, he was suffering a great deal of pain. Within hours of his Tipton stop, he gave his last speech of the day in Indianapolis and then was taken to St. Vincent Hospital for surgery to treat the abscess that had formed in his leg. After a brief hospital stay, the president called off the rest of his tour and returned to Washington. (Library of Congress and Theodore Roosevelt Center at Dickinson State University.)

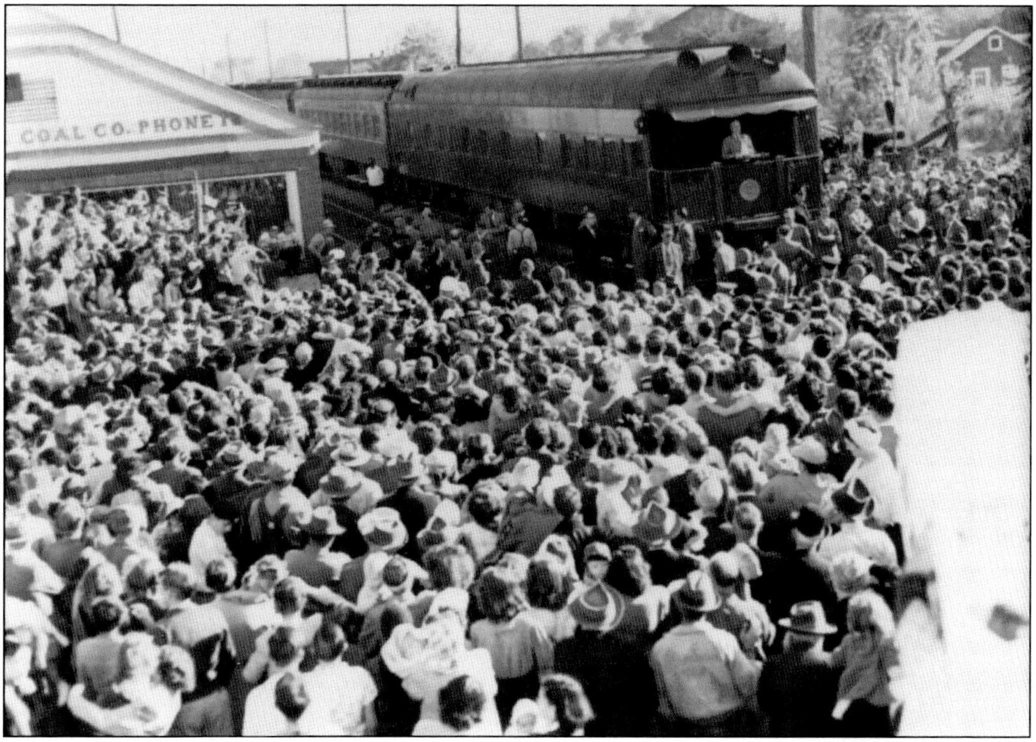

Pres. Harry S. Truman rolled into Tipton on the Presidential Special and made one of his famous whistle-stop speeches on Friday, October 15, 1948, about three weeks before the election. For the historic event, schools dismissed early, and businesses closed. As the city of 6,000 swelled to 9,000, a crowd converged around the Nickel Plate Railroad tracks where they intersected with Jefferson Street, two blocks east of the town square. The *Tipton Tribune* reports that people in search of a good view packed the second floor of the Tipton Lumber Company and the icehouse and hung out the windows. Two linemen climbed a pole, and a family sat in their car perched atop the hydraulic lift at the Marathon station next door. (Above, *Tribune*; right, Ruth Illges.)

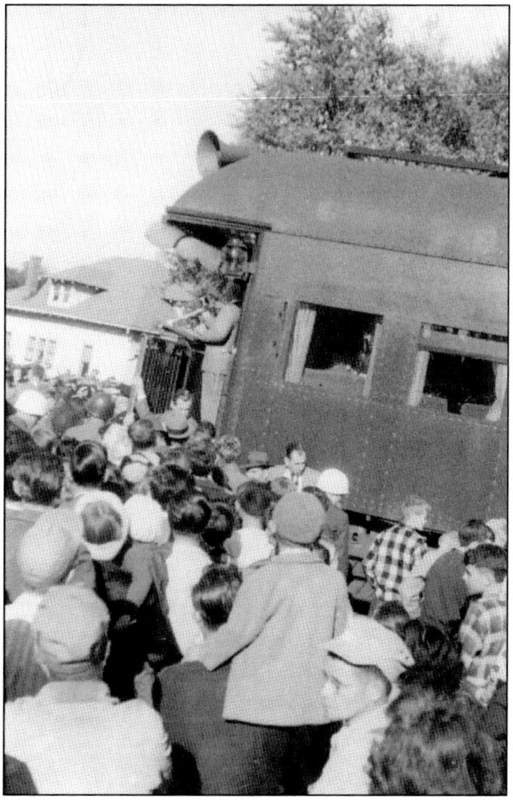

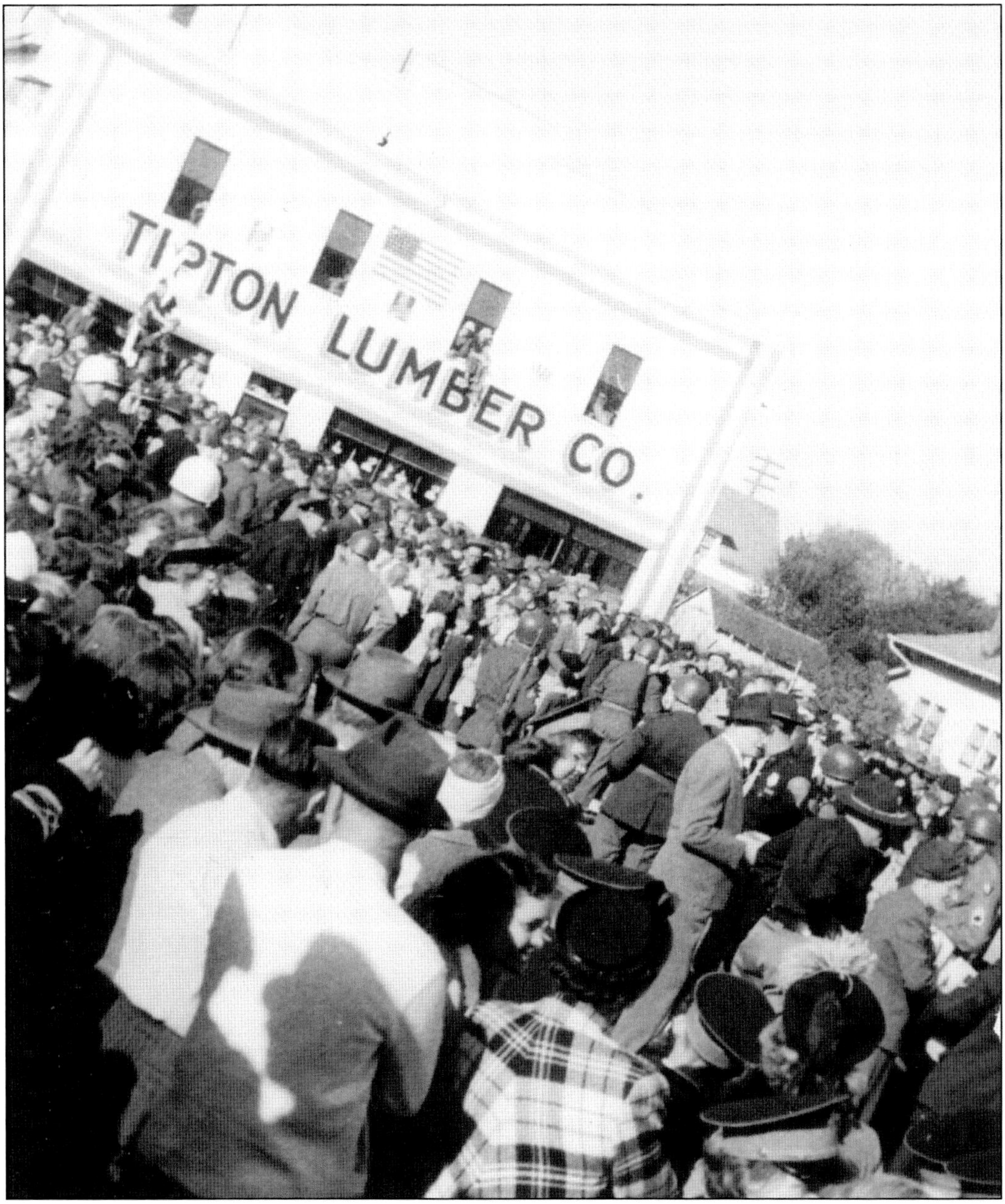

Arthur H. Noble of Hobbs, then Tipton County Democrats' chairman, boarded the train to personally greet Pres. Harry and First Lady Bess Truman and their daughter, Margaret, during their brief stop. But it was Mona Haskett, Tipton women's Democrat leader, for whom the train stopped yet a second time. Haskett had boarded the train to present the Trumans with flowers and candy, but before she had completed her mission, the train was rolling down the track. The officials quickly realized the error and stopped the train, allowing Haskett to disembark. Police Chief William Basey, his officers, local National Guard members, and several state policemen were called on for crowd control, and all complimented the orderly crowd. Some time after Truman's visit, Richard M. Nixon, then vice president and later president, traveled through Tipton. However, his train did not stop, not even once. (Ruth Illges.)

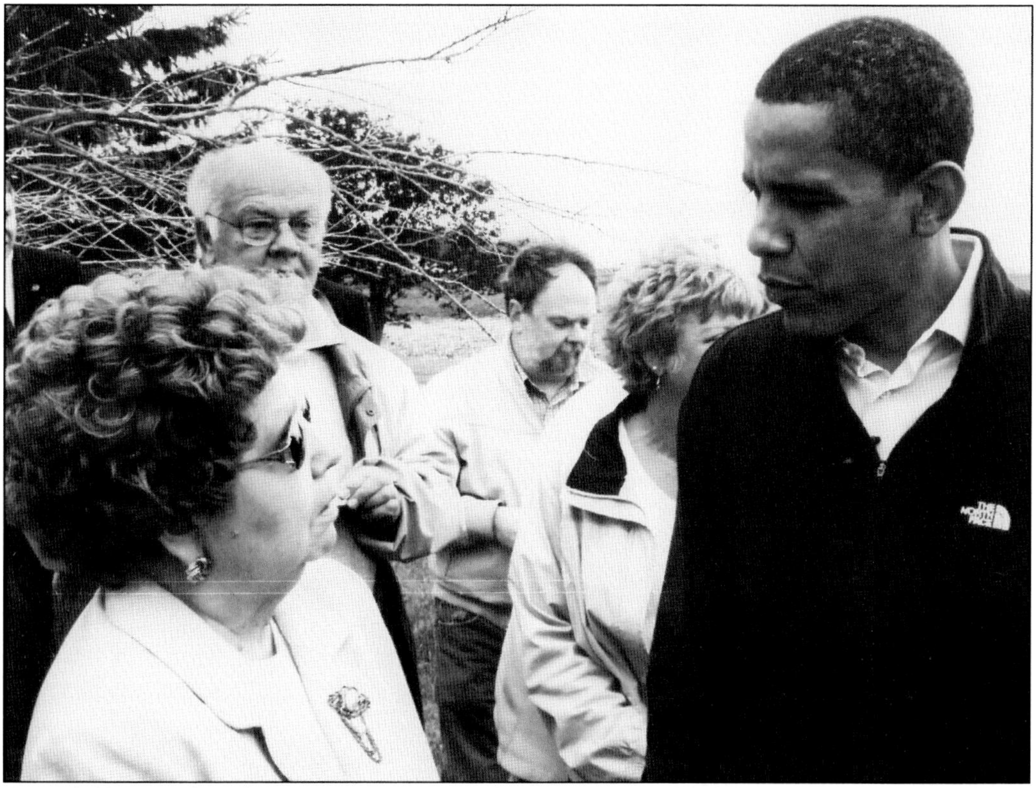

On a chilly Saturday afternoon in May 2008, the campaign trail led then senator and presidential contender Barack Obama and his family to Kempton. Obama, wife Michelle and their daughters, Malia and Sasha, were making a sweep through Indiana on their way home to Chicago. As they headed west on State Road 28, their motorcade made a stop at Kempton's century-old Dunham homestead, which links directly to Obama's ancestry. Above, Carolyn Etchison, 2001–2010 president of the Tipton County Historical Society, exchanges a few words with the Illinois senator. "I was impressed with both him and Michelle," Etchison said. "They were interested in what you were saying." Below, Obama is greeted by Shawn Clements, owner of the former Dunham house. The brief meeting garnered Clements an invitation to the presidential inauguration a few months later. (Both, Shawn Clements/Dunham House collection.)

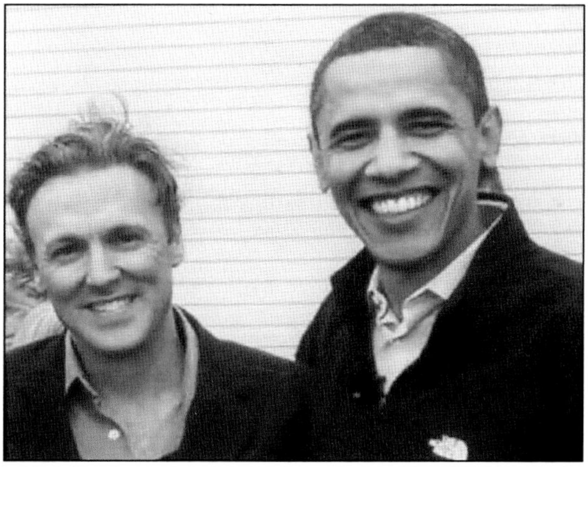

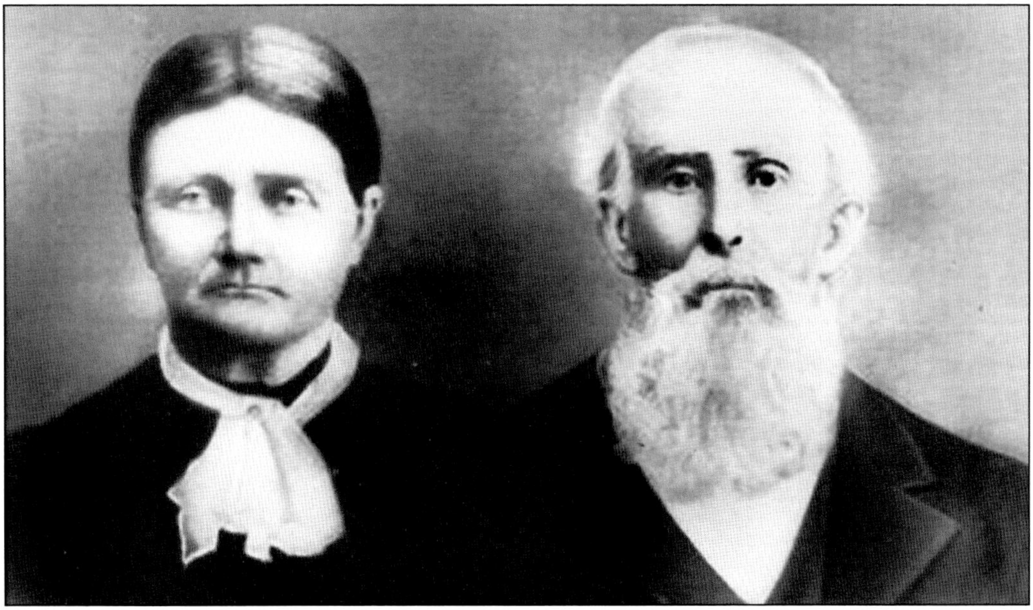

Above are Louisa Eliza Stroup Dunham and Jacob Mackey Dunham, Barack Obama's great-great-great-grandparents. They inherited the land in 1856 from Jacob's parents, Jacob and Catherine Goodnight Dunham—Obama's great-great-great-great-grandparents—who acquired the 120 acres from an 1849 government land grant. Eliza and Jacob Mackey married in Tipton County July 21, 1853, lived on the property, and produced seven children. When Eliza and Jacob Mackey moved to Kansas (producing the Dunham line that includes Obama's mother, Ann Dunham), their children joined them. Eliza and Jacob left the land to Jacob's brother Samuel Goodnight Dunham and his wife, Eliza Reese Dunham. It passed to Samuel and Eliza's son William Riley Dunham (below left), a Democratic state legislator, teacher, and farmer; and his wife, Laura Belle Allen Dunham (below right), Obama's fifth cousins, in 1891. (All, Shawn Clements/Dunham House collection.)

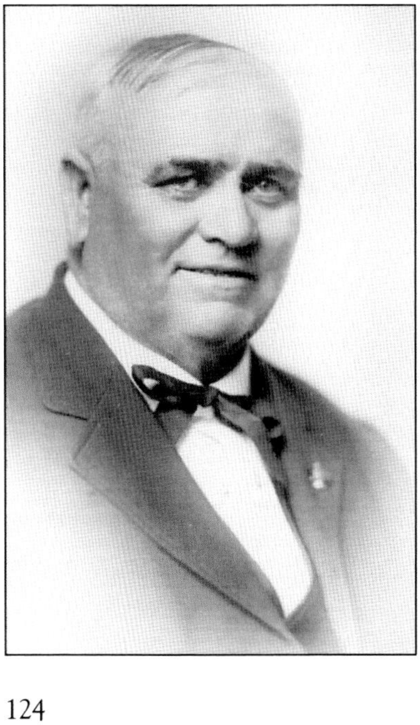

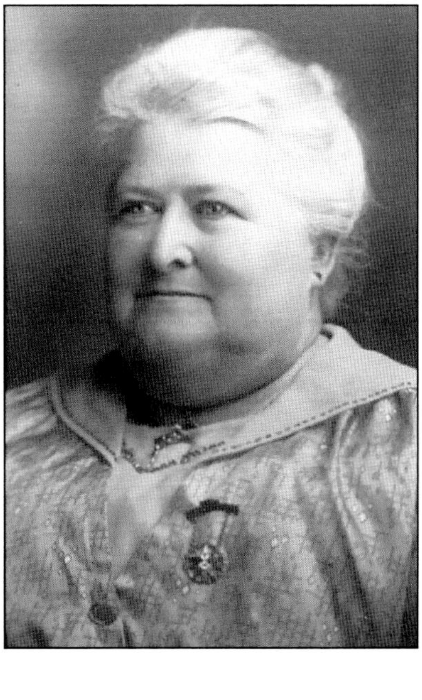

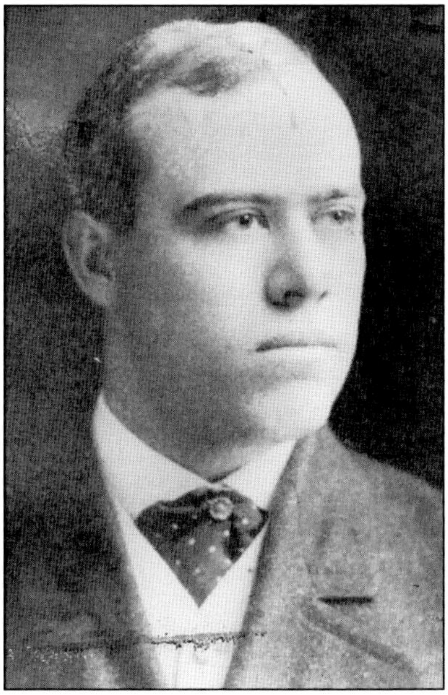

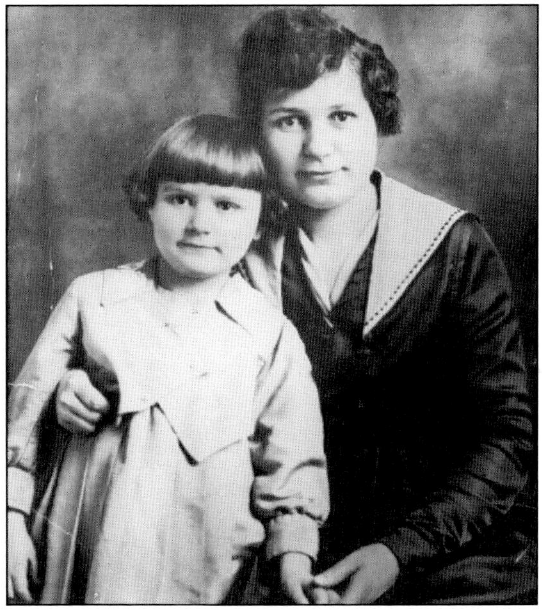

Obama's sixth cousin, Dr. Grover Cleveland Dunham, above left, took over the house after his father, Riley, died. The photograph below, dated June 1935, shows Dr. Dunham outside his Kempton office. He served patients in Tipton and Clinton Counties for some 50 years and was Tipton County's health officer around 1910. Following his death in 1956 at the age of 72, his wife, Hazel, shown above with their daughter, Melba, continued to live in the house until her death in 1969. Hazel was the last of the Dunhams to occupy the Kempton home. (All, Shawn Clements/Dunham House collection.)

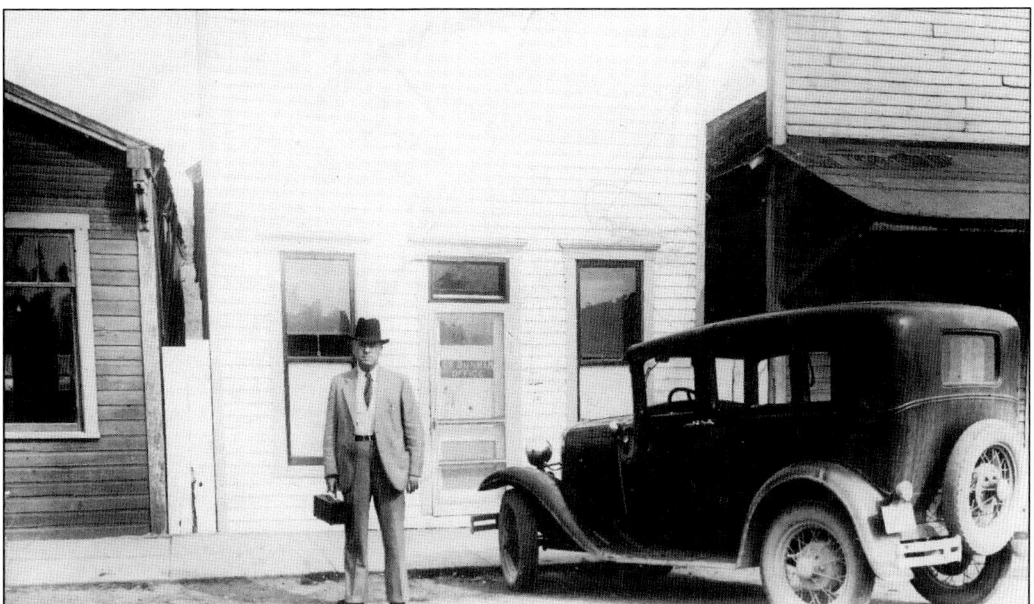

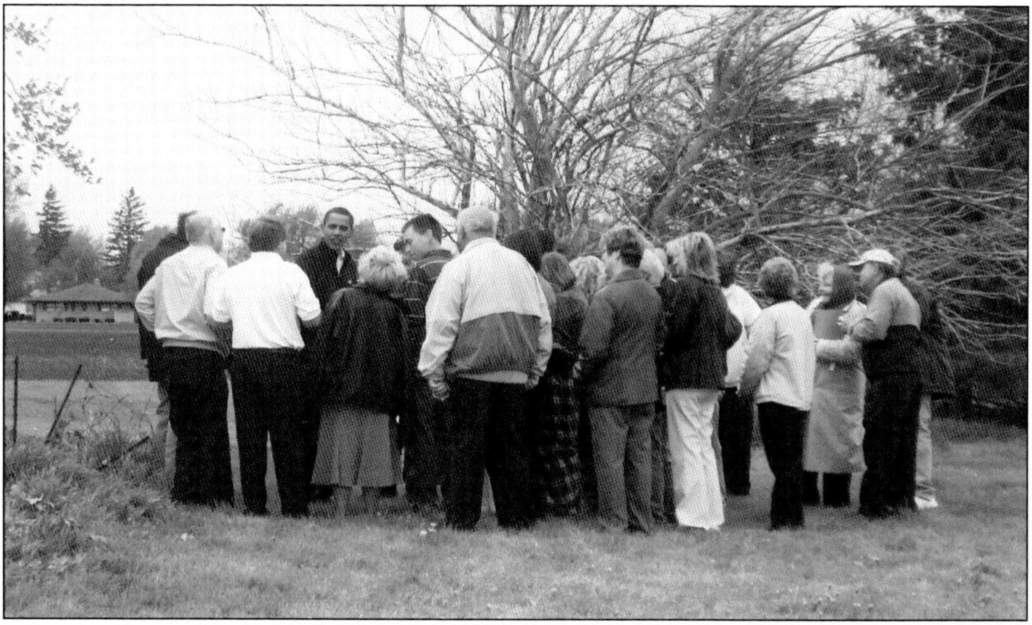

When the future president, third from the left, arrived at the Kempton home, he was greeted by several members of the Tipton County Historical Society and Dunham family descendants. They gave the Obamas a warm welcome in the midst of a chilly spring wind. Watching from a position of about 20 feet away was a press corps composed of approximately 100 journalists that included writers for the *New York Times*, *Time* magazine, and several area newspapers. Below, Senator Obama and his family head for a tour of the home of his ancestors. Looking back with a smile at the cameramen, he remarked, "It's a family affair." (Both, Bob Nichols.)

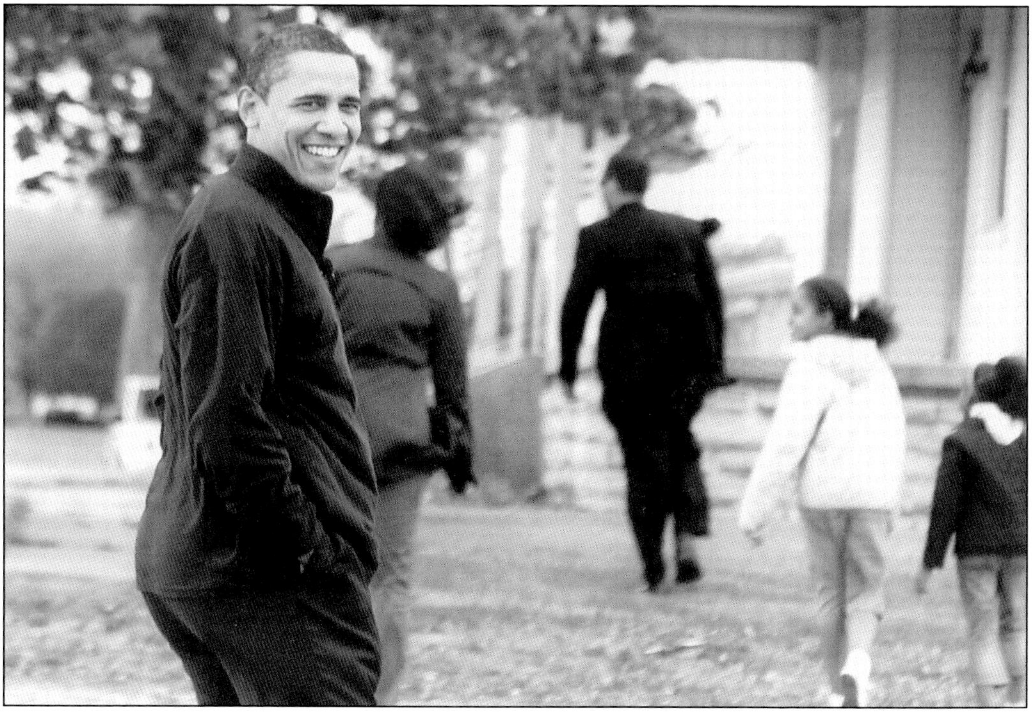

BIBLIOGRAPHY

Anderson & McCarty's Tipton County Directory. Tipton, IN: Anderson & McCarty, Publishers, 1900.

Indiana Historical Society website. "President's Shortened Western Tour." *Harper's Weekly*, October 4, 1902. http://images.indianahistory.org/cdm4/item_viewer.php?CISOROOT=/V0002&CISOPTR=2763&CISOBOX=1&REC=1.

Kemp, Gretchen, McKinny Julia, and Wimer Ruth. *Tipton County: Her Land and People*. Tipton, Ind.: Tipton County Publishing Company, Inc., 1974

Kline, George. *An Educational History of Tipton County, Indiana*. Tipton, IN: self-published, 1962.

Pershing, Marvin W. *History of Tipton County, Indiana: Her People, Industries and Institutions*. Indianapolis, IN: B.F. Bowen & Co., Inc, 1914.

———. *The Life of General John Tipton and Early Indiana History*. Tipton, IN: Tipton Literary and Suffrage Club, 1900.

"Roosevelt Reception Arrangements Being Made for Royal Welcome—Mayor's Request." *Hamilton County Ledger*, September 23, 1902.

"The President's Visit." *Hamilton County Ledger*, September 26, 1902, 1.

"This City Once Had Roosevelt as Its Guest." *Kokomo Tribune*, January 7, 1919. Newspaperarchive.com.

Tipton County Public Library Newspaper Archive. http://tiptonpl.newspaperarchive.com.